A Zany Slice of Italy

Ivanka Di Felice

For my mom

DEDICATION

I dedicate this story to all of you children of Italian immigrants—and this includes my husband, David. To you who dream about the grandeur of Florence, Venice, and Rome. Wine tastings in charming Tuscan hilltop towns. Sitting impeccably dressed in piazzas, watching the good-looking world go by.

The reality is that when you visit Italy, you'll be hijacked by relatives of all sorts; the entire family tree is waiting to meet you. You *will* catch glimpses of world-renowned monuments, but only fleeting ones from the car window, en route to the cement suburbs. You *will* eventually get a tour of all that is considered impressive—namely, the vegetable garden with its prized tomatoes. You *will* have "romantic" dinners in Rome, but you'll eat at boardroom-size tables with direct views of ramshackle sheds. You *will* return home with souvenirs from Italy: thick thighs and an extra roll around the middle.

Fear not, though—one day you'll learn to escape. Many of your schemes will be thwarted, and it may take several trips, but with persistence you can make it happen. Then you'll finally get to see the splendors of Venice and the beauty of Florence. You will sit in a piazza in a Tuscan hilltop town, though by that time you'll probably be ten pounds heavier and wearing comfortable shoes. But for now, as you drink your uncle's bad wine and listen to the sound of accordion music and roosters that never take a break, know that this book is dedicated to you.

CONTENTS

Close Encounters of the Fowl Kind.................................... 1

A Love Affair Begins 4

Byzantine Bureaucracy.. 8

First Impressions 14

Keeping up Appearances.. 19

Taking Matters into His Own Hands.................................... 26

Serenity Now! 30

A Bad Wind 37

Mining for Tomatoes 41

Manly Wiles.. 46

The Road to IKEA Is Paved with Good Intentions 51

"IKEA Can Go to Bloody Hell!"................................... 55

La Casalinga (The Housewife) 59

Sangue Italiano (Italian Blood)..................................... 63

Pink Socks and Green Pajamas...................................... 68

Where There Is Smoke, There Is Fire.............................. 75

The Road of Love.. 78

The Clash of the Fashions 82

Red "Chardonnay".. 87

SQUIRREL POWER.. 92

WAITING FOR IKEA.. 96

TOUGH LOVE TISSUES 99

PIÙ O MENO (MORE OR LESS)... 102

COZY—REDEFINED... 108

SPRING FEVER 115

FLYING THE COOP... 118

ARRIVEDERCI ABRUZZO 120

PANDA-MONIUM... 125

GYPSY KINGS.. 133

RADIATING HOPE 140

THE ROOF RACK AND A PROVINCIAL MOTHER........................... 143

SHOW THOSE EGGS SOME RESPECT!....................................... 148

REGAL LIVING, ITALIAN STYLE 157

IL VINO (THE WINE).. 162

QUEL CHE C'È C'È RISTORANTE (WHAT'S THERE IS THERE
RESTAURANT)... 167

TO PAY OR NOT TO PAY... 171

"WHICH SAINT IS LOOKING DOWN ON US?" 179

AN AFFARE TO REMEMBER.. 182

ONE BEDROOM AND SEVEN PEOPLE....................................... 187

ALL GOOD THINGS MUST COME TO AN END 193

"HOME" IS WHERE THE HEART IS 196

"STRANIERI GIUSTI" (THE RIGHT TYPE OF FOREIGNERS) 199

CRASH COURSE 209

CAREER CRISIS 220

"GET OFF YOUR BUTT!" 226

THE TRUFFLE TELEMARKETER 229

UNDER THE TUSCAN CLOUDS 233

BAR CONGO 239

FOURTEEN FERRARIS AND A FIAT PANDA 245

OCCUPATIONAL HAZARDS 253

LIVING LA VITA LOCAL 261

SEVEN DAYS, SEVEN ROOSTERS 266

REVENGE OF THE ROOSTER 271

MORE FOWL PLAY 277

RECIPES FOR AN ITALIAN PRINCE 282

CLOSE ENCOUNTERS OF THE FOWL KIND

As WE DRIVE DOWN THE winding mountain road, I see the national military police up ahead, signaling us to stop.

David hits the brakes of the ancient BMW 320. The sudden jolt sets off a round of clucking from the chickens in the backseat. The bamboo stalks roped to the car's roof slide forward but don't fall off.

"*Documenti*," orders the *carabiniere* with a sinister glare.

David reaches for the insurance papers in the glove compartment and hands them to the officer, who carefully examines them.

"Driver's license," the *carabiniere* says, leaning down to peer inside the car. The odors of chicken poop and pecorino cheese waft through the window. Just then, one of our chickens starts squawking. The officer does a double take.

David is pretty sure he left his wallet back in Tuscany, but to stall for time, he says, "I think it's in the trunk. Can I check?"

The officer nods, and David exits the car.

"*Americano?*" asks the *carabiniere*, a puzzled look on his face. With our gypsy mode of travel, I can see that we are destroying all of the stereotypes he believes about North Americans.

"Canadian," says David and asks the officer whether he speaks English.

"Not really," says the *carabiniere*, but he further explains how he speaks English like Alberto Sordi, who was the dubbed voice of Oliver Hardy in the Italian version of the Laurel & Hardy films.

David doesn't know who Alberto Sordi is but figures his best bet is to smile and assure the *carabiniere* that his English is very good.

"Thanks," the officer replies.

They walk toward the back of the car. David opens the trunk, and the officer laughs heartily to see its contents: more pecorino cheese, olive oil, numerous bags of pasta, several frozen chickens, and enough tomato sauce to last a year.

Perhaps the *carabiniere* realizes it may take ages for David to search through the trunk, or maybe he is simply pleased to hear that his English is good. At any rate, he unexpectedly tells David, "Don't worry about it. Have a nice day."

Thrilled, David hops back into the car and drives off, waving to the officer as he passes.

When we arrive home, we find David's wallet sitting on the desk. We receive more good news as we check our e-mail and learn that Kids Summer Camp did not fill enough spaces; hence, we won't have to go back to teach the "little darlings."

We put the chickens into their new home and name them Barbara and Roberta, after two sisters we have become close to here.

I glance around at the chickens, the bamboo, and the old farmhouse and reflect on our life in Tuscany. My friends think we spend one lazy day after another basking in the sun, drinking wine, and living *la dolce vita*. I try not to disillusion them. I had the same fantasies before I left Canada. Yet despite my reality—the chaotic, relentless visits from fun-loving *paesani* and relatives; dealing with Italy's Byzantine bureaucracies; the difficulty earning a living—I realize my life here is much richer than I ever could have imagined.

And now I recall that fateful peach-colored coat of long ago, which led me to my destiny.

A LOVE AFFAIR BEGINS

I FELL IN LOVE WITH Italy the minute I spotted that peach-colored swing coat in Florence more than twenty years ago. Though it was ruinously expensive, I had to possess it. Being nineteen at the time certainly helped me decide. I handed over my MasterCard, put on the coat, and pranced out onto the beckoning cobblestone streets of Florence. This coat was indeed so lovely that it caught not only my eye, but the eye of Canada Customs as well. Hence, the coat's price tag became even more preposterous.

Nonetheless, from that moment on, I was enchanted with a country that could produce such an exquisite item. Thus began my long-standing love affair with Italy.

My next inevitable step was to marry an Italian, for Italians, too, possessed an enchanting air. They were dark, handsome, and stylish beyond any North American's dreams. This goal has now been achieved, for my husband is Italian. Prior to having met me, he was adamantly Canadian, but I saw this as a mere technicality. It took some doing and a few thousand dollars, but now he is Italian.

In search of a better life, his parents, Giorgio and Maria, had moved from Italy to Toronto in 1966. David—the middle child of five children—was born in 1969. While

4

growing up, David did not always acknowledge his roots—although with a cacophony of cock-a-doodle-doos erupting from his garage every morning, his ethnicity was hard to hide.

When his parents replaced the quaint gingerbread trim and the delicate spindles of their once Victorian home with expansive brick arches and a sheet metal railing on the front porch, it left no doubt as to the cultural background of the new homeowners.

Yet there were other reasons for David's claiming to be Canadian.

For one, Caesar, their eccentric Italian neighbor, could single-handedly make Mussolini denounce being Italian. Using a roller, he painted his old Chevy bright yellow, not stopping at the tires but rolling right across half of them. One day, a calf was seen exiting his Chevy. It then lived in Caesar's basement until it was fattened up and ready to be served as "the guest of honor" at a large family gathering.

As a child, David definitely could not deny being Italian. When he was in first grade, his father received a windfall of white sacks, each depicting a potato man dressed in overalls, hands akimbo, and a straw dangling from its mouth. So, while other children had fancy lunchboxes filled with peanut butter and jelly sandwiches, David carried a Mr. Potato sack, emanating odors of sausage, cod fried in batter, homemade *capicollo*, and strong sheep's cheese. Worse still, the supply of bags was never ending, as was the trauma, because the humble potato man accompanied David to school each day right up to the seventh grade.

Above all, David was still haunted by frightening images of his hockey sticks being sawed off by his father and then jammed into the ground to serve as tomato stakes.

David did not want to end up like Frank, who, despite his Mafioso hit man appearance, broke down bawling during his wedding speech when he told his mother how much he would miss her—all the while knowing that he and his new bride would be moving into his parents' basement. Hence, fearing this same fate, at the young age of twenty-four, David proudly announced to his parents that he had bought a house.

They were impressed. "A rental property is a great idea!"

David paused, then mustered up the courage to say, "Well, actually I thought I'd move into the house."

In shock, his sweet Italian mother was reduced to tears. Her sorrow was unrelenting for the next few days, as she wondered what she had done wrong.

As a result of these childhood influences, images of Rome and its splendor went unappreciated in David's eyes. Yet just as the brick arches of his Victorian house screamed Italian, so did David's face. He could have been a model in a "Made in Italy" commercial, but he vehemently maintained that he was Canadian.

"Where are you from?" people would ask.

"Canada," he always replied.

"Really? You look so Italian."

"No. I was born and raised in Canada."

After prolonged interrogation, he would finally admit in a defeated undertone that his parents were Italian.

This self-effacing attitude was about to change. I had captured my pureblooded Italian prince, and I had a plan: to show him the beauty his ancestors had created, and surely, presto, he would lay claim to being Italian.

So it was. In 2001, we visited Italy. David's memories of lions guarding gates on suburban lawns began to fade, replaced by visions of Donatello's *Marzocco*, the heraldic lion of Florence. David recalled the brick arches his father had built onto their Victorian home, and he now saw their resemblance to the Coliseum's mighty masonry. David swiftly became Italian. That was the magic of Italy.

The broken hockey sticks, he would just have to get over.

Since I was now married to an Italian, a world of doors could open for us.

Years went by, however, and my impractical pleas to move to Italy fell on deaf ears. Meanwhile, David's parents were longing for their homeland. So, in 2003, Giorgio and Maria bought an old schoolhouse in Italy and restored it. For the next seven years, they lived in Canada from November through April and spent May to October in Italy. Three years ago, they began living in Italy year round.

Then one day in 2006, while working at the brokerage firm, I receive notice that due to restructuring, I am about to be laid off. After my initial feelings of shock and disappointment, I realize this might be my ticket out.

Still, it's not that simple. I have to fight hard against my North American mentality, urging me to find another job and feverishly save for a retirement that may never come. My years of seeing retirement charts at work have unwittingly taken their toll.

As I pick up coffee at the drive thru and inevitably spill it on my blouse while speeding away, I envision myself with David, passing a leisurely afternoon in a *caffè*. Italy is calling me.

BYZANTINE BUREAUCRACY

MY ITALIAN PRINCE HAS BEEN won over! He has unexpectedly received the most unlikely news: the furniture-making shop that employs him is moving to a new location an hour and half away. Not having the inner demons of retirement charts to contend with, he agrees to take a year off and go to Italy. His parents will soon return to Canada, so their house in Italy will be empty. We embark on the colossal task of getting the necessary documents in order, so that this dream may come to fruition.

Italy is equally as famous for its labyrinthine bureaucracy as for its pizza, wine, and grandeur. Still, a North American mind can never really be prepared.

David takes a day off work, and we spend an hour deciding what to wear to the Italian consulate. We arrive at what appears to be an opportune time: aside from workers, the place is empty.

A *signora* quickly stops us in our tracks.

"Do you have an appointment?" she asks.

"No, we called earlier and were not told that we require one." We are trying to lay the blame on this anonymous third party and thus appeal for mercy.

"I'm sorry," she says, "but you need an appointment to see me."

I surreptitiously glance around to see whether hundreds of people have swarmed the consulate. The same silence echoes, and no matter of national security appears to be looming.

We try to appeal to her sense of nationalism. Surely, the *signora* wants to help two people who recognize that life in *Bella Italia* is far superior to that in other countries. Hasn't she noticed what we're wearing? My back is already aching from the height of my heels, and my toes are squished. David is barely coping in pants far too tight, and the pastel-colored wool sweater tied around his neck is getting itchier by the minute.

"Okay," the *signora* begrudgingly concedes and lets out a loud sigh, as if signaling the nonexistent masses that they will simply have to wait.

Minutes later, she informs us with perverse joy that David is missing his long-form birth certificate, which shows his parents' nationality at the time of his birth.

"You must go to the registry office and get it done as a rush." She closes the file folder, content that we lack a vital document and no further effort will be required on her part.

"Grazie, signora. Arrivederci," we say.

We're already downtown, so we go over to the registry office and wait in the long line. Finally, it's our turn.

"I need these as a rush, please."

"No problem," the clerk says. "Do you have airline tickets as proof that you need it as a rush?"

"No, we require it for the consulate for next week."

"Then give me the letter you got from them, confirming it needs to be a rush."

"They didn't give us anything." I beg and plead to get it done as a rush but in vain.

"It's very routine," he assures us. "I get these letters from consulates all the time—the Portuguese, and so on. Go to the Italian consulate tomorrow and get a letter, then come back." He calls the number of the next person in line.

Dejected, we leave but not without hope. Tomorrow we will surely accomplish much and be one step closer to life in Italy.

I phone the consulate first, just in case an appointment is required. I explain this routine, run-of-the-mill, stamp-them-by-the-dozens type of letter we need for the registry office.

Fortunately, I'm sitting down when I receive the response.

"No, we will not be giving you any such letter," the *signora* adamantly states.

"Pardon?" I ask but soon realize this was a mistake. My inquiry changes the *signora's* mood, from being simply indignant to now plain furious.

"Madam, just because you are disorganized and leave things to the last minute, we will not be running around getting letters for you!" she yells.

Shocked, I foolishly say, "The man at the registry office said this was a routine letter and that he gets them all the time from the Portuguese consulate."

Evidently insulted, she says, "We are *not* the Portuguese, and we have matters of urgency to deal with for our own Italian citizens." She hangs up on me.

Tears stream down my face. After a good cry, I get a grip on myself and reserve a few tears for my next plan of action.

I drive furiously to the registry office. When my number is called, I march over, look at the government worker with tears in my eyes, and warn him, "I am about to cry."

He sees that I'm not bluffing, and he panics.

My tears are now flowing nonstop, and, between sobs, I explain my situation. He is sympathetic and pulls out a form marked URGENT, scribbles in the "proof of urgency" section, and presses the official stamp onto it.

"Your documents will be delivered to your door within forty-eight hours." He smiles and adds, "You just caught the Italians on a bad day; we get those letters from them all the time!"

"Thank you, thank you," I say in between sniffs. Red-eyed, I exit with soggy Kleenex in hand, hoping to escape the stares of surprised onlookers.

After a few more visits to the consulate, with me keeping quiet lest my voice be recognized, David victoriously gets his passport.

Next, we go to the visa office to get a one-year tourist visa for me. We explain our situation to the little *signora* with the dyed jet-black hair and bouffant hairstyle behind the undoubtedly bullet-proof glass.

"IM-PO-SSI-BILE!" she loudly informs us in her thick Italian accent and puts a hand on her forehead, as if about to faint at the mere suggestion of it. Not only does she have to deal with the complexity of our situation, but, to add to her woes, she notices the time. It is 11:30, and the office closes at 12:00. Like a bullet, she runs from behind the counter with an oversized key and locks the door. I feel a twinge of guilt, because, thanks to us, the next person, who has arrived in ample time, will find him- or herself locked out of the visa office, with no chance of being let in.

With visible discomfort, the *signora* pulls out a heavy, fear-inspiring manual. It's about a thousand pages thick and covered in dust, which is not particularly comforting. With a disturbed look on her face, she mumbles in Italian, while flipping pages back and forth.

As more time passes, I start to feel faint. My claustrophobia wells up, as we wait, locked in this little chamber.

"Excuse me, I must sit down as I am not feeling well," I tell the *signora*. I feel the color leave my face and sip on some water, hoping I don't pass out. Her mood instantly changes. The woman with the Gestapo demeanor on the other side of the glass now becomes compassionate—motherly, in fact.

"Here is my number, call me in a few days. I will make sure something is worked out for you," she says in a soothing tone.

I'm not sure whether this is a clever ruse to get rid of us before closing time or a truly empathetic gesture. Regardless, I hope the *signora* will work something out for us and that it will be legal.

Continuing to make headway toward living in paradise, I place a call to our friendly Italian airline.

"Do you fly to Pescara?" I ask.

The customer service person says, "We fly to Milan."

"Could we then get a connecting flight to Pescara?"

She seems outraged that I have not heard her the first time and repeats, "We fly to Milan. How you get from Milan to Pescara is not our problem."

I suspect that her ex-husband must have been from Pescara.

Convinced I must not be hearing her correctly, I say, "Pardon?"

Now, with full recognition that she is dealing with a difficult customer, she calls for back up.

Another "'customer service'" agent asks me, "Did you not hear what my colleague said?" To add insult to injury, she repeats what I clearly heard the first two times.

Just how many bad days can these Italians be having?

Days pass, and I check on the mood of those in the visa office. The *signora* who had promised to help us is not in. In her place is a man who, fortuitously, is leaving Canada and returning to live in his motherland.

"A vastly superior place to live," he declares.

We may have an ally. "We cannot agree more. That is why I am so desperate to have a one-year visa, because a few months in Italy is not nearly enough time."

We chat and find out we will be living just twenty minutes from this man's hometown.

"I can't believe that's where you're going. We'll be *paesani!*"

He cannot let down a future *paesan*, so not only will he give me my visa on the spot, but it shall be free of charge!

Triumphantly, we leave the Italian visa office. When we're certain that we're out of sight, we head straight into a Chinese restaurant for lunch.

FIRST IMPRESSIONS

WE ARRIVE IN ROME. NO taxi is available, so we walk to the bus stop and soon discover that cobblestone is no longer charming when one has to wheel enormous heavy suitcases over it. We miss our bus to Abruzzo and must wait three hours for the next one.

Regardless, we put on our new Italian personalities. We will relax, soak in the warm Roman atmosphere, and watch the world go by.

Determined to get us on the next bus, David perches directly in front of the store that sells bus tickets. I doubt that he could have found a less appealing spot to sit in all of Rome. Sweat drips down his face, and his eyes shift to and fro, as he suspiciously watches everyone who approaches to ensure that our luggage will be safe.

Three long hours pass, and we climb onto the bus. People sit wherever they want, yet one man is determined to sit in his assigned seat. Soon the entire bus is in an uproar, and I see mob mentality at work. The bus driver tries to calm everyone down and to seat the man elsewhere. Finally, the man sits down one row ahead of his assigned seat, loudly grumbling as the other passengers complain about him.

Our bus driver is on a mission, but I'm so tired, I don't care if he goes off a cliff. The lady beside me evidently still cherishes life, though. Her husband consoles her for the entire two and a half hours, as the bus driver speeds through curvy mountain roads. On occasion, the husband gets a break at the few red lights where the driver deigns to stop.

We eventually arrive at our destination, and the driver even brings the bus to a full stop. Earlier, he merely slowed down long enough for people to jump out. Yet he is still trying to keep up his momentum and chucks out our luggage with brute force.

David's father, Giorgio, and his uncle (*Zio* in Italian) pick us up. *Zio* Luigi affectionately greets me and sheds tears while hugging and kissing David. I immediately like David's uncle. He has kind eyes that exude warmth and happiness, though I can sense some regret behind them.

I repeat my name to *Zio* Luigi several times, but he gives up and finally refers to me as *moglie di* David ("David's wife"). I suspect he will do so for our entire stay.

David and *moglie di* David will go in the car with Giorgio, and *Zio* Luigi will take our luggage in his ancient little Panda.

Giorgio has assimilated well into the Italian lifestyle and is driving a Fiat Uno. The engine is equivalent to a motorcycle's—1,000 cc's. Regardless, it immediately becomes evident from whom my husband has inherited his driving skills. To add to my woes, Giorgio is similar to most Italians, who always like to look someone in the eye when conversing. David hasn't seen his father for months, and they have plenty to discuss. At least, *I* don't take my eyes off the twisty mountain road the entire trip home.

We arrive at my in-laws' house with its elaborate front gate, built slightly lower than prison walls. The setting is ideal. The ochre-colored house sits on a hill, looking out over valleys and mountains, olive groves, and vineyards. Patchwork pieces of cultivated land blend harmoniously together: the silver green of olive groves next to sandy brown soil, waiting to come to life again in the spring.

"The air is good up here. One should never be down in the valley." My father-in-law shakes his head in pity for the homes below.

David's mom, Maria, runs out and ecstatically greets us.

The men unload the suitcases, while I peek at the grounds. Naturally, there is a large vegetable garden, with teepee structures holding the tomatoes in place. Plastic covers them, lengthening the growing season. A wide balcony has an unobstructed view of the vegetable garden.

This garden has been designed according to a precise plan. Elsewhere, though, massive rocks are randomly strewn across the grass, seemingly too big and too heavy to move after mischievous aliens threw them down. The mismatch of small trees and shrubs also looks arranged by Mother Nature's furor, coupled with her sense of humor.

Maria points to where the cypress trees used to be but were painstakingly removed, to ensure enough light for the vegetable garden and an unobstructed view of the neighbor's ramshackle sheds.

There is a church up the hill and a cemetery nearby, so we will still enjoy some of that famous Tuscan view.

Maria rushes us inside to eat, where a meal awaits that is worthy of the prodigal son's return. We start with prosciutto, accompanied by juicy red tomatoes from the garden and buffalo mozzarella. Then handmade gnocchi in homemade tomato sauce. Zucchini flowers stuffed with mozzarella and fried in a parmesan batter. Roasted sheep, a specialty of the region, is next. Red and white wines accompany this feast. We finish off the meal with thick slivers of *Parmigiano reggiano*. Afterward, we have espresso *corretto*, espresso "corrected" with a splash of grappa or sambuca, that is.

During the meal, Maria watches us eat, her face beaming. She doesn't miss an opportunity to reload our plates, despite our protests. Radiant with Italian pride, Giorgio gives us a play-by-play account of each food item. The prosciutto is from Parma, the only good kind. The *parmigiano* is also from

Parma and must be aged a minimum of twenty-four months. The sheep was locally raised by *Zio* Luigi. . . .

Then Giorgio takes us on the grand tour, complete with architectural floor plans and a comprehensive explanation. A mini thesis follows on the topic of cement and its virtues.

Next is a professorial lecture on paint. "We are choking in Canada! Our walls do not breathe." I discover that it really is possible to deliver an entire one-hour sermon on breathing walls.

The tour continues, accompanied by Giorgio's pontificating on building materials.

This home is my in-laws' true love, as evidenced by the exclusive Murano glass chandelier with lights that are not energy efficient. Back in Canada, David's parents have several costly crystal chandeliers—each one, however, uses curly, energy-efficient bulbs.

Two massive brick arches lead to the kitchen. It is conveniently located next to the stairway going downstairs, which facilitates easy access for running up and down when one is cooking in the second kitchen and serving guests upstairs.

We soon realize there is no place comfortable to sit down: three large tables; a kitchen, a dining room, and a balcony on the main floor; and in the basement two more tables, with another one outside. Six tables, and not a couch in sight.

Outside, a staircase rises to an unfinished second-floor apartment, in case any grown children have a sudden need or desire to move in.

The *cantina* is stocked with at least a year's worth of food and wine, ready for any impending natural disaster, a world war, or a few typical Italian family dinners.

The grand tour finally complete, Giorgio sits down on a small stool in the living room and pulls out a fancy accordion. I have always found it to be a quaint instrument, reminiscent of old Italian movies. My love of the accordion quickly wanes, although Giorgio certainly has mastered that one beloved piece he plays over and over again.

We begin counting the days.

KEEPING UP APPEARANCES

HAVING BARELY SURVIVED OUR HECTIC existence back home, we're longing to embark on a slower pace of life here. But my father-in-law seems to be related to the bus driver; he, too, is a man on a mission. With only a couple of weeks left before their departure, Giorgio has much to show us, and time is of the essence! Obstacles such as our extreme jet lag will not be allowed to get in his way.

Day one, his first mission is to get us registered with the local police.

"We don't think this is necessary," we say.

He is determined, however, and when an Italian is determined, it's definitely best to go along with it. Having a soft spot in her heart for sleeping children, David's mom wakes us up just minutes before we have to leave.

"Where is Giorgio?" I ask.

"He's in the car, waiting for you," Maria nonchalantly answers. Because we know Giorgio does not possess the patience of Job, we down our *caffè latte* and pastry and run off in a stupor.

Sitting in the backseat, I soon realize I'll be calmer if I look sideways, rather than straight ahead. In matters that relate to speeding oncoming traffic, it's best to remain ignorant.

After traveling at a velocity I never thought possible for this poor little Fiat, through what I assume is lovely countryside, we arrive at the police station. We press the buzzer. A big, burly man glares suspiciously through a little window on the door and then lets us into a small chamber. My claustrophobia kicks in. The tiny room swims in front of my eyes, and the walls close in.

"Breathe," I tell myself. "In and out, in and out." I fear that a panic attack would not garner any sympathy but rather may get us shot. *This is a necessary evil, so just remain calm.*

The police size us up and occasionally pat the impressive black machine guns hanging on their belts. Finally, they decide that we're unlikely to be a trio of terrorists, and the chance that we'll do them any harm is minimal. We are led to a bigger room, where we wait to see the chief. Every few minutes, someone pops his head out from the adjoining room and curiously stares at us. We refrain from smiling and greeting the person and keep staring ahead. Our best bet is to look frightened at all times. We don't speak, we don't move, and we try to keep our breathing to a bare minimum.

Finally, a husky man with a big curly moustache approaches us. He's decked out in a crisp blue-and-white uniform with gold stripes. We all stand up as a sign of respect. The others join him and stand to our left. *Is this what all tourists must go through? No wonder the guidebook says that most do not bother to check in with the police.*

Giorgio explains why we are here. The chief pauses, then says, "You are at the wrong police station. This is the military station, and you need to go to the Questura, which looks after matters of immigration." No wonder everyone was staring at us; we are, after all, three very unlikely characters to join the military!

All is not lost. The town, Civitella del Tronto, is quite lovely and perched so up high on a rocky mass, it looks impregnable. With a sense of pride and nationalism, Giorgio takes us on a tour. He explains that it was the last location to hold out to Italian unification until it succumbed in 1861. We enjoy a leisurely stroll and pose for pictures, thoroughly enjoying a much-needed moment of peace and calm. I spot a bar and hope for a second cup of coffee.

That instant, a silent alarm goes off in Giorgio's brain. Like Cinderella at the stroke of midnight, he panics. He leads the way and runs to the car, cane in hand. If I thought he drove like a maniac when we had all the time in the world, that was nothing. David's father has a clock in his stomach, and he must start eating before the last echo of the one o'clock chime. My envisioned calm, nonchalant way of life will have to wait.

Despite our speed on the mountain's hairpin curves, we arrive home safely. Maria is on the porch, anxiously waiting for us. She's wearing her apron, short white sport socks, and black running shoes. Accessorizing this outfit are heavy gold earrings and a thick gold necklace. Lunch, of course, is already sitting on the table, because we're two minutes late.

Last night a friend dropped off some porcini mushrooms he had picked in the forest, though he could not divulge where.

"One does not tell," he said. "Picking mushrooms is a dangerous thing. You have to hope they don't slash your tires. There are enough people picking mushrooms, they don't need anyone else."

Visions of myself stranded in the forest, with slashed tires, quickly end any future plan I had to pick mushrooms.

Maria had dipped the porcinis in breadcrumbs and fried them. They are so flavorful that a soliloquy on the superiority of Italian food naturally ensues. *Writing a nationalistic cookbook, lesson two* . . .

At two-thirty, Giorgio's same finely tuned clock goes off. In mid sentence, he leaves the table and dashes to the bedroom for the sacred *pausa*. Do we take a *pausa* as well and forfeit the only quiet and calm time in this house? We opt for the *pausa* to inaugurate our new lifestyle. I lie down on the bright yellow-and-burgundy velour bedspread, trimmed with fuchsia pink pom-poms, and find myself face-to-face with pink and forest green angels dancing on it. I will hide this bedspread in the back of the armoire the moment my mother-in-law leaves.

We close all of the shutters, lie back in the darkness, and within minutes fall into a deep sleep.

We are awoken shotgun style, like a warning shout from the police mere seconds before the SWAT team breaks down the door.

"Hurry!" Maria yells. Five minutes to get ready—because Giorgio, naturally, is waiting in the car. We must make the customary rounds of visiting relatives. I get dressed in record time, but apparently my new top will not do. Maria says this baby-doll style might make *Zio* Luigi and *Zia* ("Aunt") Franca think I am pregnant.

"Don't you have something a bit more form fitting?" Maria asks.

The sound of impatient honking adds to my stress. I enlist Maria's help, and after several attempts, she settles on something suitable for me to wear.

This scene will be repeated numerous times, because specific rules must be obeyed concerning matters of dress, especially when visiting relatives. My outfits will be judged according to weight, length, warmness, cut, overall appearance, and so on. I feel as if I have Giorgio Armani scrutinizing me moments before his runway collection will debut. Incidentally, other rules, such as building permits, dumping laws, and driving regulations, are optional in Italy.

People seem most offended by my fashion faux pas concerning the weight of fabric.

"Those pants are too light. You should put on a sweater with that outfit, it's too summery."

I make the mistake of arguing. "Though it's October, it's still very warm, so why would I need a sweater?"

"Simple," Maria says. "No one else is in short sleeves at this time of year."

I give up and make any required adjustments, then silently swelter in the back of the Fiat.

We are briefed on what is not to be discussed in front of relatives. My second-hand shopping sprees, though popular back home, are not to be mentioned. Nor is the divorce that is taking place in the family and has been under way for several years. Thanks to my limited Italian, I can be trusted not to spill the beans on any of the taboo subjects.

We arrive at *Zio* and *Zia*'s family compound. It makes me want to call the Milan stock exchange and purchase shares in cement. It's as big as a small village, and several generations live within this area—to all outward appearances, happily. Also housed within this complex are flocks of sheep, chickens, goats, pigs, and even a pair of ostriches for special occasions when a frittata for twenty-five hungry souls is on the menu.

The old stone house has weathered slate-blue shutters, dripping with character. Sitting on a hill with stunning views all around, it is abandoned, except for a few animals dwelling in one section. Another part of the structure houses two dozen hinds of prosciutto hanging from the ceiling.

I picture what British or American expats would do to that house. They would restore it, then write a book about repairing it and their adventures with their Italian neighbors. I point this out to *Zio* Luigi, who laughs heartily and says, "Who would want that old place?" *Ville & Casali* décor magazine is evidently not on his short list of preferred reading material.

The shed-to-house ratio is in normal proportion: four ramshackle corrugated metal sheds per house.

We enter their combination dining-living room. Almost as an afterthought, the dining room is enclosed by the living room. A broad table sits in the center, and pieces of a living room set are placed against the surrounding walls.

As the non-Italian in the family, I get the quick once-over and hear the word *simpatica*. It appears that my mother-in-law's wardrobe coaching has paid off, and I have passed the test.

Course after course of fine Italian food is served. I realize that when you are full and your plate is empty, you must guard it with your life. Otherwise, it will be chock-full again within seconds.

Accompanying each course is a commentary on the superiority of Italian food, with David and I knowing full well that no one in the room has ever tried any other type of cuisine. They would most likely choose death over eating a meal in a Chinese restaurant.

Although my plate keeps getting filled, my glass does not. David, however, appears to attract a magical, ever-flowing fountain of wine. His uncle makes desperate leaps across the table, lest our Italian prince's mouth become dry. Cheese is now being served, and I long for another glass of red wine to accompany it. As if reading my mind, *Zio* suddenly looks at me.

"I didn't notice your glass was empty!" He apologizes and quickly fills it with pineapple juice.

The TV is on full blast, so everyone has to shout. A crazy game show is on. The camera zooms in on a pair of *velines'* (showgirls') breasts spilling out of their low-cut tops, as the women sit crossing and uncrossing their long legs in miniskirts, with the host laughing uncontrollably. Certain channels feature more scantily clad *velines*, offering their commentary on the soccer game. Our other option is to watch thirty-year-old-reruns of Columbo speaking Italian.

We sit upright on hard wooden chairs. I longingly gaze at the couches surrounding us, as the unsolicited double portions of pasta induce sleep.

Though I don't speak a lot of Italian, I have mastered good eye contact, a perfectly timed nod, and a warm grin. As a result, *Zio* and *Zia* regularly compliment me on how quickly I have picked up the language. Because they haven't asked me a single question I need to answer, I'm able to convey an excellent grasp of the language.

Orders for coffee are now being taken. "Will David's wife have coffee?" *Zia* asks. She serves dessert, along with *spumante* in plastic cups. This time my glass is filled to the brim, with foam.

After-dinner entertainment includes watching a cousin's wedding video. The bride poses lying across the floor like a snake in her fluffy white wedding gown, surrounded by carrots, tomatoes, and other vegetables. The background music for the wedding video is "Against All Odds."

Exhausted and stuffed, we begin to say our good-byes. We start off in the dining room, proceed to the hallway, and then, after another twenty minutes on the veranda, we take our leave. In the distance, we hear them yell, "Don't forget to come back soon!"

The Fiat groans as we drive up the mountain.

One aunt and uncle visited, only six more to go.

TAKING MATTERS INTO HIS OWN HANDS

"MARIA, PLEASE, WE NEED MORE than five minutes to get ready in the morning," I remind her the night before. She complies and gives us seven minutes the following morning.

"It breaks my heart to have to wake you," she says. I'm about to explain when I see Giorgio put on his coat and get the car keys. He has many things to show us today, and, as always, time is of the essence! *Why are retired people always in a hurry?*

Meeting the local barber is higher on the list of priorities than meeting the local doctor.

We stop at the gas station and put in a quarter tank of gas.

"Sometimes you can even fill it halfway, but never more," warns Giorgio. "It weighs the car down, and you use more gas." *No wonder he has no time!*

The stroke of twelve is approaching, and David's father speeds home, cursing all interferences. My "Italian" is becoming more prolific by the moment. Like an army sergeant, he orders David, "Quick, call your mother. Tell her we'll be there soon and to be ready!"

Maria is outside, wearing her mandatory coat despite the unseasonably warm weather, and holding gift bags in her hands. I quickly pull on my sweater, lest I get caught by the fashion police. We barely slow down enough to let her in, and off we go, to another relative's for lunch. Unless we make up for lost time, we won't begin eating by one o'clock! I wipe the sweat from my brow and brace myself for the rocky ride down the unpaved mountain road.

I survive more relatives, more superior Italian food, and four people simultaneously speaking to me in a language I can barely understand.

We arrive home, and I assume everyone will automatically run off to their rooms for the *pausa*. Regrettably, we have missed the *pausa* cut-off time. Though all of us are dead tired, one simply does not take a *pausa* after 4 p.m.

The next day Giorgio has more surprises in store for us. "I'll be waiting in the car! Hurry!" he exclaims.

We obediently get in the car, assuming there are more relatives we need to visit.

Moments before we arrive, Giorgio briefs David. Being an older Italian man, Giorgio is not in agreement with the concept of our taking a year off and scoffing at retirement charts. He decided to take matters into his own hands and has brought David to a job interview.

"Giorgio! Nice to see you. Is this your son?" the shop owner asks. "Come on in."

Because we have another five days to endure before his father's return to Canada, David plays along. He is a good actor and pretends to be an eager and willing employee.

"What would you pay me?" David asks.

"Work for me for three months, and then I will conclude what you're worth and will pay you accordingly," the man responds.

"What about a ballpark figure?" David asks.

"No," he says and repeats the three-month formula.

Fortuitously, Giorgio isn't pleased with the shop owner's ambiguity, and we leave—David and I, happily.

"I need to give you some driving lessons before I go," Giorgio says.

Our twenty years of driving experience are evidently not sufficient. After a few minutes of Giorgio's barking orders at David, we completely understand why people would rather pay a driving instructor than take lessons from their parents.

We again do the countdown.

Two days prior to her departure, Maria insists we go to the supermarket to pick up some items she urgently needs, such as a year's worth of pasta; enough meat to fill up the freezer; large quantities of various cheeses; and several boxes of laundry detergent. There is no end to her urgent needs. Giorgio, no fool, pays for everything, and we rush home again, the little engine whining with all of the excess weight heaped on it.

At home, immediately out comes the accordion! David's father serenades us. We must put away the vast quantities of groceries, and we cannot escape. *Only two more days, we can do it.* We have newfound respect for David's older brother living back at home, who has endured Giorgio's nightly serenades for more than seven years.

With my in-laws departing tomorrow, the armies of well-wishers arrive. They take turns with the plumbers in competing for the attention of David's parents. For the last few weeks, the plumbers have been installing a heat system that works in conjunction with the fireplace. But, naturally, the plumbers could not always arrive as promised, and now they are frenetically trying to complete the job while the man with their cash is still in the country. Finally, they finish, and off they go.

We test the new system and light the fireplace—foolishly, after the plumbers have left with their pay. Soon the entire kitchen and dining room are filled with thick gray smoke. Undeterred, the well-wishers toast on! People continue to come and go. We are now counting down the hours, unquestionably not being able to keep up pace with David's parents, who are in their seventies. Exhausted, David and I make our way to bed. We leave the last of the guests standing by the door, a clear indication that within a half hour or so, they, too, will be gone.

It is five o'clock in the morning. We get up to say one final good-bye and to thank Giorgio and Maria. Her parting words are "Remember to eat at least one piece of prosciutto every day."

Once they leave, we immediately decide to sleep till noon, ever grateful that we were deemed too stupid to be able to find the airport, hence were not asked to drive them!

SERENITY NOW!

THE HOUSE IS QUIET, EXCEPT for the barking of a pack of dogs. The shutters are drawn, and the room is in utter darkness. We will sleep in today. At last, no five-minute countdown. Our new life shall begin.

Soon, though, we hear a noise in the distance. As it gets closer and louder, David, half asleep, turns to me and in jest asks, "Do we need any sheep feed?"

The sheep feed truck is announcing its wares on a loud speaker system with the sound of a very ill sheep: bah, baah, baaah. I look at my poor husband, who has now placed a pillow over his head.

David, thankful that no schedule awaits him, quickly dozes off again. Yet within minutes, it sounds as if a circus has arrived, because boisterous carousel music fills the air. Again, David abruptly awakes. A truck with an assortment of kitchen wares is making its rounds. Next, droves of teenagers leave the sad little bar down the street and roar up and down the hill on their *motorini*.

Then I hear *Zio* Luigi's voice, loud and clear, as if he's in the bedroom with us. He's talking to Emma, a neighbor. She epitomizes every stereotype about an older Italian lady, having spent her entire life in a small village. She must have been quite beautiful when young. Even in her advanced old age, she has a beautiful square jaw, sculpted cheekbones, big dark eyes, and ever jet-black hair.

They continue to shout back and forth.

"I wish they would move closer and stop shouting," I say.

David cautiously peeks through the window. "They're only a foot away from each other."

"David! David!" yells *Zio* Luigi.

"We must get up," I tell him. "They know we're home." While David sleepily contemplates the situation, I see no way out.

I open the shutters and wave to them. I find that the shouting is contagious, as I belt out, "*Buongiorno!*" Emma smiles and holds a bottle in the air. I signal for them to come to the front door, which gives me just enough time to finish dressing.

"*Buongiorno,*" they say.

Emma has brought us a bottle of their newly pressed olive oil, along with a loaf of homemade bread from her wood oven. "New oil, old wine," she says and instructs us on how best to eat it. "You toast the bread in the fireplace. Then rub a piece of garlic over it and pour lots of olive oil on, add a bit of salt, and enjoy!" She takes her index finger and corkscrews it into her cheek, denoting "delicious."

"Of course, olive oil from this region is far better than other oils." A simultaneous explanation by *Zio* and Emma commences. She has about eighty trees, which are barely enough for her and her family because they use about one bottle a week. The gift suddenly becomes even more precious.

We offer her coffee, but she must rush away to prepare lunch. "*Arrivederci!*" she hollers.

"Will you have a coffee, *Zio?*"

"Yes, but make it *corretto*, because that is the only correct way of drinking coffee."

Zio has been dropping by a lot lately, especially since his last visit to the doctor when he was told to give up drinking.

"But that just means no wine. It's not easy, but I have to be very strict with myself. Not a drop!" he says for emphasis.

"But, clearly, the doctor did not mean grappa. It's good for your health, so surely it's fine to have some in my coffee," he states, rather than asks. His eager eyes win me over, and I give him the grappa bottle.

So it's no wonder that I begin to notice *Zio* arriving more frequently and at regular intervals for his *caffè corretto*. I also notice the absence of his wife on these drop-ins and wonder just how many *caffè correttos* he is consuming daily.

"I came to invite you for lunch today," he says.

It's almost noon, and I haven't brushed my teeth yet. It will take me forever to figure out what is safe to wear, now that my fashion consultant has departed.

"Maybe another time."

"Sure, no problem. See you tonight then!"

"But, *Zio*, we have lots to do. Thank you, but we really can't make it."

Zio pauses, reflecting on the gravity of what is taking place.

"Okay, see you tomorrow for lunch, then!" Without giving us time to answer, he runs off—no doubt to have his next *caffè corretto* somewhere.

Just before lunch, I really start to miss my mother-in-law, but at least with my father-in-law gone, the meal will not have to be ready pronto at one o'clock.

After lunch, I walk down to the little village just down the street, a series of pastel yellow and peach-colored homes jutting out of the mountain, incredibly with parts of them built right into it. I see Emma and thank her for the wonderful olive oil and bread we have just enjoyed. She is pleased.

"Off for a *passeggiata?*" she asks.

"Yes. I'm anxious to get to know my new surroundings."

Her face turns serious. "You must be careful of snakes. They lie in the tall grass and catch you unawares." She includes a prolific amount of gesturing, I suspect to both aid my comprehension and ensure that she gets enough physical exercise for the day.

"Sometimes you even have to be careful up above. My son once came across a bunch of them in a tree. It looked like a large ball stuck in the branches, but it was actually some sort of plastic with a bunch of snakes in it."

In a very serious tone, she explains how these snakes happened to have this fate. "When research scientists finished their experiment, they must have dropped this package from a plane, and it landed in a tree. So be cautious at all times, both below and above!"

I'm amazed at her innocence and the immense zeal she possesses while recounting this unlikely event.

As I continue my walk, I spot two older men sitting on a bench in the village. Though their clothes are older and slightly faded, they still sport the customary dark sports jackets and pressed pants that are worn when going "out."

"Who do you belong to, and where are you from?" is what I gather they are asking.

"Toronto, Canada," I say.

"Oh, America!" they simultaneously reply. I smile and realize that this will not be the last time I am called an *Americana*.

"I speak English. Oui, oui," says one of the men. Then they proceed with their interrogation.

"Do you have children?"

Surprisingly, when I say no, one man is pleased.

"Good for you, children today are so bad: drugs, crime . . ."

We continue to chat, me in my very limited broken Italian and them in the local dialect, as my brain works overtime trying to comprehend what they say. As soon as enough time passes for me to make a polite escape, I bid them farewell.

"*Uno momento.*" One man raises his finger as a warning and says, "Remember, accidents happen. Be very careful."

It takes me a moment to register that he's giving me birth control advice!

"Grazie," I say, not knowing what would be an appropriate answer. I head off, wondering who else I may meet and what other sage advice I might receive today.

I don't have to wait long.

After dinner, there is a loud, determined knocking on the door—as if the *carabinieri* are on the other side, insisting we answer it pronto. We open up quickly before the door is kicked in.

We are stormed. Unfortunately, it is not the *carabinieri*, but in come *Zio* Luigi and *Zia* Franca.

"Whew, we're relieved. For a moment there, we thought you might not be at home."

They are still in disbelief that we did not come for dinner. They have come to rescue us from our dull existence.

"No TV, no phone! How are you managing?" *Zio* asks.

Barely twelve hours have passed since my in-laws left. I look longingly at the pile of books I brought, stacked by the fireplace, which *Zio* assumes are kindling.

Zio further proves why he had to rescue us. "What could a husband and a wife talk about all day?"

We offer him a coffee, and, despite the hour, he gladly accepts. As he pours in the grappa, his wife flashes him a concerned look. Undeterred, he smiles and says a coffee "must be *corretto*."

The first hour we are cross-examined and wish it had been the *carabinieri*, because if it were, the interrogation would be over by now. We explain several times why we could not make it today. They are not satisfied. Surely, we could have squeezed in lunch or dinner—or both. David's patience is being tested. I try to distract them by taking them into the dining room.

The chance to spy on my housekeeping skills seems to intrigue them. The conversation shifts to bounteous amounts of advice. *Zia* looks at the recently purchased dining room chairs and says, "Remember, if you ever have guests, put these chairs away and use the old ones from the kitchen."

Memories return to David of couches preserved in plastic, his skin sticking to them in the summer.

We pull up our hard little wooden stools and sit by the fire. *Zio* explains that heat is a bad thing, and *Zia* nods in agreement. *Zio* Luigi has an impeccable memory, for thirty-six years ago "when I was a shepherd traveling with the sheep, six other shepherds and I used to sleep under a bridge. There was a lady who brought us coffee every morning. One day she invited us for dinner. We didn't want to go, because we were dirty, but she threatened to stop bringing us coffee if we didn't come. So we went. We ate well and then went back to sleep under the bridge. Didn't I catch a bad cold the very next day! I'm sure it was because of the heat in this lady's home!"

I fear ever visiting *Zio*'s home in the dead of winter.

They now turn their energies to ensuring that we come for lunch and dinner tomorrow. After much wheeling and dealing, we settle on only dinner. Not satisfied at having secured a visit just for themselves, they remind us, "Don't forget to visit *Zia* Giuliana and *Zio* Domenico. They are old, so go soon!"

Before giving us a chance to respond, *Zio* asks, "When will you go?"

For further efficiency *Zia* directs her questions at me, while *Zio* concurrently directs his to David.

Zia now slyly summons me into the kitchen. She leans over and whispers, ensuring that no one else can hear: "Have you chosen not to have children, or, after much trying, are they just not coming?" She points to my stomach and says, "*Bimbi.*"

While I'm being interrogated in the kitchen, David is still held captive in the dining room. I can see him squirming.

After they depart five hours later, David does an inspection and concludes, "The shutters are all closed, the car is in the garage, so how did they know we were home? They must have seen some light."

He continues his assessment, while I decide it has been a long day, a long week, and a long month. I'm exhausted, having had to concentrate so intently on trying to understand not only Italian but the local dialect, spoken loudly and simultaneously by various people. My head hurts, and I'm off to bed.

Tomorrow, surely, our new life will start . . .

A BAD WIND

I AWAKE AND ROLL OVER next to David to keep warm. He isn't in bed, and his side is cold, indicating that he has already been up for a while. I feel a chill in the air, so I put on my thick robe and go into the kitchen. David is working with zeal on his latest project. He has stayed up all night, contemplating how *Zio* and *Zia* knew we were home. He must work really hard if he is to outsmart his relatives.

I look up in shock, saying, "What the heck?" The transom above the door is now covered in dark paper!

"That way, if we're in the dining room with a light on, it can't be seen from the side entrance. I'm sure this is what gave us away last night!" David triumphantly explains.

I begin to fear for him.

"Let's go for a walk," I suggest. "It may do you some good."

We walk past the little village precariously sticking out of the rocks, and I wave at my newfound acquaintances manning their bench. Now that my husband is with me, they refrain from doling out more birth control advice.

We walk down the mountain through fields of long-abandoned corn, which was obviously planted only for the government grant.

Below the "no hunting, rehabilitation area" sign, the ground is littered with numerous yellow and red shell casings from hunters' guns, left no doubt by the same Italians who complain that the beauty of Italy is being ruined by foreigners.

We walk past the Madonna who has been not so strategically placed on a blind curve, and we see men and women crossing themselves as they drive by at reckless speed. Someone recently placed fresh flowers at her feet.

At the bottom of the hill awaits our newfound canine friend, Briciola (crumb). Weeks ago, we drove past her house, and she excitedly chased our car, wriggling her little body and barking incessantly. We stopped and, her head lowered submissively, she approached with extreme caution, but it took no time for her to trust us. Now she joyfully runs over, trying to lick our faces, and accompanies us on the rest of our walk.

We meet Antonio. He looks rather glum, as he holds a string tied to three sheep.

"*Buongiorno*," we greet him.

He dejectedly explains his plight. "I borrowed the male sheep two weeks ago, but he is only interested in satisfying his voracious appetite and is not doing his duty. I give up, so now I'm returning him. The male would only follow if the other two came, because they have been together for the last two weeks." He's upset that he has been outsmarted by a sheep.

Looking at Antonio and his sheep, I think back to the days of the FIDO advertisement, where they published ads of dogs that looked like their owners. If FIDO were doing commercials of sheep and their owners, with his doleful, droopy face Antonio would surely take the prize.

We arrive at an ancient brown stone house, only three walls now standing, completely covered in overgrown ivy. Inside are three friendly and curious *cinghiali*, wild boars, which are no doubt being raised for a special *festa*. Briciola acts tough and growls, as she stands a safe distance away behind the fence.

David's cousin lives down the road from us, and for the last half hour, she has been driving back and forth, up and down the hill, passing us each time. Her baby is in the child seat. Her mission is accomplished; she points to the child, who is now sleeping. She does this every afternoon to put the two-year-old to sleep. With gas in Italy being double to triple the price in North America, no wonder it's so expensive to have children here.

We arrive back at Briciola's home and sit on some rocks. She jumps into my lap and turns over, waiting for us to pat her belly. We do, and she outwits me by planting a big wet lick on my face. David vows never to kiss me again. Pointing *tua casa* (your home), we sternly tell her to stay. She watches us with sad eyes and walks up the driveway to her house, stopping repeatedly to look back at us.

Soon I hear little footsteps behind us. Briciola! She can tell we aren't pleased and returns home. We don't want to be like Antonio, outsmarted by an animal.

We walk back up the hill, where our neighbor Luciano greets us. Despite the beauty of the day, doom and gloom are just around the corner. Shaking his head, Luciano says, "I feel compelled to warn you."

Alarmed, David asks, "What happened while we were gone?"

"Nothing, nothing," Luciano says. "It's just that I feel compelled to warn you that the wind can kill you. A bad wind is very dangerous."

We are puzzled, but Luciano reassures us, "No, actually you are safe here now. Ours is a clean wind."

We arrive back at the house, tired and hot, but still alive despite the wind and the short sleeves we dared to wear on an October day.

Not only have our relatives outsmarted us, but shortly after we arrive, Briciola squeezes her slim body through our gate and lies on her back, paws in the air.

"Leave her be," I say. "On our way to your uncle's tonight, we can drive her home."

Just before we head out for dinner, David's cousin Francesco drops in. He isn't feeling well and is hacking and coughing.

"Do you have a cold?" I ask.

"Yes, yesterday I caught a bad wind," he says.

We drop off the dog and head out for dinner, where we are outsmarted again. After several hours we start to leave, only to find our coats and wallets hidden. *Zia* has decided it isn't yet time to go.

Poor David—despite having worked so hard to get his Italian citizenship, I now have visions of him forfeiting it, acquiring forged passports, and seeing if we can get into the witness protection program.

MINING FOR TOMATOES

I NERVOUSLY INSPECT DAVID'S "REPAIRS" to the transom and wonder how long it will be before we are caught. Miraculously, so far no one has noticed. I attribute that to the abundance of *Zio*'s *caffè correttos* and his cousin's ill state, courtesy of the bad wind.

We hear a long, loud toot outside, immediately followed by more frantic honking. I want to climb a ladder and remove the dark paper, but just as I contemplate doing this, we see David's cousin Leonardo with his eighty-five-year-old mother, *Zia* Giuliana, at the door.

We invite them in, and David makes coffee, while I scurry around the kitchen attempting to look busy, lest I appear to be a lazy wife and hostess.

Leonardo is both a shepherd and a farmer, and I soon discover his fascination with grossing us out.

"Just yesterday I had to go in and save a calf during birth." He accompanies this statement with a full game of charades for our benefit. "Yup, I had to go right up there." To paint a vivid picture, he rolls up his sleeves, points his big rough hands upward, and illustrates "Right up there!" He regards our disgusted expressions with great pleasure, evidently amused by his city slicker cousin.

"Since you didn't come on your own, we came over to invite you for dinner!"

Zia Giuliana, generally a sweet older lady, slyly asks, "Do you remember how to get there?" It's a slight jab, because we haven't visited in almost ten days.

"*A dopo*! [See you later!]," says Leonardo and winks.

Ten more cousins, and soon we should be done.

I try to finish my breakfast, although—thanks to Leonardo and his gesturing—I have lost my appetite.

We hear more frenzied honking, followed by yelling.

"David! David! It's me, it's me."

Zio Luigi is here, along with *Zia* Franca. Despite the balmy weather, she is bundled in a down jacket with a fluffy fur collar. Her hair is dyed jet black, and her gold earrings stand in stark contrast. They have been to the market; thus, he's sporting a light-blue shirt, black pants, and a navy jacket. For a man in his seventies, he's in good shape, and with his dark tan he looks quite handsome.

I make them both an espresso, hers a long one and his a short one, thus allowing for a hearty pouring of grappa. I can see she doesn't approve of his self-diagnosis and looks at me as if to say, "What can I do?" He orders another espresso *corretto* and gets to the point of his visit.

"There is much work to be done in the garden. I'll be back after lunch. Be ready!"

Zia, meanwhile, is casually strolling through the house, her eyes wandering to any spot where dust may hide. Her inspection complete, she declares with a note of surprise, "You're doing well, all is clean and neat."

Nodding, she bids us, "*Ciao*." They make a sudden mad exodus. No last-minute reminders of visits to relatives, no long good-byes on the veranda; just a quick toot and *Zio* peels out into the street with mad furor, for it is approaching noon.

Soon thereafter, I receive a call from my in-laws. They compliment me on my housekeeping skills.

There will be no *pausa* today, for I hear the frenzied honking outside the gate. Lunch is over, and *Zio*, a man on a mission, is back.

No longer the elegant gentleman of this morning, he is now wearing his farmer's attire and is ready for business, his black toque perched just a tad too high on his head. A bundle of bendable and pliable twigs hangs from his belt, to tie the vines.

David is ready, despite the fact that gardening wasn't what he had in mind when he took a year off. Not having any of his own work clothes, he is wearing a pair of his father's pants, who is three sizes bigger than him. Giorgio's shirt is extra large and hangs on David. He and *Zio* are quite the pair.

We have faithfully been carting out organic waste and placing it directly in our garden, where we had visions of earthworms working away diligently. We thought we were helping to save planet earth and enhancing the soil.

Zio disapprovingly shouts, "Santa Maria, what are these chunks of food doing in the garden?" We give him the speech we were saving for our acceptance into one of the green groups.

"*Oh, my*," he says, with an all-knowing look. "Fortunately, I came by just in time to tell you to stop this nonsense before you completely ruin the garden."

And so our "composting" and feeling in harmony with the earth come to an abrupt end.

David and *Zio* get to work. Actually, it's mostly *Zio*, because David can't keep up with his elderly uncle. As *Zio* works on, he educates us about the dangers of all food purchased at the supermarket. "Full of *chimiche*" (chemicals). Spurred on, no doubt, by the mere thought of *chimiche*, he continues to work at a feverish pace. He looks at the flowers in the garden and disdainfully shakes his head. He points to the tomato vine and says, "Now that is something beautiful!"

They are preparing a tract of land to plant tomatoes for next year. "First, we must dig a foot and a half down by a foot and a half across," *Zio* explains. "The hole must be wide and deep, so that we can fill it up with manure, cover it with dirt, and let the manure ferment for a few months. So when we plant the tomatoes in April, they will just shoot up. Then we'll dig another hole about three feet deep at each end of the ditch."

David is exhausted after a few minutes, while *Zio* digs with tireless energy as if preparing a foundation for a Coliseum-like building. David pauses and rests his hands on his throbbing back.

"Though we're simply putting in posts that will support the row of tomatoes, the winds can get pretty fierce up here," *Zio* says earnestly.

"I've been here for a couple of windstorms, and sometimes it sounds like a tornado is going by. But these posts are so far down, they'll survive a nuclear blast," David says.

Zio, certain that David is joking, laughs heartily and keeps excavating.

They are finished with the arduous portion. Next, David will prepare an area to plant salad greens and then will rest his painful back.

Suddenly, I hear him scream, "Ouch!"

I rush out and see blood pouring from David's mouth. *Zio* had thrown down a rake, and David inadvertently stepped on it. Wham, it smashed his lip in two.

"I think my teeth are going to fall out!" he exclaims. I envision a toothless husband.

"We have to take you to the hospital to get some stitches," I say.

"No, no! I'll be fine," he slurs, as he tries to stop the flow of blood.

We have been battling Italian bureaucracy for the last few weeks, and he still doesn't have his health care in order.

"We can just pay, I'm sure it won't cost much," I beg him.

"I'm not going, and I can't talk anymore because my cut bleeds when I do." He holds a rag across his mouth.

"At least you don't have to dig anymore today," I console him.

Zio feels terrible and finishes up on his own, then heads home, clearly contrite because he even declines my offer of a *caffè corretto*.

David goes to the bedroom to lie down and, with his aching back, perhaps is even grateful for the cut lip.

Meanwhile, I begin my study of Italian with *Signor* Facci, my congenial teacher (as he is described in my book on learning Italian). Lesson two promises: "In this unit you will learn how to (1) Say who you are, (2) Ask who other people are, and (3) Deny something." I am learning how to deny things when I hear a knock at the door.

The "medics" have arrived. *Zio* Luigi is back with *Zia* Franca and for reinforcement has also brought along *Zia* Giuliana.

Feeling dreadfully responsible for David's current predicament, *Zio* Luigi has brought bags full of healing cures. They pull freshly made ricotta out of the medic's bag, followed by farm fresh eggs, and more homemade cheese. They explain, "This is what he needs to eat to heal the wound."

"He needs to pour olive oil on it to stop the bleeding and to close it up."

I was hoping they would convince David to go to the hospital. "I was thinking stitches may be necessary."

"No. Olive oil," all three insist in unison. "Lots of it, and he'll be fine," is their final conclusion. They also matter-of-factly say, "David should eat lots of ricotta. It helps with any illness, mental or physical."

On that note, the medics leave their patient to heal.

Much to my surprise, David's lip is soon much better.

Oddly, other Italians tell us that no one they know goes to all of this trouble for tomatoes. They grow so easily, all they really need is sun.

MANLY WILES

SINCE THE CUT LIP INCIDENT, David is obsessed with getting his health coverage, and soon.

His Italian passport, obtained while living in Canada, has rendered him an Italian living abroad. Though I am a Canadian living abroad, oddly enough I receive full health coverage.

"Get dressed," David says, "we'll be leaving soon."

He braces himself for the bureaucratic hurdles he'll no doubt have to jump.

Last time, the *signora* in charge told David to "fly back to Canada and remove himself from the list of Italians living abroad."

"What about sending a fax instead?" David asked.

"It would be easier for you just to go back," she said.

"Me getting on a plane is easier than you sending a fax?" David asked in disbelief.

Perplexed by the question, she said, "Yes."

Another response like that, and he will have a nervous breakdown and will *really* need that health card to go to the ER.

Hence, today he is on a serious mission to get his full coverage.

We arrive at the *comune* (municipal office) in record time. The ladies behind the counter flip through dusty books as if they are sincerely trying to help. We know better; the very design of the place is enough to make one give up. Three people work behind the glass, seemingly to serve you. Yet there is only one hole to speak through, so when these three workers gang up on the poor sap in front of the glass, eventually he surrenders. This time, however, they don't know who they are dealing with.

After weeks of conflicting suggestions, two things appear certain: David has to remove his name from the list of Italian citizens living abroad, and he needs proof of residence. He confidently pulls out a letter that his father had signed prior to leaving. It says that he is sponsoring David and as his host will care for him and that he will be residing at Via . . .

The sweet *Signora* Vincenza is behind glass for a good reason, because David would have reached over the counter and strangled her by now. After studying his father's letter for a moment, she says, "The wording is not quite correct."

"Pardon?" David says, and I fear for him now because I know from experience that word has never been well received by Italians.

"What needs to be said is that he is accepting you into his family," she explains.

David reads it to her again. "That is what the paper says."

"No, this simply says he is your host; therefore, you are a guest, not really a member of the family."

"But I'm his son!"

She is undeterred, and they're wearing David out. I suspect this will not be our last visit to the *comune*.

She confers with her colleagues. The three of them huddle like a football team on a timeout, determined to win the game. They discuss and debate and occasionally refer to the big dusty book. Twenty minutes pass. I pick up a brochure on Mafia compensation law. It describes a fund for victims of Mafia crime, and while they, of course, recognize no sum of money can replace a lost loved one . . .

David waits behind what we now deduce is surely bullet-proof glass. The conference is over, and *Signora* Vincenza returns.

"We have unanimously decided that the wording is not quite conclusive enough for us. Your father will have to sign a declaration accepting you into the family."

David is not amused and is certain they are making it up as they go. The *signora* offers him another option that includes leaving the country and yet more spurious paperwork. David breathes in deeply, trying to control himself. His disdain is evident by his furrowed eyebrows and the tone of his voice, as he tells me about the fabricated bureaucratic rule they are trying to convince him of.

I decide to intervene and teach him a thing or two about being Italian. I recall how David's father, who has much more experience in this area, conducted himself with women in government offices.

Here is where the story changes. Now it really should begin, "Once upon a time, in a land far, far away . . ."

My husband is a handsome man with a full head of dark, wavy, Italian soccer player's hair. He has dimples and a charming smile. He is simpatico. Time for a quick lesson in manly wiles, and then they'll be the ones who won't stand a chance!

Lesson one, courtesy of my father-in-law. You must lean into the window. It shows the women that you are relaxed and have full trust in their competence. To enhance the leaning, put one's hand on one's hip. This is a declaration that you want to save them from the cruel confines of their dusty old law books. It denotes understanding of their plight in this office and in their lives. This is the stance one must assume.

My husband looks at me and asks, "Are you giving me permission to flirt?"

Knowing this is our only chance, I say, "You better believe it!"

"Here goes," he says. As he turns back to the window, his stance changes. He smiles and leans, hand on hip, being utterly charming, an Italian prince! I watch them from afar. *Keep leaning, keep leaning!*

Voila—it has worked! They have now miraculously come up with a simple procedure and are asking him for his phone number in case they have any questions regarding his urgent matter.

Getting things done Italian style, lesson one!

The spell has been cast. In a sympathetic tone, the *signoras* now ask, "How is your lip? Do you still have a lot of pain?"

Meanwhile, in that land far, far away, there also lived a *vigile* (municipal officer). His job is to confirm that we do indeed reside where we claim to. That papà *has* accepted David into the family. Murmurings of his appearance begin to surface throughout the village, confirming the efficiency of the Italian neighborhood watch program. It's also clear evidence that part of the beast has been slain by the prince.

Finally, the *vigile* catches us at home. He is dressed in a formal uniform, similar to something a guard in a king or a queen's service might wear. He has on an impressive cap to match. I invite him in. He sees a pot on the stove, boiling away. The house is toasty, a roaring fire blazing in the fireplace. All are clear verifications of human habitation. He registers this as part of the proof that we really are living here.

As chance would have it, he has a cousin who lives in Canada. Suddenly, the *vigile*'s serious demeanor changes, and we are now *paesani*. His cousin, needless to say, would love to return but cannot at the moment. He discusses the superiority of life in Italy, and we wholeheartedly agree, perhaps quelling any regrets this man may have had about not going abroad. He now contently leaves our place. He will be giving a full report, indeed confirming that we are proudly living where we say we live.

Shortly thereafter, bona fide evidence of the beast being slain presents itself in our mailbox. David's laminated health card has arrived.

The Italian prince is enthralled. He has accomplished a Herculean task. He has slain the evil beast: Italian bureaucracy.

Hence, the prince lived happily ever after.

That is, until . . .

The Road to IKEA Is Paved with Good Intentions

We saw many signs before this one, but we unwisely ignored them. When Sonia and Salvatore first got into the car, they referred to each other as *this*—never a good sign in a marriage.

We had recently met Sonia, an African lady, and her much, much older Italian husband, Salvatore. After years of living abroad, he wanted to return to Italy. He was getting on in years, so it was time to come back home, "just in case." One may choose not to live in Italy, but, of course, one wants to die in Italy. He was encouraged to move by the sage advice in a famous Italian saying: a rabbit dies where it is born.

His years of living abroad are immediately evident to us. Unlike his *paesani*, with their smart fedoras, his long curly white hair is now creeping out from under a baseball cap with a team logo. Unlike his *paesani*, with their polished black shoes, worn even when riding one's bicycle, his stark white running shoes add to this foreign look. He reminds me of what an old, eccentric, retired Italian baseball coach would look like, if there were such a thing.

He moved Sonia and the children into his childhood home, which clearly had not been renovated since his youth. For three years, Sonia tried to convince him that perhaps it was time for a new kitchen, and at long last Salvatore agreed.

Sonia visited several kitchen stores, but despite many promises that someone would be out to measure her kitchen pronto, no one has arrived. Months have gone by. Poor Sonia is frustrated and thinks it's because she is obviously a foreigner. We fear she may be right, so we offer to help.

This can be a tricky matter, because if anything goes wrong, we are to blame. Yet we cannot watch her waiting in utter desperation. Thus, we mention IKEA. It is known for being reasonable and reliable: two virtues the local kitchen stores obviously do not possess. Because Salvatore no longer drives, we offer to chauffeur them the 120 kilometers (75 miles) to IKEA. Not wanting any surprises, for Salvatore, IKEA, or ourselves, we explain how the process works. Great: he has no problem with that. We are relieved, and we make plans to go. Then he says, "And once it is all installed, and I agree they have done a good job, then I will pay them!"

The sad part is that we can actually sympathize with Salvatore. We see his half-painted walls and cabinets hanging crookedly and the absence of a stall for his bathroom shower: trademarks of an Italian worker who was fully paid prior to having finished the job. Having been paid, the likelihood of his ever making an appearance again were slim.

Understanding Salvatore's plight, we try to reassure him. "This is a worldwide company. They are not out to rob the little guy. They have a money-back guarantee."

Yet nothing, but nothing we say will convince him. He adamantly sticks to his guns. "Once the job is done, they will get paid!"

Not wanting to be responsible for the eventual stroke that this man is going to give himself, we back off. Sonia then starts in.

To avoid getting caught in the crossfire, we leave, saying, "Discuss it amongst yourselves, and if you're willing to pay in advance, let us know."

Miraculously, Sonia convinces him. Prior to their being picked up, Salvatore goes to the bank. We proceed on our one-and-a-half-hour trek up to IKEA.

This should have been our second clue: when Salvatore enters the store, he sees an ad for a kitchen chair and yells, "29 euros! Boy, this place is bloody expensive!"

We find it odd that David and I are the only ones taking a real interest in the kitchen showrooms. Sonia and Salvatore just seem to be out on a casual stroll, looking up at the ceiling, down at the ground, and everywhere else but at the kitchen cabinets. We keep trying to bring them back to the matter at hand—namely, that they must choose a kitchen today. Finally, they pick the kitchen they like.

Now we have to configure it to work with their existing space. We make all of the decisions for them, and they occasionally glance at the drawings. IKEA will come up with a final price, and we will return after lunch to finalize the details and pay in advance for the new kitchen.

Lunch goes without a glitch. The Swedes have given in to the Italians and have placed bottles of olive oil on the tables. At the self-serve soda section, you can also get unlimited beer, a concept that would never work in Canada! I laugh as I envision the IKEA restaurant in Canada full of drunks repeatedly toasting IKEA in slurred voices.

Seeing that we are moments away from a small victory, we send the men to pay for the kitchen components, and Sonia and I wander through the market section. We pick up some items for the new kitchen, now that the job at hand has been accomplished. But alas, it is too good to be true.

I see my husband's less-than-amused face as he races toward us. Salvatore has not brought any money with him. No bank card, no check, and definitely no credit card. On top of this, he is persistently trying to haggle the price down, insisting he has a nephew who can install it for half price!

We know that old habits die hard, but we read him the law prior to our arrival. Sonia is mortified. "He went to the bank this morning, what the hell did he do there? What do we do now?" she asks me.

I whisper to David, "Let's turn him upside down and shake him hard to see if any money falls out."

We see a sign offering an IKEA credit card and, best of all, no fee. We head to the finance section to see if we can get Salvatore an IKEA credit card. No problem. He simply needs a few documents. Well, he has only one of them, and they are sorry, but they must deny him the credit card.

Salvatore screams at the top of his lungs, "IKEA can go to bloody hell!"

I think back longingly to the unlimited self-serve beer.

The mood is somber on the way back home. We are all dejected, Salvatore included. "To think they wouldn't give me a credit card! To think they wouldn't trust me to pay after delivery! The insults I have endured today!"

"What about the insults I endured yesterday?" Sonia says.

She has been having back problems lately. Her self-diagnosis involved everything from hernias to spinal disorders to slipped discs. Salvatore had given her his own diagnosis.

After they saw the doctor yesterday, Salvatore felt vindicated and happily announced what the doctor said, loud and clear for everyone in the waiting room to hear. "She is too fat! Yes, too fat. I told you so!" he added for emphasis.

Salvatore has forgotten all about IKEA today, and he has a new rant. "I told her she was too fat."

We wonder just how long it will be before Sonia tells *him* to go to bloody hell!

To add to our dark mood, the highway signs that normally advise motorists about traffic and weather conditions now warn us to drive carefully because on this very highway, sixty-eight people have died this year. Each and every sign on the entire route home is lit up with this gloomy message.

"IKEA CAN GO TO BLOODY HELL!"

IKEA CAN GO TO YOU-know-where—just not yet.

Salvatore had left his only piece of ID at that infernal place. He blames IKEA for this as well. Those people made him nervous and upset, and under those circumstances, *who wouldn't* forget his card?

Having correctly concluded that my husband's silence during the previous excruciatingly long ride home was clear evidence that he in no way could be asked to drive them back to IKEA, Sonia and her husband wisely make the trek on their own.

As it turns out, IKEA will nonetheless deliver their kitchen to them. Salvatore has now brought the three thousand euros with him, in cash. Maybe the last time he was worried that we would rob him.

Previously, I'd insisted that Sonia call IKEA so that the plans for their kitchen would be saved. Sonia never did call, so naturally their order is nowhere to be found. Fortunately, they bring the preliminary paperwork with them that they filled out last time. IKEA now spends two hours inputting these items into the computer, one by one, which frustrates

Salvatore to no end. He is losing confidence by the minute in IKEA, such an inefficient place!

According to IKEA, we had forgotten to include the kitchen counter in the original order. Therefore, the price now is 250 euros more than the previous quote. This could have happened because they originally wanted a granite counter and would stand for nothing less—that is, until the final price was calculated. Then, all of a sudden, the laminated countertops are just as good; one can hardly tell the difference.

Given all of the confusion, it is plausible that we forgot to add in the cost of the laminated counter, once we had taken out the granite one.

"Ha! That's an unlikely explanation," says Salvatore, shaking his fist. "Those crooks are out to get me! Again!" He suspects that IKEA has joined forces with the Mafia and is out to rob innocent, unsuspecting victims at every opportunity. He goes off on another tirade.

These ideas are inculcated at an early age. Salvatore's young daughter warned us not to buy chestnuts from street vendors, because her teacher told the students that the Mafia controls them.

Better not mess with the Mafia; thus, they leave their kitchen order "as is" and make their way home.

For inexplicable reasons, nothing is ever simple with these two. IKEA is right off the *autostrada*; you can't miss it. As they exit, Sonia and Salvatore do manage to miss the giant signs leading them to the *autostrada* only yards away, and they end up on a small country road. For further inexplicable reasons, they decide it will be too difficult to now find the *autostrada* and will have to take this road instead. As a result, it takes them three hours to get home. Again, Salvatore blames IKEA for this.

Once again, we offer to chauffeur them while they purchase other kitchen items. Within minutes, though, David is wondering how they ever got together to produce offspring!

Because Salvatore knows a shortcut, we travel along a back road in Abruzzo full of prostitutes offering their services. One is about sixty-five, sitting in the driver's seat of an old VW van and wearing an overflowing black bra, proudly showing off her stuff.

At the local store we browse and compare prices, the latter being very important, because no matter how little you pay, someone will always tell you how he paid half price for the very same item, and if only he had known. In circumstances like these, every Italian is an expert, but always after the fact.

According to the IKEA drawings, there is enough space left for a standard stove that sits between two cabinets. Sonia is confused. Tears flow down her cheeks, as she cries, "I wanted the type of stove that sits in the counter! The new kitchen is ruined, completely ruined!"

She never said a word about this type of stove while we were at IKEA, yet now she is too upset to even contemplate any other type of stove. She marches off, leaving the three of us standing there in astonishment.

The Latin blood in Salvatore now boils. His face gets even more red than usual, and he loudly declares, "The old kitchen was good enough for me! I don't need this!"

David and I realize: neither do we. Sonia has already left the store, so David and I follow suit, while Salvatore slowly shuffles behind us, the whole time muttering and shaking his head and his fist. I occasionally make out the words "bloody hell!"

Once again, the mood in the car is dour. I have an inkling IKEA will be seeing the likes of these two again, and I begin to feel sorry for the Mafia.

Having dropped off a very unhappy Sonia and an even unhappier Salvatore, we are not in the mood for any visitors tonight. The car is parked in the garage, and David has frantically run around the house and double-checked that all of the shutters are closed, recalling that visitors outsmarted us several times last week.

I'll have to keep the kitchen light off, because I removed the dark paper from the transom earlier, and I hope David doesn't notice.

After our experiences of the last few days, we will put off any further blood pressure–altering events and will go to the Questura (the immigration office) next week instead.

LA CASALINGA (THE HOUSEWIFE)

AS TIME GOES ON, I fear I'm turning into my mother-in-law.

I'd packed my large suitcases with only highly fashionable items, so that I could join the young, buxom Italian women with flowing white linen skirts and long wavy dark hair. Yet instead I seem to have mastered one of the other classic, timeless Italian looks: the *casalinga*.

In rural areas, the *casalinga* is the fashion of most women who are over sixty (me now being the exception) and buxom (again, me being the exception). The classic version begins with a straight, knee-length skirt, accompanied by mid-calf black socks with closed shoes. This dowdy look almost ensures that one's pasta sauce is just so, the gnocchi will melt in your mouth, and the pizza dough will be perfect! This outfit is a virtual guarantee that a woman is a wonderful cook.

For me, this look evolved by accident one day because my jeans were too tight. I traded them in for a skirt, and with the chill in the air, the socks and the shoes easily followed. People who see me are tempted to conclude that "forty is the new sixty."

With my *casalinga* style, I'm now quite adept at being an Italian housewife. I'm able to cook in two kitchens at the same time, which means I had to learn what to cook in the second kitchen. Peeling potatoes is ugly work, thus is done in kitchen number two. Fruit salad can be made in kitchen number one. Gnocchi are made in the second kitchen. Surprisingly, pizza dough or focaccia can be made in kitchen number one. Many women are banished to the second kitchens for the entire summer, because they don't want to heat up their houses in the hot weather.

As he does almost every day, *Zio* Luigi invites us to his home. This time it's under the guise of teaching us how to make ricotta, and I convince David to accept *this* invitation. A worthy *casalinga* must know how to make her own ricotta.

Zio is waiting for us in the old house, which is now used for storage and as a third kitchen. He dons his cheese-making outfit: compulsory knee-high rubber boots, a black woolly sweater, and a black toque. We are zealous students and watch as *Zio* begins. We ask for a sheet of paper so we can write down and then follow his recipe to a tee.

"I don't think we have any paper," he answers.

We see an old shelf haphazardly covered in paper. "Could we rip off a piece of this?" we ask, only to be polite.

He contemplates this request a moment and reluctantly replies, "Well, maybe just a little." He tears off a piece the size of my thumb.

The rest of the process is no easier. His measurements consist of "fill it up to about here." He takes my finger and sticks it into the sheep's milk and says, "Then get the temperature about this warm." I'm desperately trying to figure out what to write, in the most minuscule handwriting, when he says, "Make sure you follow the recipe precisely, or it won't work."

Perhaps that's why, at the end, he uses a long wooden spoon to make the sign of the cross over the pot of ricotta, while chanting a short prayer: "in the name of . . . ,"

Zio enjoys the attention we give him and seems convinced that he manifests the creative genius of Michelangelo himself. To reward us for being diligent students, *Zio* decides to show us his secret stash. He opens the door, leads us to a dark room, and turns on the lights. Then he spreads his arms expansively like a game show hostess to encompass all of his cheeses. Rounds and rounds of cheese lay on an ancient solid-wood table.

"Can we take a picture of you and the cheese?" I ask.

Zio, now a poster boy for cheese, smiles and picks up the biggest round, then raises it in the air with one arm.

"*Grazie*," I say.

But *Zio* is just getting warmed up. He promptly heads over to several prosciuttos that are being salted and again leans across the meat, waiting for me to take another picture. The *capicollo* receives the same loving treatment. With both hands, he holds up a large jar of anchovies, accompanied by an *Italian Vogue* smile. *Zio* examines each photo, and if he isn't satisfied, he readjusts his black toque and has us retake the shot. Finally, he leads us to the room where the potatoes are stored, with shoots bursting out of them, and *Zio* poses one last time with his creations.

I guess I shouldn't fear turning into a *casalinga*. There is simply too much to learn and, with lessons like these, no real way to learn it.

I'm growing to accept this, as I get more acquainted with the world of a *casalinga*. The hours are grueling, and retirement never comes. Long after the husband has finished his duties outdoors, the *casalinga* is still inside, serving him and the children, hand and foot. While others lounge at the table after dinner, she hustles to clear it and then washes the tall stack of dishes by hand, regardless of whether or not she has a dishwasher. When she gets older, this scene does not change—only the number of people she slaves over increases. The grown children now arrive with their mates and their children and possibly *their* children.

As the family grows larger, the *casalinga* will jar that many more tomatoes, peppers, and other preserves, because surely the children cannot be expected to purchase and eat the stuff sold at the supermarket, so full of chemicals. She will do all of this while looking after the grandchildren who are dropped off at her house daily.

And, after years of saving and now with a ton of money under her mattress, she will always think twice before buying herself anything, though she willingly indulges every whim and wish of her children and grandchildren.

So, on further reflection, I realize that *casalinga* is neither a title nor a role I would choose for myself. *Americana* will suit me just fine!

SANGUE ITALIANO (ITALIAN BLOOD)

I NOW REALIZE IT'S IN David's blood. *Sangue Italiano*. I must bear some responsibility, for I'm the one who convinced him he is Italian.

The birds are having a convention outside and show no respect for those of us who are still asleep. The red sun is rising above the valley. I look forward to another day, as I hear the espresso machine grinding and David making coffee.

After I get up, I start my leisurely preparations for lunch. I mix the dough for the focaccia and survey the refrigerator. Italian cooking is liberating; one simply cooks what one has. Pasta with homemade tomato sauce, some sliced prosciutto and pecorino. I gaze out the window at the mountainside and sigh deeply, again grateful for this year off. The peace, the quiet, the stress-free life!

I walk to our mailbox, ever hopeful. There is an envelope with our car insurance renewal and an invoice. Today is February 8, and the insurance expired February 5. Everything is a little slow here.

In the afternoon we take a luxurious, yet now mandatory, *pausa*. Then later we will go to visit some new friends. I love Italy, I love my Italian husband.

Minutes after we leave our driveway, I'm brought back to reality, I *am* married to an Italian. *Almost* everything is slow here.

David, a chip off the old block, appears to have turned into his father. The driving lessons he so resented now come in handy. As he changes gears, the Fiat engine roars. David looks at me and smiles. "Just trying to keep momentum."

Bouquets of flowers placed on roadside shrines to accident victims only add to my anxiety. Just moments ago, we had all the time in the world. I drank my *caffè latte* for two hours, I baked bread. My husband played solitaire. Why now the mad rush? *Sangue Italiano*.

David drives through a small town, madly swerving to avoid parked cars that protrude into the street. The vehicles were left there by Italian drivers who apparently want to cause maximum inconvenience for others.

Miraculously, we exit the town without hitting anything. I breathe a sigh of relief. We are back on country roads, and within minutes I hear him say, "Momentum, momentum!" The engine rumbles, while I pray for a flat tire.

I'm not sure where to look. There is a car on our tail, but ahead another car is coming straight at us while passing. I opt for the side view, with its countless roadside bouquets.

We come to an abrupt stop at our first destination. Despite our begging, our hosts refused to give us an address and instead insisted we meet up with others on the side of the road.

"It will be too difficult for you to find," they said.

Due to our punctuality and David's driving, we arrive long before anyone else does.

After a half hour, we see some familiar faces.

"*Ciao!*" they greet us.

"*Ciao*," we say, trying to hide our irritation.

"So, you know where Giacomo lives?" I ask.

"No. But Daniele does, and he should be here soon."

I put on a fake smile and try to stop my stomach from growling.

We wait impatiently—David and I, that is. Emanuela is chatting away happily on her cell phone, and her husband, Paolo, is doing the same. When another one goes off, Emanuela pulls several phones out of her bag, not certain which one is ringing. With the ease of a switchboard operator, she goes back and forth between calls.

Soon, more lights approach.

"*Ciao*, Daniele," I hear. I'm grateful that our navigator has arrived, for it is well past 8 p.m., and I'm really hungry. Daniele gets out of his car and leisurely greets us, then chats with Emanuela and Paolo.

"What's going on?" I ask David.

"I don't know," he replies.

"I knew we should have squeezed the address out of them."

A shiny black Mercedes pulls up and parks in what we have now turned into a parking lot. It is the ever-fashionable and fashionably late couple Martina and Fabrizio. They recently moved here from Milan but quickly adapted to the concept of time in the south. Martina exits the car like a movie star. She has on skinny four-inch-high heels, slim-fitting jeans with sequins, a large fur collar draped around her neck, and oversized dark sunglasses perched on her head. She greets every one of us, planting a kiss on both cheeks.

After a bit more conversation, at last we are ready to go. I look at my watch and vow never to do this again.

The convoy heads toward the highway, with our poor little Fiat following a Mercedes, a Volvo, and an Alfa Romeo. These cars pull onto the road and zoom away, while our Fiat tries to keep up. The speed limit is 80 mph, though I fear the members of our party consider this merely a suggestion.

The Mercedes driver weaves in and out of the passing lane to overtake cars he deems too slow. The other three cars follow him. Our Fiat is making tortured sounds. Memories of

David's childhood return: long processions of relatives driving to Niagara Falls, arguing about who will lead the convoy, with no one wanting the blame for inevitably getting everyone lost.

Now I'm wondering whether we're even following the right car. "This is easier than giving us an address and directions?"

David is silent, perhaps secretly enjoying the fact that he can drive so fast.

With visions of my life ending before the year is up, I phone Daniele and say, "Sorry, we've lost you."

He responds as expected, but I'm adamant: "No, we will *not* be catching up! Give us the name of the exit, and we'll meet you there."

Disappointed, he tells us which exit to take. I vow that this will be the last time we travel to an unknown destination at an unmentionable velocity.

Now it's their turn to wait. After what must seem like an eternity to them, we arrive and join the convoy. Just ahead is a group of houses in a small village, and Giacomo and his family are waiting outside.

"I was worried," he says. I suspect that people will blame our slow driving for everyone being so late.

We are greeted by the entire family and perhaps the entire village. I've noticed that whenever there aren't enough family members to come to dinner on any given night, Italians will import friends, neighbors, or acquaintances to fill spots at the table. This evening is no exception.

After several hours of food and laughter, it's time to go. Now that we know where we are, we realize we could have taken a much shorter route, one that didn't entail speeding down the highway. Happy to be driving and in control again, I cruise through ancient little towns with their lights glimmering in the darkness. A light fog adds to the mystique.

Just ahead is a road check, with half a dozen policemen armed with submachine guns. *Be calm,* I think, *you have done nothing wrong. In fact, you are the only person in the whole country driving the speed limit.*

I show one policeman my newly purchased international driver's license, and he lets us pass. With two pictures, fifteen dollars, and no instructions whatsoever, you enter the world of Italian driving.

With me at the wheel, it takes us twice as long to get home, and I can tell David is exhausted when it's over.

My only consolation is that even after our high-speed chase, David isn't fantasizing about a new sports car. In the morning, he tells me that if we ever decide to live here permanently, he would like to buy a tractor.

"A big powerful tractor," he says—as if there was any doubt about that.

Pink Socks and Green Pajamas

Feeling cut off from the wider world and going slightly stir crazy, we decide to buy an old computer. Our friends know just the man, but they warn us that he is rather peculiar and lives alone, way up in the hills. As usual, we are not given an address but meet him in a parking lot.

I'm surprised to see that Mike is a tall, well-dressed, handsome American man—not what I had expected. We make a deal and choose one of the ancient computers in his trunk. The three of us go to have coffee in the piazza. Mike appears uneasy as we sit in the bar, but nonetheless he stays and proves to be a wealth of information on where to find brand-name items for next to nothing.

"What made you move to Italy?" I ask.

"Let's say, American law made me move," he answers with a wink.

"Oh," I say. Lovely —the man we just bought our computer from is an American fugitive.

"Listen, let's get together again real soon and hang out," says Mike.

Not wanting to encourage any further friendship or business dealings with Mike, we tell him that we'll be leaving town for a while. This inspires us to finally visit Rome.

"Ah, a vacation from your vacation," our friends remark.

We had been to Rome several times in the past but merely spent time visiting relatives and eating double helpings of pasta in the cement suburbs. We'd missed the historic city center, the museums with their awe-inspiring art, the grand piazzas, the world-famous monuments, and the *caffès* with their chic clientele. This time will be different.

To save money, though, we nonetheless ask *Zia* Rosa if we can stay with her.

We drive through winding mountain roads for two and half hours and finally arrive in the countryside just outside the city. Umbrella pine trees jut from hilltops. We pass old villas that have seen better times, before the land around them was swallowed up by highways and subdivisions, and before the advent of graffiti artists. One of the taggers' more profound lines reads, "Every time you drink Coca Cola you are their accomplices." En route, we find many similar philosophical statements.

We are abruptly introduced to driving Roman style as we enter the Grande Raccordo, the highway that encircles historic Rome. David politely tries to merge into the circle. After several failed attempts, he remembers our friend's advice: "Close your eyes, pray, and go for it." I open my eyes, and, unharmed, we have now merged. The speed limit is fifty km (31 mph), yet every car on the road is driving at least twice that fast. To keep up, we are forced to speed as well.

Our exit is just ahead, and David must cross over several lanes. Ignoring our pleas, cousin Francesco had refused to give us an exact address. "It will be too hard to find. *Zia* will meet you at the Sma supermarket instead."

We now search for the Sma, again without an exact address. We eventually find it and see *Zia* standing outside. It is unseasonably warm, yet she has on far too many clothes. She has pitch-black hair freshly done in rollers, heavy gold earrings on that make her earlobes droop, and the same black running shoes that my mother-in-law wears.

"Ciao, *Zia*," we greet her, with the customary double kiss.

Yet she has no time for pleasantries. "Dinner is on the table. *Zio* Mario is waiting."

Quicker than a twenty-year-old, she hops into our car. We drive down steep hills, and two miles later we reach her home.

I ask, "Who drove you to the Sma?"

"I walked," she says casually.

I want to strangle Francesco for assuming it's easier for a woman in her mid seventies to walk two miles up steep hills, rather than to give David and me directions.

I've always dreamed about going to Rome: *We arrive at the Ritz Carlton Roma and check in. The hotel is gorgeous, luxurious, and grand. A bellhop takes our luggage to our room. David and I go down to the bar for a vodka martini and the best appetizers we have ever eaten.*

Reality at Hotel *Zio* and *Zia* is slightly different. We arrive at the gray compound, consisting of six apartments protected by an impregnable gate. The only grandeur is displayed in the travertine stairs and the granite floors, each room in a different color. We carry our own luggage to our room and then hurry to the small crowded kitchen to eat good food, accompanied by terribly bad, almost undrinkable wine that *Zio* praises as if it is the elixir of the gods!

While *Zio* pontificates on the virtue of his wine, *Zia* gives me a lesson in the saints' names.

"*Santa Maria, Sant' Antonio!*" she yells and rushes me back to the bedroom with the speed of an Italian ambulance driver. There, she gives me a pair of home-knit socks.

"How could you come out with no socks on?" she asks, shocked at my blatant disregard for the precious life God has given me. She puts the baby-pink knit socks on my feet, all the while shaking her head. "The bladder, the bladder!"

She hustles me back into the kitchen. *Zio* is at the table, knife and fork in hand, his patience being tested because it is minutes past the hour when he normally eats.

Zia has made enough pizza for a dozen people and is determined that we eat all of it. Not even my used and scrunched-up paper napkin, strategically placed in the center of my plate, is enough to discourage her.

"C'mon, you must eat more!" She shakes her head in disdain, removes my dirty napkin, and puts down another large slice of pizza.

"Children today are so spoiled, they won't even eat the fat on a piece of prosciutto," says *Zia*.

I glance down at my plate and the pile of white fat I have removed from the meat.

We discuss inheritance laws. Under Italian law, the surviving spouse *and* the children are automatically entitled to a fixed share of the deceased's assets, regardless of his or her wishes as stated in the will. We find it odd that you and your mate could work for something your whole life, and some derelict child could end up with a sizable portion of the estate while one mate is still alive and kicking. Italians find it normal, though, unfortunately, inheritance disputes often occur.

Over the horribly bad wine, conversation revolves mainly around the superiority of all things Italian—this despite the TV news blaring in the background about government corruption, angry protesters in Rome, the deplorable living conditions of some of the elderly in Milan, and countless other stories of violence, racism, unemployment, drugs, and scandals. Intermittently, between proclaiming what vastly better lives David and I would have if we stayed in Italy, they shake their heads in disgust and yell various saints' names at each news clip.

According to *Zio*, when he was on death's door a few months ago his life was saved by a miracle straight from heaven. He is always just moments away from being made a saint; for this reason, he naturally has a lot to say before this happens. "There must be a reason why God himself spared my life at the very last minute."

Zia Rosa is not paying him any mind, so poor David is held captive as *Zio* competes with the blaring TV.

My head is aching, so I excuse myself to go take a quick shower. I was informed that *Zio* may have to use the bathroom at the same time, so all of my visits there need to be quick. In my haste, I reach for some shampoo on a high shelf and almost knock over a glass holding a set of false teeth. I wonder whether the price we're paying to stay here is too high after all.

We offer *Zia* the gift baskets we brought. She surveys them and says, "You shouldn't have," then remarks, "Fine, I will give these to my daughter tomorrow when I visit her."

She takes us on a thorough tour and shows us the old, crusty-looking cloth we must use before sitting on the toilet. "My husband has a tendency to sprinkle," she says, then shrugs and raises her palms upward. "I can't kill him, so I have to put up with him for now!"

Several evenings pass, and David devises a plan to avoid being held hostage for hours again. He avoids eye contact with *Zio*. It works, and *Zio* now tells his stories to me. The fact that I don't speak much Italian doesn't faze him. He tells me story after story. Looking for sympathy, he explains how he has wasted away to nothing since his illness: he is now half the man he used to be. Judging by his current weight-to-height ratio, he is still vastly "under tall."

We are woken abruptly in the wee hours of the morning. *Zia* and *Zio* are having some work done in the apartment above us. I lie still and enjoy the warmth that can only be found in a bed here. Precious money is not spent on frivolous things like heat.

Due to the construction, we don't see *Zio* in the mornings, and he is terribly apologetic. He leaves at an ungodly hour as the plumber begins demolishing. He supervises the workers the minute they arrive and right up to the minute they leave. He waddles back and forth, watching them with eagle eyes. He knows little about their trades but has perfected the art of hovering.

Zia, too, has been enlisted to work, because *Zio*—being an older Italian man—has to eat pronto at twelve. Yet he cannot leave the workers unsupervised upstairs even for a minute, so *Zia* will cook for all of them, and they must congregate to eat in her tiny kitchen.

We leave for the day. When we return, I discover that my bed-making skills must not be up to par, because the bed has been completely remade. Our pajamas are no longer under the pillows and are laid across the not-so-toasty radiator.

While we were out, *Zia* evidently studied my nightgown and decided it would not do. "Your nightgown is not warm enough; you need pajamas so that you can tuck them into your pants and protect your back." I am chastised again for my disregard of both external and internal organs. *There are an awful lot of body parts one needs to protect in Italy.*

The next day, two presents are sitting on our bed—for me, a pair of bright-green fuzzy pajamas. I put them on and bear a resemblance to a giant frog. I show them to *Zia*, and she is pleased.

"You just need to tuck the top into the bottoms," she says.

I obey and now resemble a giant *pregnant* frog. With my new pajamas and my baby-pink wool socks, I am informed that my insides are now safe. David, too, has received a pair of pajamas in a ghastly color, suitable for arctic conditions. Romance in Rome will just have to wait.

After a couple of days, *Zia* anxiously rushes into our room and says, "I'm so sorry, I forgot to tell you not to use the pink hand towel in the bathroom." Indeed, the very one we have been using for the last few days!

"My husband has a very contagious eye infection, and that's his towel, so make sure not to use it."

Mortified, we now carry our hand towels in and out of our bedroom, not sure whether *Zio* might also be color blind, along with his other problems.

Time passes, and we survive life at *Zia* and *Zio*'s. We do the math for the cost of a hotel in Rome and are grateful for their hospitality. Thanks to the unsolicited wake-up call each morning, we always got an early start and saw a lot of the city.

After a week in Rome, we are in total agreement with our guidebook: "Rome is probably the most fascinating city in Italy—which arguably makes it the most fascinating city in the world."

WHERE THERE IS SMOKE, THERE IS FIRE

WE RETURN FROM ROME TO a cold welcome; inside our house, the thermometer reads fifty degrees Fahrenheit. Our breath is visible in small clouds. I keep my coat and hat on and prepare for the cold evening ahead. David starts the fire, hoping that before we go to sleep, the house will warm up, at least slightly.

We seek the only reasonable course of action and plant ourselves on two hard stools near the fire with glasses of wine. To distract myself from the cold, I get my mystery novel and mentally travel to Bologna with Marco. I picture myself there, walking under the porticoes, stopping for a hot cappuccino in a hip bar to warm up.

Possibly distracted by Marco or carbon monoxide, neither of us gives heed to the warning signs. It's a bit smoky in here; we will simply close the hallway door when retiring.

By morning, the fire has gone out, and all that remains are some hot red coals. Despite our having stoked the fire all evening, the thermometer reads a cool sixty degrees Fahrenheit, outright balmy by *Zia* Rosa's and *Zio* Mario's standards. David adds some kindling and awaits the roaring flames. I now see David through a haze.

"Is everything okay in here?"

"Yes, just a bit smoky," he says and adds some heavy logs.

Soon the entire villa is filled with thick smoke. In true form, a car from the neighborhood watch program pulls up and stops outside. Two unknown ladies rush to our aid. The chimney pipes are glowing bright red. Carrying a ladder, a neighbor runs over, ready and willing to help. Within minutes, we have a full team of "firefighters" who are prepared to save our villa.

David runs to the roof. We all rush up and down ladders, carrying buckets of water to throw on the red-hot flames. As the water hits the blistering hot pipes, it evaporates. Our volunteer firefighters valiantly continue their battle, buckets in hand. After much heroic effort on everyone's part, the chimney cools down, occasionally hissing as the flames in it die.

With trepidation, I survey the dining room. It's filled with water and dark smoke, but nothing that a mop and a good cross breeze cannot fix. I'm suddenly a great fan of cement and ceramic.

We offer our "firefighters" a coffee and some sweets, and they gladly accept. We sit and chat in the smoke-filled kitchen and drink espresso. Smoke swirls around our heads, and every so often we wave it away. Soon we are the best of friends. As people leave, they give us their phone numbers and insist that we come for dinner. Our neighbor profusely thanks us for the coffee and our hospitality, then ventures home.

Emma has seen the smoke and comes to our aid, in her own way. She brings us lunch: homemade focaccia from her wood oven, polenta smothered in a creamy porcini mushroom sauce, and a cake.

When I contemplate today's events, I hope that *Zio* Luigi and *Zia* Franca don't get wind of what happened. I'm certain they will, however, so I wait in dread for the inevitable phone call from my in-laws.

THE ROAD OF LOVE

WE TAKE OUR *PAUSA* IN the only room that doesn't smell of smoke, our bedroom, at the opposite end of the house.

After our nap, we get ready to go out for dinner. Word has spread that *Americani* are here, and though they abound in Tuscany, they are rare in these parts. Hence, some friends want to introduce us to the De Lucas, members of a local family who are learning English. Our clothes smell like smoke, but we put them on anyway and leave, reeking of *eau de campfire*.

Surprisingly, our friends give us directions to the house. Yet although these seem straightforward, we get lost. We see a lady ahead and slow down to ask for directions, but then we notice several more "ladies" on this remote industrial street. White women on the left, black ones on the right. Roaring fires burn in barrels, warming their scantily clad bodies. Some of the women jump in front of our car and shake their half-naked butts at us.

We cautiously approach a man exiting a factory. He confirms that we are going the wrong way and must turn around. This gives hope to the ladies on the other side of the street, who see our car lights approaching. I authorize David to speed up.

We notice an older gentleman on his balcony and say we are looking for number 30. He yells to his wife, "Maria, these people are looking for number 30! Where is number 30?"

She runs out, keen to help. "I don't know," she replies.

"Well, what number are you?" I ask.

There is silence. She runs inside to get a piece of mail. Much to everyone's astonishment, she declares, "Oh, we're number 30!"

So we have found our destination. Indeed, now we see our friend standing outside the main entrance of the building, frantically calling us on his cell phone. He no doubt regrets having given us an exact address.

"*Ciao!* Sorry we're late, we went left when we should have gone right and ended up on a road full of prostitutes."

"Oh, the Road of Love," he says with a laugh.

He invites us in and introduces us. Massimo, the father is dark, well nourished, and, despite looking like someone out of a *Godfather* movie, sweet and jovial. His wife, Sofia, is a bundle of energy, with fierce dark eyes, her Latin blood evident. She laughs hysterically no matter what we say. Their teenage daughter is text-messaging, giving her parents a false sense of security. They assume she could never be up to any no good on a phone. Regardless, she takes time to greet us. Alessandro, their son, is nine years old and looks like the boy in the film *Cinema Paradiso*. With ardent brown eyes, he holds out his small hand for us to shake and asks, "How are you?" in a thick Italian accent. We cannot help but smile. He collects soccer cards and is fervently scribbling down numbers that are duplicates, ready to trade these in for new heroes.

We laugh all evening. Everyone is highly amused by my husband's made-up words. Italians living in Canada Italianize a word by adding a vowel at the end. Hence, *truck* becomes *trucko, front room* becomes *fronta rooma*. David is certain these words are Italian, having heard them spoken by his parents his entire life. Alessandro, though, is quick to complement us on our Italian.

The children stay with us the entire evening, eating what we eat and joining our conversation.

Sofia's tone turns serious as she notices David's lip, which is still a bit swollen and hasn't healed perfectly. We relate the story of planting tomatoes deep under the earth's surface.

Massimo understands, for he, too, wanted to provide healthy, *chimiche*-free food for his family—the only problem being that he doesn't own any land because they live in a small condominium.

He winks. "I took a piece of city land near where I work, so that I would have lots of time to care for my garden."

The plants soon sprouted, and he waited for his first harvest. But Massimo wasn't the only one watching and waiting. He gave the sweet peas a few more days to fully ripen, but when he returned, the sweet peas were all gone.

"The thief didn't even have the courtesy to just pick the peas, but ripped out the whole plant, probably because he was in a hurry. I was so mad!"

That thief must like to live dangerously. *I* sure wouldn't want to mess with Massimo.

He hoped this was a one-time occurrence and that the thief's tastes would stop at sweet peas. Yet with each new harvest, the thief helped himself to the fruits of Massimo's labor.

"I thought about putting a fence around the garden, but since I took the city land illegally, I figured I'd better not. So I put the word out that I didn't mind if they stole some of it, I'd still do the garden, as long as they left me a little."

Apparently, however, there is no honor among thieves. They continued to steal fruit and vegetables from Massimo's garden plot.

Watching the melons grow and mature and knowing he would never enjoy their sweetness, he devised a plan. He arrived early and, making sure no onlookers could see, he took out a syringe full of a clear liquid. He injected every melon with his concoction.

Massimo left his garden wearing an evil grin. His face lights up now as he recounts the story's happy ending.

"Revenge would be mine at last, as I pictured the thieves at their next destination . . . the toilet! The clear liquid was a laxative, a very effective one, the best on the market! I'm sure that to this day, those thieves do not eat melon!" he says and roars like a madman.

We, too, laugh until it hurts. It is now late, so we tell everyone good night. They beg us to stay longer. We are exhausted and insist we must leave. They refuse to let us go, literally clutching onto us. After all, *Americani* are very rare in these remote parts. We promise to keep in touch, and after a half hour of chatting by the door, we kiss them one last time, the other good-bye kisses having expired by now.

We remember to take the right road home and avoid the Road of Love.

THE CLASH OF THE FASHIONS

TODAY I CONVINCE DAVID TO accompany me to the market in the well-heeled coastal town San Benedetto del Tronto. We can also thank his cousin Simona and her husband, Gabriele, for prompting this shopping excursion, because they both asked David, "Whose suits are you borrowing?" The "comfort fit" is not appreciated in Italy, and they described his current suit as "scandalous." With that moniker popping into his head every time he donned his suit, David finally agreed to purchase a new one.

We aren't the only ones heading to the market—for many, the Italian social event of the week—and traffic is horrendous. The neighborhood bakery certainly attracts its share of people dressed by *Italian Vogue*. Arriving on ancient bicycles, older men wear fine jackets and hats, some with ties, and shoes just polished. The elderly ladies have freshly coiffed hair and fur-adorned puffy jackets; both men and women wear large sunglasses. They carry hot loaves of bread in the baskets of their bicycles, next to other items purchased for today's menu. Waiting in line, mothers dressed like fashion queens toss their long thick hair and push fancy strollers showing off their children; the two-year-old *bambina* in her stroller also wears big sunglasses.

The fashion show continues at the bar, which is crowded with people fighting their way to the counter to place their orders. Then they stand there, each downing a shot of espresso accompanied by a pastry to begin the day.

Attired from head to toe in the latest colors of spandex, cyclists take over the road and block traffic. David's patience is tested.

It is eighty-four degrees today, but Italian fashion is evidently not dictated by the weather but by the fashion season. Thus, everyone is wearing the fall/winter collections: puffy parkas, layered scarves, and boots. A priest walks by, and even he is dressed in the de rigueur black puffy jacket with a fur collar on top of his long black cloak.

An eighty-year-old with deep wrinkles in her bronzed skin happily drives her *motorino*. Her long gray hair sticks out of a helmet, and her scarf flows in the wind. I would like to grow old in Italy, for there is something dignified about it. Despite keeping up with the latest fashion trends, women don't seem to be on a mad quest to stay young. I notice new wrinkles on what was previously my fresh youthful skin, such a short time ago. Time goes by all too quickly, and it's comforting to accept aging gracefully. No botox—all I need to do is buy a big fur collar and oversized sunglasses.

Pet owners, too, are out for their strolls, many paying no mind to the gifts left behind by their animals on the cobblestone streets. An older *signora* hangs her laundry on long bamboo sticks, resting the other end on her neighbor's window, several feet across from hers.

Finally, we arrive at the main piazza. The parking lot is paved in travertine, so our little Fiat should rest happily there for the next few hours.

We head to the market. The regulars are here: the Senegalese selling their fake brand-name purses and pirated CDs and the Chinese with shoes and clothing. The Italians profess great disdain for the latter, though I suspect that some of their newly purchased items are indeed from the PRC. The Italians barter with everyone, except with other

Italians. Handwritten signs proclaim 100 percent made in Italy—ironically, even at the Chinese stall.

I buy a lovely pair of patent leather boots and wait for my receipt, having heard many frightening stories about the Guardia di Finanza (Finance Guard). The saleslady digs into a drawer, grabs a receipt, scribbles something on it, and hands it to me. After I leave, I notice the date has been changed, and the receipt for my one hundred euro boots reads twenty euros. If I get stopped, I hope the Guardia di Finanza know nothing about the cost of boots these days.

Despite the market still being full of people, it is nearing twelve-thirty, and the sellers are packing up their stands to go home for the sacred lunch hour and *pausa*. I think back to my working days on the Canadian equivalent of Wall Street and my boss repeatedly chanting, "Money never sleeps." I imagine the look on his face as all of the stalls close and the workforce goes home to eat and take a nap. Then I picture the cardiac arrest that would surely follow.

We return to the ancient square that is now completely vacant. Moments ago, it was teeming with life, with groups of older men huddled in the piazza. We eat our *porchetta* sandwich—slices cut off a whole roasted pig—and enjoy our private piazza, ever grateful that money *does* sleep here.

Since we have not accomplished our mission, David calls Simona to ask where else we can go to buy a suit. Only too happy to accompany us, she will take us to her husband's favorite store—called, oddly enough, Sonny Bono.

Anxious to give her "American" cousin a makeover, Simona drives with reckless speed while text messaging. I'm envisioning one of those tailored suits that makes everyone here look slim and trim.

Though David's blood may be 100 percent Italian, the fact that he was raised in North America soon becomes evident. He picks a dark suit with light gray pinstripes and comes out of the dressing room wearing a jacket that fits perfectly. The slim fit looks good. *We will soon be able to join the ranks of the fashionable masses sipping wine in enotecas* (wine bars). Then he tries on the slim-cut pants. From the dressing room, he asks, "Can you bring me another pair of pants, one size larger?"

I bring him the next size up, and he tries them on.

He emerges from the dressing room, and Simona, who has been talking on her cell phone, now urgently tells the caller, "I have to go," and hangs up. The pants do not match the jacket; they are loose and out of proportion to the suit.

"Yes, these feel much better," David happily says, pulling them out in front to show us he has plenty of room to grow.

I apprehensively say, "The other pants looked better."

"The other ones fit just right, but these are way more comfortable," he protests.

Simona is a young, hip, fashionable Italian girl who does not mince words with her cousin. "You already have your dad's suit at home. Get the other pants." She grabs the smaller size and takes them up to the cashier.

Outnumbered, the poor guy who just wanted a bit of "breathing room" doesn't stand a chance.

Simona now brings him an extra-large pair of black sunglasses. "Try them on."

Surprisingly, he does, then looks in the mirror and says, "I already own safety glasses, so I don't need a second pair."

To finish off the day on a pleasant note, we go for a gelato. We join the throngs in their winter coats lining up for ice cream. Remembering the slim-fit pants, I forgo the medium and order us two small ones.

The gelato is wonderful, and so is the ambiance: funky modern crystal lights suspended from ancient vaulted ceilings built of bricks, a perfect blend of new and old.

A man of about fifty wearing construction clothes comes in. Judging from his proportions, this is not his first encounter with ice cream shops. He carefully evaluates his choices as if contemplating the solution for world peace. The look of delight on his otherwise tired and hardened face as he eats his gelato makes me smile. We watch the happy throngs of teenagers, families, and elders come and go.

One man is particularly distinguished. His pressed shirt is tucked beneath a handsome suit jacket. His tanned skin stands out against his shocking white hair. He is old, yet he seems content. He is out for an afternoon stroll with his grandson, to meet friends and have a gelato. I watch him as he walks with difficulty. Yet I don't feel sorry for him, because, despite his age, he is still very much alive.

For many people here, life does not derive meaning from a powerful corporate job. Their lives are their families, their land, and their food, none of which are taken away on retirement. Older people now have the luxury of time to devote themselves to the things they have always loved; thus, the golden years bring contentment and happiness. They are happy when their children marry. They are thrilled to become grandparents. Their prime of life has passed, and in their own dignified way, they accept aging, content to turn beauty over to the next generation.

We accomplished a lot today. Happy, we make our way back up the bright green hill.

The following week, David's cousin gives him a present: a beautiful box containing a pair of sheer knee-high nylon socks, black with red stripes, to go with his new suit.

Then, while shopping at a small supermarket, I stumble on a pair of shoes for David.

"If my husband doesn't like them, can I exchange them?" I ask.

"Of course, bring them back, and we'll exchange them for a prosciutto," the clerk responds.

I hope David likes them, because it's the final touch he needs for his total makeover.

RED "CHARDONNAY"

"WE'LL WAIT FOR YOU, THEN." David hangs up and turns his palms to the ceiling, as if to say, "There was nothing I could do."

We need new tires, and two *stranieri* (foreigners) cannot be given directions to the tire shop, nor can we go alone. David's cousin Francesco will pass by the house to pick us up, even though the tire shop is down the mountain and around the corner from where he lives.

Knowing this is a battle we cannot win, we wait for him.

Our neighbor Luciano is in his garden. Today is not unlike other days, for he always has some theory that involves impending doom and gloom to share with us, in the resigned tones of a man who is certain the world is about to end. Luciano is a true connoisseur of woe. Each declaration of calamity is accompanied by a bit of history.

Because the weather has been so mild this year, we say, "What a beautiful day it is."

He responds, "Ah, yes, but since it is so warm, we must be on the alert for earthquakes! Yes, in 1984 . . ."

"Nice day, eh?"

"Yes, but if we don't get more rain, we will have no water this summer. Yes, in 2002 . . ."

However, should it rain, we must be on the alert for hailstorms, hail the size of . . .

Remarkably, even though Luciano is quite adept at being a doomsday crier, he always wears a broad, jovial smile.

Today earthquakes are his favorite subject. His lecture includes full historical details, as well as the dates of occurrence and the vast damage left in their aftermath.

We tell Luciano *arrivederci*, and I nervously say to David, "It might be a good idea to have an earthquake plan."

He stares at me.

I protest, "But Luciano says . . ."

We see Francesco pull up in his tiny ancient Fiat 500, honking his horn several times to announce his arrival to the neighborhood.

"So, you are finally at home!" he says.

Innocent as doves, we ask, "What do you mean?"

"The barber passes your place on his way home each night, and he never sees your car, nor are there ever any lights on. He says you guys are never home!"

David suppresses a smile, realizing that his plan of living in stealth mode seems to be working.

We are now to follow Francesco back down the mountain to the *gommista* (tire man) to get winter tires.

"Don't speak to him," Francesco warns. "We don't want him to know you are foreigners."

David and I vow to be silent. We get into our car, and my hopes that the Fiat 500 cannot go fast are shattered the minute we turn the first corner. We try to keep up as Francesco hurtles down the mountain.

Soon we are on the Road of Love. The tire store is at the end of the road. Despite its being only ten in the morning, numerous enterprising women are already at work, showing off their merchandise as we drive past.

At the tire store, Francesco says, "Remember, I will do all the talking."

Mute, David and I follow him in. The *gommista* greets us, and David and I nod and smile. Francesco, of course, is trying to get a good deal, and some bartering will be necessary. They finally agree on a price, and we are told to park our car in the garage and to stay in the waiting area.

We flip through ancient magazines when suddenly Francesco jumps up and disappears through a door marked "Employees Only." He is gone for a while.

I whisper, "Where did Francesco go?"

David nonchalantly says, "He noticed that they started work on our car, so he is in the garage, hovering over the worker while he changes the tires."

"Why?" I ask.

"To ensure that he's putting on the promised new tires and giving us back our old ones," David says, evidently in the know.

I peek through the glass and see Francesco pacing back and forth next to our car, ready to pounce if necessary. The worker, though, appears to pay Francesco no heed, and soon he has the four new tires on, and we have the old ones.

On our way out, David and I are finally allowed to speak, and we tell the tire man *"Grazie"* and *"Arrivederci."*

It is approaching noon, and Francesco insists we come to eat at his place.

"Thank you, but we have too much to do."

Our gracious refusals fall on deaf ears, because Francesco sees this as a reason to come to his place. "Good, then you can save time cooking."

Despite our protests, he hops into his little car, waves his arm, and says, "Follow me."

David looks at me again as if to say, "What can I do?" I know the answer: nothing. It must run in the family; we cannot ever escape Francesco's pleadings or those of his father, *Zio* Luigi.

Like a madman, Francesco drives home so we can eat lunch on time. His wife has prepared pasta with a creamy porcini mushroom sauce, and there are several bottles of wine to choose from. As I pick one of them to try, Francesco makes the decision easier for me "They are all the same wine, I just put it in different bottles."

We eat and chit chat, with Francesco filling us in on all of the latest goings-on with the family.

"*Zio* Vito has just given up smoking and drinking because the doctors told him it will kill him if he doesn't stop."

"How old is he?" I ask.

"Eighty-two," Francesco says casually.

We make small talk, hoping to avoid the inevitable interrogation. Francesco finally asks, "So, have you been to see *Zia* Giuliana lately?"

"Why, yes, we visited just two weeks ago," David answers.

"Two weeks ago! She's getting old, she may die soon; you need to visit more regularly."

I can see that David is biting his tongue. The interrogation continues.

"What about my brother Bruno? Maybe on your way home, you can stop in on him."

David changes the subject, as Francesco tries to fill our social calendar for the next several weeks.

Remembering his new line, David says, "Sure, but I'll have to get back to you."

Francesco concedes. "So, are you planning to stay in Italy forever?"

"We're definitely staying for one year; then we'll see," David answers.

"That's good. Your parents will be happy to have you living with them."

We've been waiting for an opportune time to break the news to the family that when David's parents come back, we'll be going to live in Tuscany for five months. We figure this is as good a time as any.

"Tuscany?" Francesco asks. "Why would you go there when you can stay here? Your parents have three bedrooms; you can all stay together."

We don't know how to reply. Sensing our awkward silence, Francesco says, "No worries, no matter where you go, we'll come and visit you often!"

On that note, I pour myself another generous glass of red "Chardonnay."

SQUIRREL POWER

"ONCE UPON A TIME, IN a land far, far away, there lived a Prince and his Princess. In their wondrous land, life was idyllic. Beauty surrounded them, each day had a *pausa*, and their only stress was the Prince's ongoing battle to outsmart the "squirrels." Yet something was amiss. Yes, they had left many friends behind, in the land beyond the sea. These friends missed them greatly, but every week the friends received updates on life in paradise. These friends wished they had something equally interesting to write back to the Prince and his Princess, but in reality, life beyond the great sea was, for the most part, routine and often rather dull."

—excerpt from a letter by Colin and Esther, our friends in Canada

***

David's waves have turned into long dark curls, like an Italian soccer player's. It is with great dismay that I snip off the curl I hold in my hand.

Now that David knows the barber is keeping tabs on us and reporting to the family, he will no longer have his hair cut by the man. "The less he knows about us, the better," David assures me.

And so I am forced to take on the role of hairdresser.

Though quite fussy about his hair, David is more fearful of getting caught. "What does a hairdresser in a small village do?" he asks and then answers himself, "He makes small talk."

David doesn't want to face the gauntlet of questions from the local barber.

We've been warned, "If you cut your hair with the moon rising, it will grow back quickly. If you cut it with the moon waning, it will grow back slowly." I cut his hair anyway, even though the moon is not right.

Despite my lack of training, his hair turns out quite good, though probably because it is curly and thus forgiving of any major mistakes.

However, "he who laughs last, laughs best."

The two of us are relaxing at home. There are no knocks, no phone calls, no need to fend off dozens of invitations; the interrogations have miraculously ended. One would think David has succeeded.

Yet one can never count one's success too soon, as David learned last winter back home in Canada.

Because he took great delight in bird watching, he decided to build the Ritz Carlton of birdhouses. He drew "architectural" plans and bought white oak. He painstakingly hand-carved the trim work. A five-star birdhouse was finally finished. He strategically placed it and carefully chose the birdseed, wanting to attract only the noblest of birds. Now he could sit back with a sense of satisfaction and watch a variety of birds flock to his house.

Weeks passed, and the birds did not come. David soon discovered why: in their place was a squirrel. Slightly dismayed but still very determined, he relocated the birdhouse. Yet as David repeatedly repositioned the birdhouse, we learned that this was no ordinary squirrel but rather a flying, jumping, acrobatic squirrel that was even more determined than David was. Waxing the roof and watching the squirrel slide off gave David fleeting moments of joy, until the squirrel caught on. Nothing could deter this little superhero from getting at the birdseed. The squirrel even ate away the hand-carved molding.

Finally, he gave up—my husband, that is, and not the squirrel. In a last attempt to outsmart the squirrel, David chucked the birdhouse into the back of our woodshed.

A hole the size of an orange suddenly appeared in the door of the shed. Inside, we saw that the birdhouse had been overturned, and every last seed had been polished off! Having lost the battle and been outsmarted by a squirrel, my distraught husband gave away the birdhouse. To add insult to injury, our friends have taken to teasing David about this squirrel that outwitted him.

As I sit by the hot fire and look out at the shining lights of the hilltop town across from us, I'm happy and I feel a sense of peace overtake my over-anxious mind. I pick up *Under the Tuscan Sun* and begin to long for our days in Tuscany.

David comes back, arms full of wood and out of breath from the climb up the stairs. He looks at me, so happily warming myself by the fire. Though he doesn't want to ruin the moment, he says, "We're going through wood pretty quickly, and it's not even very cold yet. I think we'll have to order some more."

It seems like only yesterday when he was stacking it three rows deep. Thinking the solution is simple, I reply, "Could we just ask Francesco to get us some more?"

"No, I can call the wood man myself," David says and makes the call. He is quoted an outrageous price. He asks for a better price.

"What are we, Moroccan?" the guy says. "The price is the price!"

I'm certain we're being ripped off because the man thinks we are rich *Americani*, and I beg David to call Francesco.

"I don't want to bother him. Besides, you know what an ordeal it is here."

The last time we needed wood, Francesco took a day off work so that he could be present when the wood for delivery was put on the scale and weighed. Then he followed the truck to our house, ensuring that there would be no illicit stops en route.

"But we'll freeze!" I say. "What other choice do we have?"

Realizing that I'm right, David calls Francesco.

I watch David's surprised face as Francesco replies, "You guys are never home. You will never use up all of the wood!"

There is a long silence on our end. Outwitted again! We have two choices: to let our subterfuge be exposed or spend the winter shivering. I'm not sure which one David will decide is worse.

WAITING FOR IKEA

I PUT ASIDE OUR WORRIES about the diminishing wood pile and call Sonia to see how her kitchen is coming along.

After a week of resisting the idea of a freestanding stove, they again made the trek up to IKEA. While they changed the order, it seems IKEA discovered another mistake: only half of a counter was ever ordered! It would cost another one hundred euros to remedy this newfound error. We, too, now begin to wonder: could the Mafia really be running things up there?

Close to a month passes. Salvatore has long ago handed over three thousand euros to someone he's never met, and he is sleeping uneasily, wondering whether he'll ever see this kitchen. His friends in the village mock him, saying how stupid he was to give them all of the money up front. They back up their claims with one story after another: "Remember the time Gino gave them all the money first? How about Luigi, has he seen his painter again?" His friends assure him he will *never* see this kitchen. Given Salvatore's bad heart and the added stress of this ordeal, we begin to think the same thing.

As time passes, we start to avoid him—for his sake, not ours. We know IKEA will deliver their kitchen soon, we're almost certain the Mafia isn't running IKEA here, but the mere sight of us seems to remind Salvatore of his anguish.

With deep regret, he repeats, "I should have known better than to give the money up front. I should have stuck to my guns! Once delivered and installed, *then* payment! Had I been firmer, they would have done it my way! This is Italy! This is how it's done here! You can't trust anyone, anyone!" He then quotes all of his friends and the long succession of rip-off artists they have personally known.

His face changes color and is soon bright red. We switch topics and are amazed at how long we can discuss prosciutto. The red gradually returns only to its rightful place, on Salvatore's cheeks and nose, and we bid him farewell.

Please, IKEA, please!

The long-awaited phone call occurs. There was a delay, because the countertop they ordered was out of stock. The kitchen will arrive next Tuesday. One week is a long time for all of us to hold our breath.

Tuesday comes and goes. No kitchen, no phone calls. Salvatore and Sonia's relationship, already precarious, is becoming more so by the day. We wonder if their marriage can survive this crisis.

No longer fully convinced ourselves, we unwaveringly assure them that IKEA will deliver the kitchen soon.

Precisely one month after the promised due date, the kitchen arrives. Four men work nonstop all day to install it. We drop by in the evening to see how things are going. The kitchen looks pretty good—from afar. As we approach, though, an agitated Salvatore points out the deficiencies. On closer examination, I try to keep a straight face—no easy task when I contemplate what the Swedes would think if they saw this.

The kitchen components form a perfect 90-degree angle; however, the walls do not! Shaking his fist, Salvatore says, "These crooks wanted to come back another day after I had the walls fixed, but they would charge me for their travel time today. Nobody is pulling the wool over my eyes! No way! I said it wouldn't matter, the kitchen would be installed today!"

And it was, with all of the components lining up at a perfect 90-degree angle. The problem is, the walls recede about eight inches behind the cabinets the closer you get to the room's corner. There is enough room to drop a small child between the counter and the wall. Yet these ingenious men didn't want the overhead cabinets to be out of line with the bottom ones, so they screwed a few rough planks behind the top cabinets to make them hang evenly over the bottom ones. The workers didn't take the side view into consideration, though.

I am horrified, but I fear reporting this to the Mafia— which, we are now certain, *is* running IKEA in Italy.

Salvatore is tired. Hovering all day *is* exhausting. We join him and Sonia and stand over the four men, watching them work, yet they don't seem to notice. They continue to smoke, dangling cigarettes out of their mouths and dropping ashes on the counters.

Salvatore points at two of the men and in a loud, accusing voice tells us they are *Marocchini* (Moroccans). He then shrugs and makes a face, as if to say, "What can you do?" He reassures us that "the other two are Italian."

The men work until nine o'clock. They still need to finish a few things, such as fixing some items they have broken, but they are tired and promise to come back tomorrow. If Salvatore would just sign right here on the dotted line, acknowledging that all is complete and satisfactory.

So he signs . . .

And tomorrow never comes.

TOUGH LOVE TISSUES

OUR SOCIAL CALENDAR IS GETTING filled up, and we now seem to rush from one place to another. Later today, I'll meet Sofia in the old square of Ascoli Piceno, one of the most beautiful yet relatively unknown piazzas in Italy. We'll go to my favorite spot, Caffè Meletti, situated in the arcades of the Piazza del Popolo, and have a hot, thick, rich melted chocolate with whipped cream piled high on top.

Sofia will practice her English, while I stumble through my Italian, occasionally sending her into fits of laughter. She is tiny but feisty. She finds it funny that I'm so amused and intrigued by what to her are everyday sights. We always have a great time together. As we chat, I suddenly notice the time. David will soon be picking me up outside the city walls, because we have another appointment.

"But you'll come for lunch first, right?" she asks.

"Sorry, but we won't have time today. We brought our lunch with us. We'll just eat it on the run."

She is confused—I assume, due to the language barrier. As we approach the parking lot, she gasps in shock to see David in the car, eating a sandwich. She stares in disbelief at two cups and another sandwich on the dashboard.

"My heart is broken and absolutely torn to pieces!" Sofia dramatically says, fighting to hold back tears. "Come on. Please, just come to my house for some pasta."

She has me by the sleeve and will not stop inviting, begging, imploring. David, now rather adept at ignoring incessant pleading, nonchalantly chomps away at his tuna fish sandwich.

I look at Sofia's face, and now my heart is broken too. I fear we have hurt her feelings, and I even contemplate canceling our appointment.

"Please forgive us," I say, breaking out of her grasp. I get into the car. David finishes his sandwich, waves good-bye, and hurriedly drives away, while I do a balancing act of eating and drinking without spilling anything on myself. Hot pasta, a glass of wine, and a dining table start to look good to me. Slow food, Italy's slogan, seems rather sensible.

This scene, along with many events of the last few months, makes me recognize our need for outside help. I email my friend Melina, a *thin* Italian, currently living in the United States, who has mastered this game.

Melina's reply is instantaneous: she recommends tough love.

"It's not that Italians don't understand the word *no*, they simply don't believe you. Everyone eventually gives in, so they'll have their way if they pester you enough. You must let your *yes* mean *yes* and your *no*, NO! When they fill your plate again after you've said no, you must not eat what they've given you, even if they cry and plead. It's all an act. When they pester you, simply change the subject, repeatedly. They do eventually stop. Don't be afraid of hurting their feelings. Eat *what* you want, *where* you want, and if someone starts crying when they see you eating a tuna fish sandwich in the car, simply hand the person some Kleenex and keep eating!"

I find her approach a bit harsh, but as we continue to fight the same battles, I realize that her tough love measures will have to be implemented.

I print up Melina's advice and purchase a box of tissues.

The next time Sofia pleads with us to eat, I simply pull the email out of my purse and read it to her. I then hand her a tissue, which she gratefully takes, as she wipes tears of laughter from her face.

Now Sofia and her family have miraculously been transformed into a family of white knights, ready to jump to our aid. When in the vicinity of others who are pestering and begging us to eat more, they pull out a tissue, wave it, and laugh heartily!

PIÙ O MENO (MORE OR LESS)

I DECIDE TO HOST A dinner party, and I want everything to be perfect— meaning it will *have* to be Italian food. Months of brainwashing have taken their toll.

When we invite our guests, they all protest that it will be too much for me. No one feels it's too much for David's eighty-four-year-old aunt to cook for all of us, but it's too much for me. After much coaxing, they reluctantly agree to come.

I've been slaving over a hot stove all day, and the floor is in desperate need of cleaning. The ceramic tiles show every speck of dirt. I left the task of cleaning the floor until the very end, to ensure that it would be spotless for our guests and their not-so-subtle searching eyes.

The moment has arrived, or, as the Italians like to say, *più o meno*. I'm in the kitchen, finishing off a couple of items, when I hear the familiar long, impatient triple toot. Who could it be? It's not even 6:30 p.m.! They were invited for 7:30.

I am frantic and also filthy, as are the stove and the truly unforgiving ceramic floor, which can't be disguised by dim lighting because that is reserved only for churches here. I send David to greet our guests outside, while I get on my hands and knees and hysterically wipe the floor. I hope he can make idle conversation before allowing them in.

In his quest to get out before they get in, he slips on the wet ceramic and either breaks or sprains his toe.

Broken toe or not, you keep them out until the floor dries in here!

He does, and they all eventually hobble in together— David, thanks to his newly broken toe, and the others, due to a combination of age and too much pasta over the years.

I will have to adjust my carefully planned menu, because the words *more or less* now equally apply to the number of our guests who have arrived. The other half still have that window of appearing either any minute or up to 8:30 p.m.

One of our guests has not shown up with her husband.

"How is Martina?" we ask.

"She's at home, guarding the house," he says. "We don't like to leave the house alone."

Other than livestock, David and I haven't seen anything that one might, or even *could*, steal in there.

We try to seat them in front of the fireplace. Any friend of mine back home would be thrilled to sit down and relax in front of a fire with a glass of wine. Not so in a land where hovering is an art form. Perhaps it was my offering of a glass of wine *prior* to dinner that made them suspicious and convinced them of my need for constant supervision. Although I can barely understand their heavy dialect, David and I decide I should stay with them as a defense, while he takes care of the meat.

Soon we hear the triple honk of a car horn. The rest of our guests have arrived, more or less. David's aunt is alone. We inquire about *Zio* Luigi.

"Oh, he has just gone to visit a friend and should be here in a little while."

I let out a "Yeeesh!" but since it is with a big smile on my face, they all simply smile back.

I strategically whisk *Zia* into the dining room in front of the fireplace and hope they will find a controversial topic to debate and thus occupy themselves while we finish in the kitchen.

This plan seems to be working. Yet unbeknownst to us, what occupies them is a quest to satisfy their love of roaring fires. Like pyromaniacs, they have opened the door to the fireplace halfway and thrown in every possible bit of kindling, wooden crates, and firewood, stopping just short of the new dining room chairs. Now they sit smugly, pleased with themselves, watching the towering inferno. Perhaps the carbon monoxide has begun to dull their senses.

What they don't realize is that if the fireplace door isn't fully opened, the flue remains half closed, and smoke shoots back into the room.

This is how we notice our guests are out of control. Not only is the dining room full of thick gray smoke, it has also infiltrated the kitchen. We rush into the dining room and rescue everyone by throwing open the doors and windows, and even they recognize that the draft we create will be the lesser of two evils. You'd think that with an average age of seventy-five, our dinner guests could be safely left alone for a few minutes!

We hear three more loud honks of a horn outside, and I assume the last of our guests, *Zio* Luigi, has arrived. That is true, more or less.

Because it's now freezing in the house, we all sit down to dinner wearing our winter coats. A haze of smoke fills the air. The culprits are quiet, and despite suspiciously surveying the open windows on opposite sides of the room, no one dares mention the imminent pneumonia they are certain to catch.

David and I, still wearing our coats, start to serve dinner: a *torte* consisting of layers of grilled vegetables and ricotta. *Zio* Guido seems to be enjoying it until I list the ingredients.

"Oh," he says and quickly puts it aside. "I did not know it was made with ricotta. You cannot mix ricotta and wine!"

I guess if he has to give up one of the two . . .

Fortunately, the others had finished eating prior to my listing the ingredients and, despite having drunk wine with the ricotta, are alive and well. The pasta is served next, *penne a la vodka*. They have no problem mixing their liquors as they all load up on the pasta dish.

Outside, we hear another impatient triple toot of a horn. Who could it be now?

Martina has arrived, after all. Her son has come home and can now stand guard at the family compound. I immediately bring back the extra set of plates I had whisked away, and I serve her. She is a gracious guest, and I'm happy she was able to hand over the guarding of the house.

Conversation up to this point has been lagging, but that changes when Martina explains why she had to stay home. "Romanians are doing some work down the road. You cannot trust them—though they are not as bad as Albanians."

Zio Luigi, otherwise meek and mild, starts his rampage. "A family of Albanians just bought the house down the road from me. This house does not even have a bathroom, so they just go outside." Apparently, this is much to the disgust of *Zio's* cows, because now they won't go into the field bordering the Albanians' house. *Even the cows here are prejudiced!*

"There are at least a dozen of them living there. Like mice!" he emphatically says. When Italians live together, it is an extended family, but when immigrants do this . . .

"Was it an old, rundown home they bought?" we ask.

"No. It is a beautiful, newly renovated home," *Zio* says in a huff.

Newly renovated, but they omitted to put in a bathroom? We are even more dubious.

One thing is confirmed and agreed on: that it is getting more difficult to purchase Parma prosciutto. "The Chinese, who are everywhere, have taken a real fancy to it and are buying it up and transporting it all out of Italy and over to mainland China!"

"A few have even been spotted strolling near our village," they say in amazement, as if reporting a UFO sighting.

The conversation now gets quite bizarre. Apparently, when the Chinese are not gobbling up all of the prosciutto, the next course in their meal consists of their own dead.

"How can you think that?" David remarks in utter disbelief.

The indisputable "proof" is given: "We have never seen a Chinese funeral here."

I don't bother mentioning that it isn't the elderly Chinese who are immigrating to these small Italian towns, my guess being because they know better.

Gino next tells a joke. "Two Albanians come home after a morning of begging and count their money. The first one counts sixty euros.

"'Only sixty? What did you write on your sign?' the second one asks.

"'That I have a sick child, and can they please help?' he replies. The second one now counts his money. 'One thousand!' he happily says.

"'What did you write on your sign?'

"'That I would like to go home, and can they please help?'"

Everyone roars in agreement.

With all of the talk of rampant crime in Italy, the Mafia has not been mentioned once.

David and I are appalled and try to change the subject, but everyone has something to say on the topic of immigrants ruining Italy. The echo in the dining room is now unbearable, and for respite, I go to wash the towering pile of dishes, by hand, because there is no dishwasher. After a few moments of peace—wait, here comes my posse. I insist I can do the dishes by myself, so they pull up chairs, and the three of them sit directly behind me, continuing the conversation and watching me. I feel grateful for the loud clinking of dishes in the sink.

After my dishwashing performance is over, they take Martina on a tour of the house. I have foreseen this and am ready. Tomorrow will no doubt bring a phone call from my in-laws, complimenting me again on my housekeeping skills.

The dinner proves to be quite profitable in the end. We receive a freshly killed rabbit, two large salamis, two dozen eggs, a duck, sausage, cauliflower, fennel, enough lettuce for the next month for a family of ten, and a home-baked cake, because Italians always bring dessert.

As our guests leave, we endure the customary "What are you doing tomorrow, the day after, the next day? Just for lunch, then! Just for dinner. Don't be a stranger, drop by, we miss you!"

David, now a pro, gives them his latest line: "We'll see."

Cozy—Redefined

OUR CURRENT SURROUNDINGS COULD BE described as cottagelike, albeit Italian style, with a high security gate and plenty of howling dogs—nonetheless, almost ideal. The setting (without a soundtrack) conjures up words like *serenity* and *solitude*. Yet in Italy, these expressions carry negative connotations.

Spring is in the air, so we plan to celebrate its arrival and the even warmer weather that will soon come. We'll have a cozy evening with a few newfound friends and relatives. I see us chatting away, jazz music playing in the background, the fireplace lit, and shimmering lights from the hilltop town over the mountain adding to the evening's mood.

We call *Zio* Natale and his wife.

"No, *Zio*, we want to have you over. No, we don't want to go to a restaurant," David explains. "We'll cook for you. It's not too much trouble."

Zio continues to object, but David, having recently learned a thing or two about pestering, continues.

"Good, we'll see you then," David finally says.

"How did you convince him?" I ask.

"Simple. He said they will come if they can bring the pasta, the meat, some wine, and a bit of dessert."

"Are you kidding?" I exclaim.

"That was where the bargaining started. By the end, I got him down to just dessert and wine."

We next call Sonia and Salvatore. She, being close to forty, accepts readily. He, being closer to eighty, begins his resistance. Tired of debating, we leave out the rest of the aunts and the uncles and stick to our younger friends. After a few phone calls, text messages, and bartering for the right hour—we had wanted seven o'clock, they wanted eight—we manage to invite everyone over.

The day arrives. I prepare some pizza as an appetizer, and then we will have a barbecue. I look forward to a cozy evening spent with good friends, food, and wine.

At three o'clock the phone rings. It is Manuela. "Listen, would you mind if I brought my parents? If I go out, they'll be all alone at home."

How can I resist a young person looking out for her elderly parents? "Sure, no problem."

I go back to mixing my dough. The phone rings again. I motion that my hands are sticky, and could David pick it up?

Holding his hand over the receiver, he asks, "Could Daniele bring his brother? He says his brother is not well."

Not exactly sure what this means but caught off guard, I say, "Yes." I pull another package of sausages out of the freezer and put them in cold water, hoping they will defrost in time, because, naturally, my in-laws do not possess a microwave.

Incredulously, within the hour we receive a call from another person, asking to bring some friends. I contemplate turning off the phone—which I should have done, because around five we hear the familiar ring again, and Paolo is "Just checking to see if it's okay to bring three friends who have dropped in?"

Originally, we could hardly convince anyone to come, and now we will have throngs of people. We say no to him, because there is no way to defrost anything else at this late hour.

"Paolo was evidently quite surprised at me having said no," David says. "He kept pausing and repeating his request, because he thought he must have heard wrong."

Gianni calls next. "Our plumber is here from Milan doing some work on our house, so, of course, you understand we must bring him. I mean, we cannot leave him home alone."

Since this was a statement and not a request, the plumber from Milan will also be joining our "cozy" group of close friends.

There will now be twenty-one of us at a table that comfortably seats twelve. I pray that the pizza dough will behave and rise accordingly.

Soon the guests start to arrive. *Zio* Natale and his wife have managed to control themselves and have brought only five liters of wine but, fortuitously, enough dessert for more than twenty.

Stefano, Mirella, and their children arrive next. As I am now familiar with their acclimatization theory, I know not to offer to take their coats right away. I wait the customary fifteen minutes or so, when Stefano will announce that they have acclimatized, and it is now safe for them to disrobe.

The guests continue to arrive, and our kitchen table looks as if we have just gone grocery shopping.

In between greeting guests, I'm trying to finish off the pizza, but with so much help, it's difficult. All of the women are gathered in the kitchen, and chaos now reigns. Sofia and Mirella keep checking the pizzas, while happily chatting, each time inadvertently leaving the oven door open so long that the temperature cools down, yet they can't figure out why the pizza isn't cooking.

I notice that someone has blown out the candles in the dining room, and the dim mood lighting has been replaced by bright lights. My soft jazz music has been traded in for a blaring Italian radio station. I look at the culprits, and they innocently ask, "Where were we, in a cemetery?"

David and all of the other men are standing round the ancient barbecue.

"This is how a barbecue should be done, with wood, not the way we've seen it on American TV."

David hates the work involved with a wood barbecue, though, and prefers the gas one we had in Canada—with a click of the switch, it was ready.

"Of course, everything is better the old-fashioned way," *Zio* says. "Can't you just taste how delicious prosciutto is when cut by a knife versus being sliced by a machine?"

The wood has now burned down sufficiently, and hot coals await our thick, juicy steaks.

David asks how people would like their meat done. This appears to be our guests' first cause for alarm, the question being sufficient evidence that perhaps we know nothing about cooking meat.

They all move closer for further inspection. Soon thereafter, David removes our two medium-rare pieces of meat. The others gasp!

"Raw! You will be very sick if you eat these!" warns Massimo, as he grabs our two steaks and puts them back on the grill. The gasps are now ours.

Trying to save our meat, we mention that the Tuscans eat their steaks as we do: *Bistecca Fiorentina*, rare char-grilled steak. It is world famous.

"Ha!" they all declare, mocking the Tuscans. "We still know how to cook meat here, unlike the Tuscans who have sold their souls to accommodate suicidal Americans!"

Massimo guards the barbecue with his burly body, while the debate continues. We watch our meat shrivel. By now, all traces of whatever they are trying to kill must be dead, but their philosophy is: just a bit more cooking to make sure.

We are now ready to eat our very dry steaks. Hopefully, one of the dozen women in the kitchen has kept an eye on the pizza.

We try to seat everyone. After much yelling and shouting, Silvano finally gives a loud whistle and gets everyone's attention. The pizza is miraculously done to perfection, and Sofia insists she needs the recipe this minute. Massimo is happy because he starts his diet tomorrow, so today he'll eat as much as he wants of everything. I hope there will be enough.

"Help yourself," I say.

With a broad smile, Massimo picks up his plate, turns to his wife, and says, "You heard her. That means you can serve me now." Though the pizza is directly in front of him, she stands up and heaps slices onto his plate. Putting his plate down, he looks at me and winks.

They eye the potato salad suspiciously.

I list the ingredients: potatoes, peppers, carrots, green onions, and mayonnaise. Regardless, they unanimously agree that they don't think these foods should be mixed together. My salad with honey mustard dressing is received with an equal lack of enthusiasm.

Many of the women have scarves wrapped around their necks, as does Stefano. I comment on this current fashion. Yet that is not the case; rather, they all have slight colds.

"I work in a very dangerous environment, a very unhealthy one," Stefano says, feeling quite sorry for himself. "Yes, where I work there are very dangerous air currents."

Since none of the others work there, I assume they have simply caught a bad wind.

After dinner, David gathers the dirty dishes. I sit there as the women and the men watch him in shock.

Finally, Sofia says, "Leave them, your wife and I will do that."

David insists and continues. Sofia, being Sofia, cannot sit down and gets up to help him, along with the other women.

Now I tell them, "Oh, by the way, David also does our laundry." I hear loud gasps and, feeling devious, I say, "I don't even hang it up—he does."

More gasps.

"But what do the neighbors think?" Mirella asks.

They now tell me stories about their husbands. "One night after company, I was so tired I told my husband I cannot do the dishes. He led me to the bedroom and said, 'Then go to sleep, my dear, you don't have to do the dishes tonight. You can do them in the morning.'"

Stefano proudly owns up to being this kind to his wife.

We discuss and debate many subjects, mainly their disdain for radar traps and police, with their absurd regulations about speed limits.

"An invasion of privacy," Massimo says. "Last week I was caught by them, but they were hiding. That is illegal. I will fight this one!"

Having driven with Massimo, I wonder just how many tickets he has fought.

It is time for dessert. Almost everyone has brought some, and we have enough for a large Italian wedding feast. Tiramisu, sweet deep-fried ravioli filled with a chestnut cream, beautifully wrapped boxes of assorted pastries. They all sample a bit of each. I am in awe, because, aside from Massimo, not one of them is overweight. Perhaps the secret lies in evaporating all of the fat from the meat.

We serve the after-dinner drinks, and they ask whether we know how to make grappa or any other liquor.

"No, except for wine and beer, it's illegal in Canada to make your own hard liquor."

"Illegal? How can it be illegal to make your own alcohol?" they proclaim in unison.

We try to explain, but finally, to calm them down, we confess that "many Italians do it on the sly." This appeases them somewhat. It's illegal in Italy, too, but I guess that's a fundamental difference between Canadians and Italians: generally, when something is illegal, we simply don't do it!

It's late, and I'm getting tired, but I seem to be the only one. The ceramic floor does nothing to insulate the loud echoing sounds of the dozen or more people who are loudly speaking at the same time. Nor is distance a barrier to conversation; lengthy discussions take place all evening between the two people farthest away from each other.

Perhaps next time we can keep it cozy, invite only two other couples, and insist on keeping it that way. Yet despite my headache, I quickly dismiss the idea. Eating nearly raw meat, men clearing dishes and doing laundry, not making illegal moonshine, and only six of us at dinner may cause them to feel justified in thinking that we *Americani* are a very different breed indeed!

Spring Fever

Spring really is in the air. It appeared as if overnight. The howling winds, allegedly responsible for a host of illnesses, are gentle now. The colors of the mountainside are transformed from dreary brown into vibrant greens. Gleaming white and pink blossoms cover the almond trees. The mimosa trees, with their tufted yellow cotton-candy flowers, release their sweet perfume into the air, attracting honey bees by the hundreds.

I look out the kitchen window and smile to see Luciano up on a ladder, ruthlessly pruning his olive trees. Short in stature and slightly round, with a jolly red face, he looks like a little gnome sitting in the trees. The fires burning on the hillsides, emitting thick smoke into the atmosphere, provide further evidence that spring is in the Italian air.

The roar of tractors driving up and down the surrounding hills has replaced the chirping of birds that usually serenades us each morning. I see people's dependence on the earth, with the elderly industriously preparing the land for their families. Even those who have no intention of reaping their crops but who plant them only for the government grants are busy working now.

Franco, a neighbor down the mountain, is ambitiously planting many olive trees. For years, he refused to let the township run natural gas lines through his land, but now he has lost the battle. The township will soon appropriate part of his acreage. They will have to pay more if it is cultivated land, however, so he, too, joins in the planting fury.

Our pet friends have taken quite a liking to us and our taxi service. They seem to think we're running a shelter for them. David and I both grew up in a large city and never owned pets, so this is a new experience for us.

Outside, I see Leone, the giant white sheepdog from our walks. I assume he is with someone, because he never comes here on his own.

Suddenly, I hear wild yelping. We open the door to find another pet friend, Bambola, the little lap dog, shaking like a leaf. She looks up at us with large brown eyes, as if begging for help.

David goes to pick up Bambola, but Leone viciously growls at him. We're quite confused about what is going on. Leone has always been so gentle, so sluggish. His angry growling continues, and he lunges at us. Doing the unthinkable in an Italian house, especially my in-laws', I call Bambola, and she runs inside with lightning speed.

David arms himself with a large stick. Miraculously, Leone returns to his calm, docile self. Could rabies cause symptoms one moment and then show no sign the next? We wait to ensure all is normal again. We apprehensively pat Leone, and he lies down, not a care in the world. We decide to walk the dogs home.

I go inside and pick up Bambola, who has recovered from her trauma and licks me appreciatively. I take her outside, but the moment Leone spots us, he makes a beeline for the little dog and again manifests the ferocity of his name, "lion." He roars at us as we try to separate him from Bambola. Even my normally fearless husband is now scared.

I run back into the house. The only way to keep Bambola safe is to take her home. Thanks to our "living in stealth mode," the car is parked in the garage. We take her down the back stairs through the house to our escape vehicle. Feeling like bank robbers, we look around to make sure the coast is clear. We don't see Leone, who is undoubtedly trying to knock down the front door, so we quickly drive down the mountain and deliver the little dog to its grateful owner, David's cousin, who will keep Bambola safe in her bedroom—this, of course, hidden from her father. We are pleased with our rescue mission.

We venture ideas about what, exactly, the problem may be. Observing our naiveté, the dog's owners smile. We're embarrassed to find out that it isn't nearly as complex as we'd thought. Leone's behavior is simply one more sign that not only spring, but love, is in the air!

FLYING THE COOP

WORD IS SPREADING THAT WE will soon move to Tuscany, so we start breaking it personally to the rest of our family and friends.

For most of the world, Tuscany conjures up images of rolling hills, golden fields of sunflowers, clusters of dark green cypress trees, abundant vineyards, and quaint villages with lovely stone villas. For us, it means no relatives!

The news of our moving is not well received by family members. We encounter confusion, disbelief, and even a bit of hurt. "Why would you ever leave here? This is where all your family is! Why would you leave for Toscana in May, since that is when your parents arrive? They have three bedrooms; you could live with them forever," they logically remind us.

Our friends react with equal shock, hurt, and disbelief. They, too, cannot believe we would ever purposely want to leave. Perhaps we want to get away from family but not from them. They offer to help us find a place to rent on our own here.

Next, they try to deter us.

"There are speed traps everywhere up there, and they are enforced!" they warn. "And what about all of the Americans who have purchased isolated homes in the middle of nowhere?" They try to make us fear that another WACO is in the making.

Seeing their dejected looks, I think quickly and add, "By living in Toscana, we'll be closer to my family in Croatia."

They realize it's only fair to share us between families, and with great relief they declare, "Ah, so that's why you're moving!"

The one person who receives our news with great enthusiasm is little Alessandro, the nine-year-old. His big eyes open wider and, in accented English, he says, "I have heard that Toscana is very, very beautiful! It is very, very far away, but very beautiful!"

Finally, someone understands our reasons for going!

Our friends back in Canada also understand and are already lining up to visit us. According to them, this is due to our charming personalities and is in no way related to our new postal code.

Arrivederci Abruzzo

SOFIA IS BARELY FIVE FEET tall, and when she drives, her head is just visible above the dashboard. I brace myself nervously as she revs up the roaring engine to 6,000 rpm, over and over again.

"There is a slight hesitation problem with the car, nothing to worry about," she says with utmost confidence.

I offer to take my car; however, for inexplicable Italian reasons, she feels it is better that we take hers. Knowing there are no air bags in this seventeen-year-old Fiat Panda, I brace myself again, as she presses on the gas.

We take off like a jet. Our wheels lay rubber as we peel out and maneuver into the traffic. I am terrified. Sofia is calm, smiling. I monitor her driving and the other cars, because she is doing neither. She is happy to be with her *Americana* friend and is frenetically using all of her energy and concentration to speak English. I point out the rear end of the shiny new black Mercedes we are about to slam into.

"Oh," she says and hits the brakes hard, barely stopping in time. She cringes and appears annoyed, because she has lost her concentration and must start her sentence again. She is intent on speaking correctly, and traffic shall not be allowed to interfere with this.

120

I see a red light ahead and hope Sofia will also notice it and stop. Then I'll prepare myself for the frenzied revving and peeling out that follow, due to the "slight hesitation problem." All of my worst nightmares are combined in a single afternoon.

To add to my misery, we have taken the wrong road and must return along the highway to make up for lost time. I say a silent prayer as we merge into traffic. Sofia never once takes her eyes off me, determined to continue her story. She nonchalantly drives 60 kilometers an hour (37 mph), as traffic speeds past us at double or even triple our speed. We do pass one vehicle on this highway: an *ape* (a mini-truck on three wheels) driven by an old man in a suit.

Again, Sofia is calm, while I'm shaking in fear. My only consolation is that there are no red lights on the highway. Due to her struggle with a difficult sentence structure, we miss our exit, and I wonder if this day will ever end.

To add to my woes, her cell phone goes off.

"Pronto," she answers and flashes me a bright smile, her fierce dark eyes gleaming. "It's my husband; he is with your husband."

I avoid making eye contact, subtly trying to encourage her to keep her eyes on the road. She chats away.

"Isn't it illegal to drive and talk on your cell phone?" I hint. She again laughs, though I do hear her finally say she is on the highway and must go.

"Are you nervous?" she innocently asks. I smile back at her, albeit mine is fake.

Alessandro is sitting in the backseat, urging his mother to drive faster. "Like dad!" Proud of his father's Schumacher-like maneuvers, he eggs his mom on, calling her a *lumaca* (snail). Naturally, she must turn around to speak directly to him and fully explain the dangers of driving too fast. While this serious conversation is taking place, I console myself that at the speed we're traveling, it won't be possible to rear-end anyone, because everyone else is far ahead of us.

"*Lumaca, lumaca!*" he chants, then, "Schumacher, Schumacher!"

Fortunately, we can also get off at the next exit. As is the case with most Italian drivers, she slams on the brakes, comes to almost a complete stop on the highway, and then simply makes a ninety-degree turn onto the off ramp. No need whatsoever for the merge lane. I stop paying attention to her story and instead sneak peaks in the rearview mirror.

We are leaving one village, as is indicated by a prominent sign with the name of the village crossed out. Just ahead will be the name of the new village.

"Do you use the same system in Canada?" Alessandro asks, pointing to the sign.

"No, we only have the name of the new village," I reply. "Once we see that, we know the other one has ended."

He looks up at me as if important new discoveries have just been unveiled and says, "You people in America are very intelligent."

We run a few errands and soon are back at her house.

Despite her fatigue, which is caused by working full time, raising two children, and an inner Italian voice compelling her to iron the dishtowels and the sheets, she will do all of the cooking tonight. My attempt to introduce the concept of "pot luck" proved unsuccessful the last time, because I entered her home carrying the main course and noticed the aroma of another main course coming from her kitchen. The movie afterward was a failure as well. It was not a documentary, but Sofia's running commentary throughout the movie made it one. Thus, tonight she will cook, and we will not watch a movie.

Over a plate of pasta and a glass of red wine, Massimo explains his day. "The real life of an Italian," he tells us slowly and deliberately. We listen closely.

"This morning, I already wake up tired because of a 'short' condominium meeting last night that lasted from nine until two in the morning, discussing a very simple issue. You see nothing *really is ever* simple here."

Fortunately for him as a contractor, the concept of *fai da te* (do it yourself) has never taken off. Italians always hire a *maestro* to do their work.

"I've seen those shows on TV where even women are working on their own places. I'm not worried, that will never catch on in Italy. And this new generation knows nothing about working with their hands."

Massimo pours himself and David more wine and continues, "So we are restoring this old house. Each time we dig, of course, we find an old artifact, jars, broken clay pieces, and so on. I'm supposed to report these to some historical society, which will do an investigation and will likely shut down the project for months. I figure they have enough old vases, so we keep digging."

He wants to keep his clients happy, because they are *stranieri* (foreigners) and may recommend him to their friends.

"Sure, they don't know how to make a decent espresso, but what I like about them is that they only come in once in a while to give me a drink, not like the Italians who stand over me all day, watching my every move!"

He looks at us for understanding. "The Romans have had their day and their museums, and enough is enough!"

Astonished, we remain silent.

We chat over our next course, *pecora* (sheep)—well done, naturally—with fennel-roasted potatoes and more red wine for Massimo and my husband. We discuss his work and the superiority of Italian construction over Canadian methods. He shakes his head in disgust and looks at us with intense dark eyes and a smile that produces deep dimples. "Two thousand years later, it's still here, isn't it?"

Feeling chilled, I ask him about insulation and why Italians don't use it.

"We don't need it," he says. "Look how warm it is in here, despite it being cold outside."

"How much does it cost on average to heat this home?" David asks.

"About one hundred euros per month—that is, if you're not the fussy types who always need hot water just to wash your hands."

I go to the bathroom and peak at his thermometer; it is a toasty sixty degrees. Not wanting to be the "fussy type," I wash my already cold hands with ice-cold water.

Alessandro has been sitting quietly and listening to his father's rants and our debates. I smile at him and at our surroundings: the tablecloth is old, stained, but nonetheless ironed. Slices of bread are placed in piles directly on the table. Four of the six plates match, the napkins are paper, and there is not a candle in sight. The six of us are crammed into their tiny kitchen, yet we are all so happy.

"It's late now, we really should go," I say.

Trying to control their yawning, they insist we stay a bit longer. We are tired and know it will take at least another half hour and an exit into three more rooms before the final goodnight.

We have already made many fond memories with this family. Our time together is becoming more precious as our departure draws near. Sofia's eyes fill with tears each time she thinks of us leaving. Alessandro's as well. Then mine. We insist they come visit, because they have never been to Tuscany, have never seen the grandeur of Florence, despite its being only a three-hour drive. With Massimo's driving, no doubt he could shave it down to two.

They assure us they will come. They assure themselves we will return.

"Go to Toscana, but you will come back to us!" are Sofia's last words to us.

PANDA-MONIUM

WE ARE DESPERATE. OUR FRIENDS from Canada will be here in a few days, at which time we'll leave the region and relinquish our faithful Fiat Uno. We have not yet found a suitable vehicle for the five of us and our accompanying luggage—which eventually will amount to enough suitcases for the caravan of a royal dignitary.

Francesco repeatedly calls us to describe various deals on Fiat Pandas, the twenty-year-old kind that painfully putter along the highway and are usually driven by an older *signore* with his hat grazing the ceiling—a small car similar to Sofia's, but hopefully without the "slight hesitation problem."

Picture the five of us in this tiny car with luggage piled on top. Then visualize us meeting our untimely demise, as suitcases crash through the light tin roof onto our tightly packed bodies.

We suspect that Francesco is a part-time used Panda salesman and not a very effective one, for he says, "No one actually ever sells a *good* used car." Oddly enough, he has recently purchased a "good used car," one that is four-door, roomy, American-style.

The phone rings, and someone has found us a car! The man has tried to sell it for a while and has finally come down in price. Off we go, full of hope. Despite being eighteen years old, the car is in mint condition.

"You can have it for six hundred," the man says.

We examine it and decide it will suffice for five months, so David says, "Okay, we'll take it."

"Fine, but actually it is now 1100," he says, no doubt after hearing our accents. Interrupting our dazed silence, he adds, "Take it or leave it."

We may be desperate, but we still have our pride, so we leave it.

Later we learn that he's been trying to sell the car for two years, the same amount of time it has been sitting idle in his front yard.

Next, we hear of a mechanic who has a car for sale. We arrange to meet him and then make the forty-five minute trek down the mountain to the coast.

While driving, we call him and say, "We're ten minutes away."

"No problem, the car is nearby, and I'll take you to see it."

I tell David, "Maybe this will be the one!"

We arrive at the mechanic's shop and enter. Blank stares and silence greet us. We ask one of the onlookers, "Is Guido around?"

He looks at us with stunning steel-blue eyes. Nice and slow, he says, "I am Guido. I will take you to the car in just a moment."

We wait and wait, then wait some more. Guido offers neither an apology nor an explanation.

Blue Eyes is quite handsome, and I suspect he has grown accustomed to getting his way all of his life. He continues to work on an expensive black Mercedes as if we don't exist.

I look at my watch and realize that my mother and her cousin will soon arrive at the train station. They have been traveling fifteen hours from Croatia, and we don't want to keep them waiting. We explain this to Guido and ask, "Can we meet you on our way back?"

He gives us the address where the car is parked and says, "I'll meet you there in half an hour."

It must be his blue eyes, for I'm convinced he will most assuredly be there. His blue eyes don't have the same effect on David, who says, "We will see."

We arrive just as my mother and her cousin step off the train. Tears of joy fill my eyes. We kiss them and break the news that we won't be taking them to their guest bedroom to rest but rather to meet Guido, the mechanic, at a parking lot.

I add, "He does have lovely blue eyes, though."

David is not amused.

We risk life and limb in busy traffic to reach the parking lot on time. Half an hour comes and goes, yet Guido does not. At least, the car is there. We give it a quick once-over and decide it will be good enough. We continue to wait. After several phone calls and empty promises that he will arrive in "ten minutes," we make one final call to Guido.

Evidently perturbed, he snaps, "If this isn't a good time for you, we can make it another day!"

We trudge off with our visitors, who have just had their first introduction to the Italian south.

Miraculously, we are not yet jaded. We buy a politically incorrect weekly journal offering all types of goods and services and take it home to help with our car search. Both personal ads and prospective employers clearly state the race, maximum age, and gender they seek. Prospective landlords are generally looking for Italian tenants and, on occasion, will concede to their being Polish.

David makes one phone call after another. I worry about his blood pressure and our phone bill. Finally, I hear hope in his voice.

"Great, I live about ten minutes away. If you'd like, we can come right away or later today." David's face suddenly droops. "In three days would be more convenient for you?"

Because we have no choice, we wait.

After three long days, David calls the seller. "Sure, we could make it three hours later."

Shortly before the designated meeting time, we head down the mountain. The hands on the clock in the square approach twelve-thirty, as we anxiously await the arrival of the black Alfa Romeo.

Twenty minutes later, a black Alfa Romeo enters the parking lot. The car is much nicer than we'd anticipated. We approach the driver and start talking about his car.

He is confused. "My car is not for sale."

Disappointed, we realize he is not our man, nor will that be our car.

We keep phoning Alfa Man, but his phone is turned off. Finally, as we are about to admit defeat, a text message appears. "If you are serious about purchasing the car, show up Monday afternoon at the same spot."

David is now furious, and I bear the brunt of his mood as he speeds home up the mountain.

Our desperation has reached new levels, so we give Alfa Man another chance.

"See you tomorrow, but please don't stand us up," David says.

"I would never do that to you," the man says, despite being guilty of that very act.

Days pass, and the Alfa Man does not materialize with his black Alfa Romeo that is supposedly for sale.

My mother and her cousin cannot believe the absurdity! We aren't randomly surveying people to see whether anyone will give us a car for free. Instead, we are calling the very people who have advertised their cars for sale. My otherwise cool, calm, collected husband is falling to pieces. He is completely out of his element.

Now frantic, we swallow our pride and call Blue Eyes again. He should be pleased by our call, because if this car isn't sold soon, it will go to the wreckers, and one must pay for this service.

"We're coming from far away, so please ensure that all will be in order for us to purchase the car."

"The owners will be here, and we can take care of everything face-to-face," he assures us. "That's the way I like to do things, face-to-face."

Down the mountain we go and arrive forty-five minutes later. The owners are not there.

Not understanding our impatience, Guido calmly says, "No problem, they will arrive shortly."

And more or less, they do. The husband does. We must now pick up his wife at home and follow them, race-car style, to the government office. We arrive with cash in hand, ready to buy the car.

The wife is decked out in the latest fashion and manages a condescending hello. On our way into the office, she yells at her husband and at us. She doesn't like the terms of sale we have agreed on with her husband. She looks at us with utter contempt and complains to him, with matching gestures for emphasis. The deal goes sour, and we leave despondently.

We try every used-car dealership around and now even begin to visit scrap yards.

My mother and her cousin are no doubt worried about us, because we left them more than ten hours ago. When we return, they are shocked to see us exit the Fiat Uno with no other car in sight.

In utter desperation, I beg David to call Guido and agree to any terms. For the first time in our married life and probably *ever* in his life, I hear him say, "I wish we were rich."

Blue Eyes is not surprised to hear from us. "All will be in order tomorrow morning. If not, I'll call you."

There is no phone call the next day, so we drive down to Guido's shop, walk right in, and greet him, thereby depriving him of the chance to ignore us.

"Are we ready?" asks David.

"The owners of the car have gone away for the day, so come back tomorrow," says Guido coolly.

We manage not to throttle him and agree to come back tomorrow.

And just as tomorrow never came for Salvatore and Sonia and the workers who were supposed to finish their IKEA kitchen, neither will it come for Blue Eyes or his customers.

Months ago, Francesco had mentioned a man who was selling an old BMW. We tried to get the telephone number several times from Francesco, but he was so intent on our purchasing a Panda that he never gave us this information.

Our friends will arrive tomorrow, and we will leave for Tuscany in a few days—possibly on foot, it now seems. Sheer desperation has transformed David, and he will not take no for an answer! Perhaps sensing danger, Francesco gives us the phone number. The car is parked in a tire shop, and the gentleman who is selling it lives a short distance away.

Just off the highway, we see Roosevelt's tire shop and the car. We also spot Roosevelt, who sees us at the same time. Roosevelt looks about eighty and has a full head of thick, long, shocking-white hair, which stands out against his forest green T-shirt worn under Christmas-red overalls. All of his moves are slow and deliberate, and he has a voice to match. We discern that time is not of the essence for Roosevelt. He meanders over to us and proceeds with his best sales pitch.

We examine the car and note that it is a six-cylinder, and with the price of gasoline in Italy, we put on a concerned look. Roosevelt, though slow, is motivated and assures us that a six-cylinder car actually consumes less gas than a four-cylinder. At this point we decide to consult the owner, Bruno, for more information.

Bruno's home is a short distance away in a beautiful country setting. Well-maintained gardens surround the property. Bruno invites us to sit on his terrace under the palm trees and offers us drinks. He treats us like long lost friends, and we chat about a number of things, none pertaining to the car.

Time being of the essence to *us*, David finally brings up the BMW. We state our price and add that we don't wish to offend him with such a low offer. Bruno, having taken a liking to us, says, "With an offer that low, I would prefer to just give the car to you."

In disbelief and with slight suspicion, David begins to protest, but Bruno insists.

"It's been sitting there for months. Please take it, gratis. We can go to the motor vehicle registration office to take care of the paperwork. It's closed now, so let's have some lunch together."

There *must* be some catch.

Hours pass, and we feast on delectable pasta with sweet peas from their garden, seafood, cheeses, and fine wine, finished off with an assortment of pastries and an espresso.

Bruno and his wife have children our age, and they show us the family photo albums. They give us an extensive tour of their home and gardens. They load bags with produce for us. They give us recipes for fava beans. Each subject is broached with equal enthusiasm and a zest for life. We are even given a roof rack for our car. Understandably, we become attached to the man and the woman from whom we attempted to "buy" a car.

The motor vehicle office will soon reopen. Bruno accompanies us back to Roosevelt's. As we pull up, Roosevelt, now decidedly quicker, rushes up to Bruno and announces, "Just minutes ago, someone else came and wants to buy the car."

Disappointed, we tell Bruno to go ahead and accept the cash offer. Perhaps suspecting that this is a plot of Roosevelt's, Bruno says it does not matter. The car is ours, and he would rather give it to us than sell it to another. Our hope is restored, if only for a while.

The car has been sitting under a tree for months and will not start. Resuming his previous pace, Roosevelt slowly brings out a replacement battery, face scrunched as if he's carrying a two-hundred-pound boulder. The motor eventually comes to life, and even though it only has the *sound* of a Ferrari, we are ecstatic.

The windshield is covered in dirt and sap. Roosevelt, acting as if he's performing a Herculean task, lifts a bucket of water and proceeds to wipe down the windshield. I worry that the motor vehicle office will close by the time Roosevelt is finished, but I soon realize the windshield will remain filthy, except for a spot the size of a dinner plate that he has diligently cleaned. He looks at this clean spot with great satisfaction and nods that we can now drive away.

At the inspection station, the car passes with flying colors. Apparently, the loud rumbling that mimics a fighter jet is nothing to worry about. We arrive at the motor vehicle office but are afraid to turn off the engine. Thus, we leave it running for the entire three hours while we complete the paperwork. For once, we are grateful to have a nineteen-year-old vehicle that no one wants to steal.

We drive Bruno home and thank him profusely. We kiss him and his wife and promise to keep in touch. We depart in a state of disbelief. David drives the "new" car home with a beaming smile.

As for me, I soon grow accustomed to wearing earplugs in the BMW.

GYPSY KINGS

OUR FRIENDS FROM CANADA WILL be arriving momentarily. To greet them, David puts on a "tuxedo" undershirt (commonly called a "wife-beater"), a gold chain, shorts, black socks, and sandals. This is the look that old Italian men in Canada are famous for, and it gets a big laugh out of our friends.

Now a proficient *casalinga*, I have made gnocchi with homemade tomato sauce, and I cook sausages in the fireplace, using it as a barbecue.

We feast and laugh about old times and new times as David sits in his undershirt. Exhausted, we all finally head off to bed.

The next day, David takes them to the local *cantina*, which dispenses wine out of a nozzle like a gas pump, thus ensuring both parties know exactly how much of the ridiculously low-priced wine is portioned out. Free samples consist of eight ounces of red wine that contains 13 percent alcohol—enough to make you blow over the limit as you drive away.

I stay home to prepare lunch. First course will be *Caprese* salad: buffalo mozzarella, cherry tomatoes, and basil with a hearty drizzling of olive oil, served with rosemary focaccia, fresh from the oven. The meal will continue in traditional

Italian style, with fresh pasta next, lamb shish kebobs, and salad at the end of the meal, followed by a pecorino (sheep) cheese made by *Zio* Luigi. *Spumante* accompanies dessert; I serve the *spumante* in plastic cups for an authentic Italian experience!

The next few days we visit quaint villages and stroll through narrow cobblestone streets. We watch a spectacular sunset from the ancient courtyard of a wine bar, high on a hill in Ripatransone, overlooking the valley. There, we enjoy a full-bodied Italian red, accompanied by local sausage and pecorino cheese with acacia honey on top. We finally feel completely at home in Italy.

Our time in Abruzzo is coming to an end. Next on the agenda is a one-week stay at a holiday rental in Siena, then a cruise with our friends Colin and Esther along with my mother and sister. After that, we'll head to our future home in Tuscany.

The five of us will travel in our "new" nineteen-year-old, two-door BMW 320. The men survey the car and the pile of luggage. Soon I hear hammering as they make drastic adjustments to the roof rack, miraculously transforming it into something resembling a pallet. Judging by all of the suitcases, this is a fitting addition, only we are missing a forklift to load the luggage. I had pleaded with everyone to pack light, but next time I'd better be more specific. David and I, who must pack for five months, are able to bring only one suitcase for the two of us, despite the new roof contraption.

Curiously, I have yet to discern what Colin has in his suitcase; he practically wears the same clothes every day. He assures us that it's full of his undergarments.

The men press bravely onward. Within a few hours, they've loaded and tied down all of the suitcases. We're about to leave when we hear a loud crackle, followed by a thunderous boom. The sky darkens.

It hasn't rained here in months. A letter enclosed with the last water bill even suggested that we try to conserve by draining hot pasta water into the sink and using it to wash the dishes. I've been dousing my plants with the water I use to wash lettuce.

After a short huddle, the two men untie the rope and take down the suitcases. They wrap each one individually in assorted colors of plastic and painstakingly reload them onto the roof rack, in case the clouds follow through with rain. We are worthy of being called the gypsy kings. As we drive away, I glance back at the house one last time, now bathed in sunlight.

We soon discover that Italian safety standards for vehicles aren't as stringent as ours back home. Our headlights had been tested, but now that it's nighttime, we see that they're as dim as parking lights. We inch along through the darkness, with bare visibility and barely visible, and the men endure screams from their three female passengers.

We cannot find the villa. Tiziana, the owner, is on the phone directing us, mile by mile, but still no villa. We begin to wonder if Tiziana's Bella Villa really does exist. We should have known better; the price was too good and the pictures too perfect. We console ourselves that at least she only scammed us out of a one-third deposit. My mom, meanwhile, is secretly relieved that no one can see us and our gypsylike car.

Aware of my husband's Italian blood, the women had voted that Colin be the driver. Poor Colin—we're all yelling at once, urging him to drive in different directions.

In the dark, each post and pole appears to have writing on it. Esther, most likely delirious by now, sees Bella Villa written on all of them and urges Colin to drive down every possible road. The rest of us, able to see only slightly better than her, scream in unison "NO!" for it is not a road, and we fear ending up in a ditch. It's late, we're tired, and there is no villa.

Tiziana calls and gives us new landmarks, and we realize we're not far away. Soon we drive up to Bella Villa. We simply forgot to apply the *più o meno* (more or less) formula when following an Italian's directions. The villa is exactly as described, newly restored and complete with antique furnishings. A bouquet of roses and a cake are on the table waiting for us, and we laugh at our adventure, again the best of friends.

Our hosts arrive soon after we do. The husband, Renzo, looks like the star of *Il Postino*. Having run out of questions and answers, we all simply stand there and smile for what seems like an awfully long time to us *Americani*. Relaxed, the Italians keep smiling and *finally* tell us goodnight.

After a sound sleep, we're eager to explore Tuscany. Unfortunately, though, our first visit will be to a dentist. My poor mother can no longer tolerate the pain, nor can she bear to watch the rest of us eat focaccia. In her very best, completely nonexistent Italian, she explains in lengthy detail what is wrong with her tooth. The dental assistant patiently listens.

My husband, not as patient, interrupts and translates: "The bottom line is, my mother-in-law wants drugs. No dental work, just drugs."

The dental assistant is fine with that and prescribes some antibiotics. We pay the bill, leave, and make it to the pharmacy only minutes before one o'clock, closing time.

Days pass, and my mother's toothache gets better, as her supply of antibiotics diminishes. With the agonizing pain still etched in her mind, along with the thought of a ten-day cruise ahead, she finds another drugstore in the next hilltop town we visit. She exits the pharmacy smiling and shows us her stash. She has, despite her rudimentary Italian, managed to convince someone to give her antibiotics, without a prescription this time!

"Just in case," she says, patting her purse. David and I shake our heads in disbelief, though grateful to see her happy again.

Because this is now our country, David and I feel obliged to act as hosts. I cook hearty meals, accompanied with abundant wine and finished off with grappa and chilled *limoncello.* I assume that our guests are in food heaven, but it's not long before I overhear murmurs about "the Italian Spa Diet."

David and I have adapted to the Italian way of eating: a croissant and coffee for breakfast and two rather substantial meals each day: one at twelve or one o'clock, pronto, and one at eight in the evening, with generally no snacking in between.

I should have noticed that at 6 p.m. Colin went out and bought a large slice of pizza. As the days go on, our friends still don't adjust to our eating habits. I spot them sneaking food at regular intervals throughout the day. For North Americans who normally eat dinner at six and have a few snacks in the afternoon, it seems like a long time between meals, and they're starving by the time I give them dinner. I put up with their comments about how I can make a fortune by opening an Italian spa, while they keenly count the days before the cruise, which will end their so-called hunger strike.

Together, we explore the glorious Tuscan countryside. Bright red poppies dot neon-green fields of wheat. Vineyards are sprouting, returning to life. Purple flowers carpet the hillsides. Driveways lined with cypress trees lead to ancient stone villas perched high on hills. From hilltop villages, we look down on splendid views of valleys. We discover the mystical, almost lunar landscape of the Crete Senesi, the area just south of the medieval city of Siena.

Each day we find more beauty than the last, and our guests don't want to go home. They prefer the sights and pleasures, if not the diet regimen, of Italy.

We also discover that Colin is, first and foremost, a photographer and only second, a trusted chauffeur. On more than one occasion, he abandons car and passengers parked on a blind curve and darts out to get *the* shot, too consumed to hear his wife yelling in the background.

Alas, we have only one more day here, and it will be time to move on. Our landlords suggest having dinner together on our last night. Because they have been so gracious, we wholeheartedly agree.

Their parting words are "Great, we'll be at your place at eight o'clock." This leaves us a little shocked. Being *Americani* and not Italian, we can think of better ways to spend our last day in Tuscany than cooking and cleaning for guests.

"But they said they're coming to our place," I tell David. "That must mean we're eating here." We discuss and debate how to get out of this dinner. I finally think of a plan, and detective David calls them.

"Ciao, listen, just checking if you or your wife are allergic to anything?"

"No," Renzo replies. As David is trying to figure out what to say next, Renzo asks, "Why?"

Grateful for another chance, David says, "Since the ladies will be cooking for you, they want to ensure you don't have any allergies." David's relief is evident on hearing the surprise in Renzo's voice, as he says they will bring dinner.

The time is approaching. David and I are thinking about the grand Italian meal, and the others, already starving an hour after our last meal, can hardly wait, either. Eight o'clock comes and goes. Finally, we see them coming up the driveway, after eight, *più o meno*.

David runs to the car and offers them a hand.

"Oh, no, this is light, just a tiramisu," Tiziana says.

Of course, Italians always bring dessert! How could David get it so wrong? Now what can we serve everyone? We invite them to sit at the table. We chat for a long time, trying to figure out a plan. We have no food left in the house. Do we take them to a restaurant that may end up being prohibitively expensive, or do we just pretend we've already eaten and try not to devour the tiramisu as if we were ravenous beasts?

Renzo eventually stands up and goes downstairs to the kitchen in the apartment below. We keep chatting with his wife. My stomach growls, but the smell of hope is now in the air. Renzo is cooking, and in no time, he carries up platter after platter of the delectable Italian meal we were expecting.

He starts with various homemade cold cuts: *cinghiale* (wild boar), as well as a *tartufo* (truffle) one. An assortment of pecorino cheese is accompanied by a long explanation of its origins and how it made its way to our table. Next is homemade lasagna, noodles and all: Tiziana's mother's specialty. We feel like heels, embarrassed by their generosity and hospitality and our lack of the same, although that will remain our secret.

They are no longer our landlords but new friends. They invite us back for the *Palio* in Siena in the summer, and we thank them for a truly memorable vacation, right up to the dubious end.

RADIATING HOPE

IT'S MORNING AND TIME TO depart for our cruise. We'll sail from Civitavecchia, an estimated three hours away.

"Uh-oh," I hear from outside, and the men tell us, "The car radiator hose is leaking water, and the car is overheating."

During our entire stay in Italy, this was the first deadline we ever had to meet: being on time for the ship's departure. In whispers, the men devise a plan. Phone calls are made, with David pacing back and forth, waving his arms and raising his voice.

He packs a dozen water bottles into the trunk and disappears. After what seems an eternity, though in reality is only one hour, he returns. We are all hopeful.

"I have good news and bad news. I was able to get the part from BMW, but neither they nor any other mechanic here can install it for us immediately. But I've found a mechanic in Civitavecchia who can do the work."

I fail to understand what the good news is, as I look at the car, hood open, with steam billowing from it.

Because the cruise is nonrefundable, my husband is motivated. Despite being a cabinetmaker, he suggests that perhaps he and Colin could install the hose themselves. We women freeze in fear. I visualize pieces of the motor strewn across the lawn, the men scratching their heads, and the cruise ship departing.

"Is there another plan?" I meekly ask, as David and Colin survey the engine. The men stare at us without responding.

They suddenly run inside. "Hurry, we must go! If we drive slowly, and every twenty minutes stop, refill the radiator, and let it cool down, then perhaps we can make it."

With no other option, we fill another dozen bottles with water, load our suitcases, and the gypsy kings are on the road again.

David is our chauffeur, while my mother preoccupies herself with the temperature gauge. The moment the needle moves toward red, she hysterically alerts us to stop the car. We pull into a gas station, the boys open the hood and refill the thirsty radiator, and we ladies nonchalantly head for the bathroom with our dozen empty water bottles.

On the road again, my mother continues her vigil. Aware of impending danger and no longer even trusting the temperature gauge, she undertakes her own inspection. At regular intervals, she runs her hands across the jet-black dashboard and tells us the engine is getting hot and we must stop immediately. David, no longer amused, gives her a lesson on where the engine is actually located and why the black dashboard is broiling hot in 105 degree Fahrenheit weather.

We stop at a gas station, and a paddy wagon pulls in after us. Out charge six *carabinieri*. We chat with them and learn they are from Naples.

"We're transporting a prisoner from Florence to Naples."

"What has he done that so many of you are required?" my husband half-jokingly asks.

"He killed American tourists," says the *carabiniere* with a sly look, then laughs heartily.

We don't find that funny. Perhaps he realizes this, or maybe he developed a soft spot for us, after remembering he has a distant relative in Chicago. "Drive within the speed limits," he advises us, "or else you will be ticketed in these regions."

A man from Naples, of all places, telling us to drive with caution, *what next?*

We wave a last good-bye to the green fields with red poppies poking through: the epitome of Tuscany in the spring.

The breeze turns cool, and soon thereafter the temperature gauge stabilizes. We begin to believe in miracles.

We're almost there, our exit is next! We arrive at the port and spot our massive ship, regally docked and waiting for us.

With time still of the essence, David drops us off and prays for his second miracle of the day: to find a street in a city that doesn't post street names. Miracle number two: he finds it and drops off the car and the part with the mechanic.

David makes it back to the ship just before departure, as does my sister, Vesna, having caught the last transfer bus from the airport. Now that we're all here, I hug them, my eyes overflowing with tears.

All's well that ends well. On the top deck, with a martini in hand, my husband gives us some good news: "The mechanic will only charge thirty euros to install the part, and the car can stay there ten days until we return, so we won't have to pay the hundred euros to park the car!"

The stress we endured has undoubtedly taken years off our lives, but I let David believe in modern-day miracles as we sail into the sunset.

THE ROOF RACK AND A
PROVINCIAL MOTHER

WHEN THE CRUISE IS OVER, we bid a teary farewell to Colin
and Esther and head to our new place in Tuscany with my
mother and sister. David goes to the mechanic's shop to pick
up our car, which mercifully is still there. My mom mutters
under her breath, "Who would steal that car?" David,
fortunately, doesn't hear her and parks on the main road,
where he loads our suitcases onto his homemade roof rack.

My mother stands at a distance, waving one last good-bye
to fellow cruisers. Afraid of destroying her image as a jet-
setter, she hopes no one will notice the car she gets into.

We leave the port and drive along open fields, red poppies
still peeking out from the now yellowing wheat, albeit in
fewer numbers. We're anxious to get to our place, because
the hot midday sun is taking its toll.

David brakes suddenly, and we swerve at high speed. "Did
anyone see that curve coming up?" he asks.

We look at him incredulously, for the road signs couldn't
be more obvious: giant black-and-white stripes with yellow
flashing lights, preceded by warning signs of the impending

curve. Perhaps the heat has gotten to him, or maybe it's the champagne from breakfast.

Red, blue, black, and green, our suitcases sit piled high on the makeshift roof rack. Roaring like a Ferrari, our old BMW is covered in dust, with guts from dead bugs splattered across the windshield. Picturing our arrival at the villa, I now understand my mother's embarrassment.

My mother and sister will live with us for the first week, a detail I omitted mentioning to our new landlords. Thus, it's with a measure of trepidation that we approach the iron gates. Behind them stands a stately stone house done in typical Tuscan style, surrounded by large clay pots overflowing with red geraniums. The yellow and pink homes on the hillsides of Cortona are directly behind us. We are awed that this will be our residence for the next five months—until we step out of the car and smell the unpleasant aroma.

We ring the bell and are greeted by a family of four, everyone enthusiastic to meet the new tenants. The two daughters are incredibly beautiful and well dressed, Ava Gardner–like: tall, tanned, with prominent cheekbones and long dark curly hair cascading down their backs. Linen dresses hug their perfect bodies.

They stare at the luggage and then at us. I feel like a frump and wish I'd dressed up for the occasion. The girls have to rush off, though, and Antonietta, the mother, leads us to our apartment in the house. She gives us a brief tour of our lodgings: a kitchen with a couch in it, a spacious bedroom furnished in Florentine-style furniture, and a bathroom. The floors are new but done in an antique terra cotta brick look. The ceilings throughout are exposed brick, with heavy beams running across them. The pantry is fully stocked with pasta and jarred tomato sauce.

"There is no microwave, because in my opinion it's like getting an X-ray done," Antonietta explains, no doubt because we are *Americani*.

Annoyed, she shakes her head and points to the fireplace, which sounds as if something haunted lives in it. She casually opens the door, and a frightened creature flutters madly about and just misses my head on its flight out the door to freedom.

"Every so often, you will have to let the trapped birds out," she says matter-of-factly. "And you cannot drink or cook with the water."

A car drives by, playing barely audible music.

"What is this, a discothèque?" she yells at the driver, far louder than his music.

Antonietta disappears, then soon returns with everything required to make a proper Italian lunch. We say that we'll find a restaurant, but she refuses to let us do any such thing. Perhaps judging by our car and our appearance, she'd rather we have enough money to pay the rent first.

Again, she gives us the once-over and yells on her way out, "You're all invited to our place for dinner tonight." She doesn't even give us a chance to reply.

"Hurry and get dressed!" she hollers at her husband, Rocco, who has been working in a garden the size of a football field.

He looks at us, shrugs, and says, "*L'orto vuole l'uomo morto*" (the garden wants the man dead). Judging by his slim figure, dark tan, and noticeably tired face, I guess he is correct.

"Hurry! Hurry!" Stefania shouts to her father from the window upstairs.

And they're up in arms over soft music coming from a car?

They pull out of the driveway, and once the coast is clear, we haul our luggage inside. We make lunch, open the bottle of red they left, and eat our pasta, laughing hysterically at how we must have looked and their surprise as we drove up. We don't fit their image of the rich *Americani*. David doesn't join in our laughter, insisting that his roof rack is an ingenious invention. My mother, whom I now realize is rather provincial, pleads with David to remove the rack before we go anywhere else. Yet I can tell he'll leave it on a few more days just to be naughty, because he openly relishes the thought of seeing his mother-in-law beg.

Being bona fide Italians, after lunch David and I must take our sacred *pausa*. My mother and sister will watch the world go by from our Tuscan porch. They find two dirty white plastic chairs and sit outside.

On awakening, we see my mother and sister still guarding the house, despite this home being fully protected. All of the windows and doors are barred, which must be against fire code standards—and if not, it should be—and a tall stone wall with an elaborate iron gate surrounds the house. There are also motion detectors and video cameras. With all of these security measures, I wonder about the crime rates in Tuscany.

Despite the possible security risks, David and I go for our customary walk. We stroll down our street and pass one beautiful home after another, none of them barred like ours. Perhaps the criminal element is not hard at work here after all. Before long, we discover that our landlords are from Naples.

Their being from Naples also explains why they told us it takes about twenty minutes to get to Arezzo from Cortona, when it takes us forty-five. Although the entire family is undergoing physiotherapy after being in car accidents, they nonetheless poke fun at us for driving so slowly.

We walk past a pig farm, overcome by the smell. Next door to the pig farm is a vacation rental property. I pity the poor unsuspecting tourists who check into the "beautiful Tuscan villa, complete with in-ground pool." We hope the winds change direction soon.

When we return home, my mother and sister are still on the porch. Every so often, a car drives by, and they mimic our landlady, saying, "What is this, a discothèque?" Compared to the rap music blaring from cars back in Toronto, Tuscany is idyllic.

As the days pass, we discover that aside from putting bars on their homes, driving fast, and constantly yelling, Neapolitans are also famous for their generosity. Our landlady regularly leaves packages of food items on our doorstep. She picks fresh produce from the garden and brings it to us.

Neapolitans are also warm and friendly. When we're sitting in our kitchen and one of them passes by, they would consider it rude not to peek in and greet us. At first, we feel as if it's an invasion of privacy, but now, as their car rolls into the driveway, we prepare to ask how their day was.

Thus, despite our initial reserve—and theirs, too, no doubt, when they saw us drive up—in a short period we become not only the best of friends but, possibly worse, like family. My mother really had no need to worry about the roof rack, after all.

SHOW THOSE EGGS SOME RESPECT!

NOW WE HAVE NEW FAMILY and plenty of old family. My mother and sister recently left, and we're enjoying a break from our role as tour guides. But David's parents, Maria and Giorgio, are back from Canada and have missed us dearly.

Perhaps to rescue us from our "loneliness," Maria and Giorgio insist they will soon visit us and, secretly, Tuscany. They'll take the bus to Perugia and from there catch a train. We're surprised that they're willing to make all of this effort, for they're generally not the adventurous types. I get the place ready, and, being a dutiful Italian woman, now I even iron the sheets and the pillowcases.

"No, thank you, Ma, they have eggs here in Tuscany, too." A pause, then, slightly irritated, David says, "Yes, I think Tuscan chickens can be trusted." She continues with her shopping list. "They also have cheese here, try to enjoy some regional specialties. We really don't need anything, just bring yourselves."

Those were his last words to her on the phone. We pick up his parents at the station the following day, and we can immediately tell that his mother isn't a good listener. Strange odors are escaping from their suitcase, and when they open it, it becomes evident that many things in Tuscany could not be trusted, hard-boiled eggs being just one of them. Cheese, lamb, veal, bread, garlic, basil, fruit, peanuts, cookies, olives, tomato sauce, and assorted other food items have safely made the journey from Abruzzo to Toscana. Maria and Giorgio unpack a virtual grocery store, along with a few clothing items that have shared the space and now smell like hard-boiled eggs and garlic.

Campanalisti is what many Italians are accused of being. They believe that the spot right under their church bell is the best place on earth, Giorgio and Maria being no exception. They have made a long journey, and we hope they will be able to enjoy Toscana.

They are most impressed with the Tuscan-style house and how it has been restored. Papà hits the wood beams on the ceiling with his cane and remarks on how sturdy they are. They examine the terra cotta floors, done in a herringbone design. He gives his seal of approval and states, "Good workmanship and good taste these Tuscans have."

After lunch and the mandatory two-hour *pausa*, we take them up to Cortona, a Tuscan hilltop town so classic that it's almost a cliché. Cortona holds a wealth of history. Built on a high hilltop, it offers amazing views of the countryside—the Valdichiana valley stretching westward, and Lake Trasimeno visible over the low hills to the south.

They take it in, examining everything. Giorgio raises his cane and hits an ancient stone wall with it. Part of this five-hundred-year-old wall immediately crumbles and falls down, just missing me.

"Shabby workmanship," he explains.

David is mortified and makes a quick escape, leaving me behind with the culprit.

Still in the park, Maria is excited to find a plant she likes. She picks seeds from it and fills her pockets.

We walk up the steep hills, and soon we're all out of breath. We stop for a few minutes to rest and watch an elderly lady with a cane walk past us, greeting us without a hint of difficulty in her voice. As she passes by, I glance at David with a wry smile.

He dismisses her vigor. "Ah, she's used to it; she probably does it every day."

We make our descent and walk past many quaint restaurants, knowing we'll have to wait to eat there until the in-laws leave. The owner at one restaurant is not pleased. Someone has stolen one of the seven dwarves from the building's steps. He placed a large sign where, I assume, the dwarf used to stand: "You who have stolen my dwarf have stolen a very precious gift from me, made by someone very dear. So if you have even a little heart, bring it back. P.S. To steal a dwarf does not bring good luck."

Though my in-laws are not from this province, they are from this country, and their pride is evident as we take them through Cortona and the outskirts, admiring the villas and the beautiful piazzas full of people and life.

It's now time to go home for dinner. We need to hurry to make certain the table is set and we are seated before the internal clock of David's father begins to chime. David drives exceptionally fast, and his parents, though somewhat frightened, also beam with delight that their son has truly become Italian in this last year. I mention that even other Italians have noted his driving, giving him the ultimate compliment by asking, "Are you from Naples?" Again, they burst with pride.

Dinner goes well. I have prepared everything in advance, so it can be put on the table pronto. David's father is impressed that I've quickly caught on to what an Italian man needs: food at the proper time.

After dinner, David's mom spends hours gossiping with me about how she can't stand all of the gossiping in small towns and the excessive doting on children and grandchildren.

At our "hotel," we routinely give up our bedroom to our guests, so that they receive five-star service, while we sleep on a pull-out couch with a lumpy mattress in the kitchen, which at best could be considered two star. I toss and turn all night, and so does David. We finally doze off in the wee hours of the morning, still exhausted. We aren't happy to hear the tap, tap, tap on our door at 7 a.m.

David's father was well-behaved this morning; his internal clock is finely tuned, and he wakes up at six. He waited in the bedroom for more than an hour, finished several crossword puzzles, and kept his patience for as long as he could. Thus, despite pleas from his wife, who has a soft spot for sleeping children, he had to wake us. Besides, today we'll go to Florence, and we must get an early start.

Minutes later, still in a stupor, we're on the highway heading to Florence. His parents have never been there, so we reserve tickets to Accademia for them to see Michelangelo's *David*. While traveling, I notice a persistent odor in the car. Maria has brought the hard-boiled eggs with her.

"Just in case we get hungry," she says.

David drops off his parents as close to the center as possible and parks the car in his secret spot. They are impressed; their son even knows where to find free parking in Florence!

We take them to the Piazza della Signoria. They note the statue of *David* outside in the square and ask whether it's pretty much the same as the one in Accademia. My husband says yes but stresses this isn't the original. However, it's good enough for his parents.

"Then no need to spend our time and money going inside," they insist.

We take a few pictures of them under the fake *David* and purchase postcards of the real *David* to send to family and friends.

We walk past fancy windows, taunting me with their wares. I stop to look at the beautiful, exorbitantly priced lingerie. A special shaped bra promises "minimum coverage with maximum support." The Italian women walking around Florence all seem to have discovered this bra.

Watching the fashionable Florentines inspires me to buy a pair of big sunglasses for David. He begrudgingly puts them on, and, despite the dark tint, I can see him rolling his eyes. He doesn't really want these extra-large sunglasses that men wear here. They're too similar to the ones that women wear.

The African says, "Twenty euros."

I say, "Too much."

He says, "Fine, give me fifteen because I'm closing the store now." His little cardboard stand has a sheet over it, and it's not even noon. I tell him to take five.

"Done deal," he says.

David isn't too thrilled that I've won the barter, but he puts on the sunglasses to appease me.

We must hurry to the Duomo if we want to make it to the restaurant by twelve. David videotapes his parents as they approach the Duomo. Aware of the camera, they stop bickering and hold hands, suddenly transformed into lovebirds.

I'm overwhelmed by the grandeur of the Duomo, along with its beauty. As I seize the moment, I overhear an American kid whining, "Mom, how much longer do we have to stay in this place?"

"Two more days," she impatiently answers.

A man balances a pizza in one hand, while holding a camera in the other, trying to take a shot of the pizza with the Duomo in the background. I wonder what the Florentines must think of us tourists.

Enough of the Duomo; the internal clock is ticking. We must eat, because soon it will be *pausa* time. We find a restaurant that appears to have a good menu and seems reasonably priced. We are seated, and we order pasta, pizza, wine, beer, and *digestivos*. When my mother-in-law learns that we'll have to pay for water, she thinks this is unjust, so out comes the water bottle from her purse. With a big smile, she fills our glasses and brings out the indestructible hard-boiled eggs. Yet after devouring everything we ordered, we're full, so the eggs remain uneaten. The bill arrives, and David and I try to grab it, but Giorgio insists on paying, but not without a soliloquy on how we could have had a much better meal at home for far less.

They have seen the highlights of Florence in two hours, and it's time to find a place to observe Italy's favorite ritual. Recognizing that the *pausa* is never to be forfeited, we're prepared. We have brought some blankets and will try to find a spot along the Chianti road. Surely, it can't be that difficult to find a nice cypress tree to lie under.

We drive and drive. My in-laws are getting more exhausted by the mile and the minute and are soon ready to sleep under the next grapevine, even though it's close to passing trucks and within breathing distance of their diesel fumes.

David is determined to continue providing five-star sleeping arrangements. In and out of driveways he meanders. Finally, his efforts pay off, and we see a row of cypress trees beckoning, with stunning views all around. We lay the blankets down. Maria and Giorgio instruct us to wake them in two hours, and within minutes they are asleep.

"If you can't beat them, join them," David says, and soon we fall asleep, too, with the scent of pines the last thing we remember.

The heat wakes us up—the sun has changed position and is now beaming down on us. We continue our tour of the Chianti region.

As we drive along the SS222, a famous scenic route, David's father surveys the many villas completely surrounded by cypress trees.

"It's not good for their foundations," he informs us.

"Then there are a lot of Tuscans who hired bad architects and misguided landscapers," I say.

Maria explains that the Abruzzesi are superstitious and think that a tree that surrounds a cemetery should not surround your home. That would denote impending doom. Recognizing, however, that the Tuscans are not dying at a quicker rate, she decides that the trees are a good thing and is glad we planted two seeds beside their home. We agree, and in thirty years we shall see just how beautiful they will be.

We drive through several villages and stroll the ancient streets. Along with an abundance of wine souvenirs and postcards for sale, there is also a bubble gum–style machine dispensing thong underwear.

We take David's parents to *Le Cantine di Greve*, where you can try more than 150 wines. You purchase a card for ten euros and insert it into various slots. Each bottle is labeled as to type and how much a sample costs.

"How many cards should we get?" I ask.

"We don't need any," Maria says. "We shouldn't spend our money foolishly."

"This will be a treat," I say and buy two cards, despite her objections.

There is also olive oil tasting, free with the wine-tasting card. My mother-in-law's eyes suddenly light up. She samples the most expensive ones and decides the olive oil from Abruzzo is far superior, regardless of cost. Giorgio is enjoying the tasting and moves on to the more expensive brands. He soon realizes what all of the fuss is about Tuscan wine.

We take the long and beautiful drive home through the Chianti region, with its expansive vineyards on tranquil hills.

As the sun goes down, David tries to put his sunglasses on top of his head. The entire lens comes off in his hands. He is transformed from a hip Italian to a nerdy welder wearing thick black frames.

"Well, I guess that's what you get for five euros!" he says. He puts the lens back on the frames and realizes that a magnet allows you to take off the lens, while keeping the empty frames on your face.

"For this feature, I would have paid even ten euros!" David says.

We arrive just in time for dinner, and I put out my already prepared food. I turn my back for a moment, and the traveling hard-boiled eggs miraculously appear on the table. I cannot win this battle, and besides, now I'm certain these eggs have toured more of Italy than your average Italian and deserve a little respect. So, while most normal people would chuck them out, we eat them, proving we have stomachs like catfish and can digest anything.

After dinner, our landlords come to meet the family. In no time, they are all the best of friends, the men refilling one another's wine glasses, while the women converse on their own. I'm exhausted and can't understand where these older people get their energy. I long for the lumpy couch. The night edges on, and they keep talking with unrelenting vigor. I stare at the clock, knowing that soon I'll hear the familiar tap, tap, tap on our kitchen door at an impossibly early hour.

The following day, we take Maria and Giorgio to Montepulciano, one of the highest Tuscan hilltop towns. Built along a narrow ridge of limestone, it's a stunningly good-looking town, with expansive vistas, dozens of Renaissance palaces and churches, and many *cantinas*.

At one *cantina*, we wait in line for a tasting. A rather odd British lady ahead of us is blocking the entire aisle with her cumbersome knapsack and is annoyed each time someone wants to pass by.

"I would like a good but cheap Brunello," says the British lady.

"Madam, a Brunello di Montalcino, by law, has to be aged a minimum of five years," explains the ever-patient *signorina* behind the counter. "Therefore, a Brunello is not cheap. The youngest Brunello you can purchase is a 2002."

"Then just give me a younger Brunello that's cheaper."

The *signorina* repeats her explanation, in perfect English. Perhaps this lady isn't aware that we're living in 2007 or she has had one too many samples. Finally, it's our turn, and my father-in-law tries many samples himself. He is quite taken aback with the fine wine and purchases several bottles of Vino Nobile di Montepulciano and Brunello. I hope one will be opened today with lunch.

"Would you like to see the church of San Biagio on the hillside just below the town?" David asks. "It was the second largest church project of its time, after St. Peters in Rome, and is beautiful, as is the scenery."

"No," they say in unison and opt for going home, to ensure that they have time for their *pausa*.

We eat, we sleep, and soon we're ready to take them to the bus station in Perugia, because they have too many bottles to carry and cannot take the train.

Living in Italy hasn't cured my phobia of fast driving but has only intensified it. I see electronic signs on the highways stating how many have died on this very highway, flowers along the roadside, and a banner that states, "Fabio, we will always remember you," wrapped around a tree.

Nevertheless, recognizing they must not miss their bus, I whisper to David, "By whatever means necessary."

"Our car can go two hundred and forty," he teasingly says.

We arrive within minutes of their bus's departure. We wave; we throw kisses and act as if we'll never see them again. As the bus pulls away, Maria's eyes fill with tears. Another farewell, Italian style, though we'll see them again in three weeks.

It's 10 p.m., and David's father calls to let us know they made it home safely. David is astonished to hear his father thank us profusely and say that he enjoyed every minute of it, best vacation he ever had. We suspect that he opened one or more of the bottles of Brunello on the bus ride home.

REGAL LIVING, ITALIAN STYLE

SHE LOOKS LIKE A PRINCESS with long dark hair and perfect skin and features. However, she doesn't act like one. Despite her refined air, she is in no way pretentious. When she invites us for brunch and to spend Sunday at her Tuscan villa, we gladly accept. Brunch is a North American luxury we miss. She belongs to a generation of new open-minded Italians.

"Bring your bathing suits. After brunch, we'll go swimming."

In 105 degree Fahrenheit weather, it's comforting that she doesn't subscribe to the deeply ingrained belief that one must wait the obligatory three-hour period after eating to take a swim.

We enter the property through an ancient stone wall and pull into a long driveway, lined with cypress trees. There is an imposing villa and a guesthouse, we assume. Chiara is in the kitchen, cooking, with printouts of recipes scattered about, and she appears stressed and flustered. She's the first Italian I have ever seen using a recipe and exhibiting less than Martha Stewart–like calmness in the kitchen. She will attempt to make pancakes with maple syrup, quiche, and a cheesecake. For the die-hard Italians, there is an assortment of Italian cheese, prosciutto, and stuffed tomatoes.

Barbara has also been invited. She recently moved to Tuscany and is having a hard time finding work. She started including her photograph with her resume, as suggested, and since then has not received a single response, despite leaving dozens of resumes with various businesses. She feels dejected, so Chiara thought that a little *festa*, a party, might cheer her up.

Barbara is a decade younger than I am, slim, beautiful, with long blond hair, big blue eyes, ever-youthful skin, and perfectly chiseled features. As if that weren't enough, she speaks Italian and English fluently.

If no one will hire her, who is going to hire me? I thought.

It's eleven o'clock, and everything is prepared.

"Are we ready to eat?" Chiara asks.

"Of course!" I say.

However, Fabiano feels it's too early to eat such a meal.

The warm pancakes and my growling stomach indicate otherwise. "This is brunch," I say.

He argues, "The word *brunch* has only two letters from the word *breakfast* and three from the word *lunch*, meaning it should be eaten later."

Ignoring his "logic," Chiara says, "We're ready to eat." She calls the others, while Fabiano, defeated, goes for a swim first.

"Otherwise, I'll have to wait three hours after I eat," he woefully explains.

We thank her for her bravery and her good cooking.

"No, thank you!" she says. "I like to try new things, and it's hard to find someone who will appreciate them. Once I made sushi for my parents, which they thought were beautiful little cakes. As they bit into them, I explained what they were. My parents spit them out and put the rest in the oven, saying that I was going to make everyone sick serving raw seafood."

She should have known you can't serve sushi to an Italian who is older than fifty!

"So I'm happy to have you as my guests or, as my father calls you, my latest victims."

We figured she was rich. Her driving a $100,000 car gave us the hint, but how rich we could only guess. A large key hangs on the wall, so David asks what it is for.

"That's for our castle," she nonchalantly says and shows us a picture of an imposing castle, complete with towers, a vast courtyard, and a chapel within its protective walls.

"We can go and have lunch there sometime, if you like."

"That would be great!" I say, wondering what one wears to lunch at a castle.

Rachele suggests that she and I go for a stroll. Moments after we leave, her cell phone rings. We walk with Rachele loudly talking on her cell phone the entire time. At the end of the walk, she thanks me for my company and finishes her conversation with her mother, whom she speaks to at least a dozen times a day.

The boys, meanwhile, are in the garage eyeing a shiny new red Ferrari F40. I no longer recognize my otherwise camera-shy husband, as he poses next to it. He talks passionately about the engine, *sangue Italiano* showing.

"Our car sounds like a Ferrari!" I tease him.

All fired up, David jumps into the Olympic-size swimming pool. The conversation changes from what's the fastest car they have ever driven to who is the best diver. The girls do the judging, and despite having the worst car of the lot, David is happy to walk away with a diving average of 9.

The girls shed their cover-ups and emerge with thin, trim, bikini-clad bodies. Are these the same girls who eat big plates of pasta? Who drizzle large quantities of olive oil on their pizzas? The same girls who have two scoops of gelato, while I have the baby cone?

I take off my dress and, when no one is looking, slide into the swimming pool. Thankfully, it's so terribly hot outside that no one suspects a thing, while I stay submerged the entire time.

Noemi, the baby, watches us longingly. She smiles and puts her pudgy arms out, wanting us to pick her up.

However, she has just eaten a yogurt and is forbidden from even sitting in waist-high water in her little blow-up pool.

I lather on sun block and take respite from the blazing sun under an oversized white umbrella. Italians have no fear of the sun and turn over regularly, ensuring an even tan. I put my hat on and remind David to wear sunscreen. They humor my paranoia with knowing smiles.

While they bake in the sun, we discuss the dangers of using a microwave, the perils of air-conditioning, the fact that the Chinese are definitely buying up all of the Parma prosciutto, and how one can never trust a meat sauce in a restaurant. The conversation is regularly interrupted by at least one person's cell phone ringing and then the conversation of that person. I point out that they are in far more danger from using a cell phone than from using a microwave.

Their quest for the perfect tan is interrupted while they take pictures. I escape to the bathroom, as they sit on the steps of the pool, posing. I hide inside and hear them ask, "Where did she go?" I exit, assuming they have taken more than enough pictures by now.

"Hey, there you are!" They pull me by the arm, forcing me to join their photo shoot. I try to suck in my stomach, while hoping the photographer's camera will fall into the swimming pool. They laugh as I try to escape.

Our laughter is drowned out by the roaring engine of a gleaming silver Porsche coming up the driveway. A handsome Italian man casually greets us and heads into the house. Soon, another prohibitively expensive car rolls into the driveway and more people exit. A Mercedes SUV pulls up next, and I finally ask Chiara, "Who are all these people?"

Puzzled, she says, "They are all my family: my aunt, uncle, cousins, my parents and grandparents." Then, evidently for our benefit, she adds, "They all live here."

I try to conceal my surprise, as I realize that although this is a filthy rich family, it is, first and foremost, an Italian one. Another lesson in what it truly means to be Italian. We assumed that families live together because they have no other choice; that compounds were built out of necessity, but that this wasn't actually Italians' preference.

I fantasize about what type of villa David and I would buy, were we to sell just a few of this family's cars: a private one with acres of land a safe distance from family. North American blood is evidently not always as thick as Italian blood.

I feel a twinge of guilt for being happy that my in-laws departed so soon. Fortunately, though, I am truly North American, and the slight guilt disappears quickly.

IL VINO (THE WINE)

THE BOTTLE OF 1999 CORTONA Chardonnay chills in our refrigerator. I recall its near fate, but it's safe again, having been returned to its rightful place: waiting to accompany a special dinner.

We received it during one of our walks. The walk in itself was a reward. Privileged, we witnessed the glory of sunflowers in full bloom beside bales of hay on gently rising Tuscan hills.

In a field of rustling wheat, we saw two men brave the scorching sun while harvesting. We chatted with one of them, named Bruno. He was a striking man with dark skin and a full head of thick curly gray hair, stylishly unruly. He was pleased to learn we were Canadians and didn't say, "Oh, *Americani!*" Due to his business of wheat farming, he had visited cities all across Canada. He said, "Your country has ruined the price of wheat for us!"

Nonetheless, he still liked Canada very much, although his favorite city happened to be the most European one, Quebec City.

He had stayed at the Chateau Frontenac. Having enjoyed a fine meal there ourselves, we ask whether he'd eaten there.

With a wave of his hand and a big smile, he said, "Oh, no! I wouldn't eat there! In fact, that was the only bad part of Canada, the cuisine! This sauce, that sauce, all these different-flavored sauces, I couldn't wait to get home and have a real meal!"

We nodded and agreed that Italian food was the best.

"Of course, it is," he said, "and I'm not saying that just because I'm Italian!"

Consequently, just before leaving Canada, he phoned home and ordered the menu that was to await him. With the enthusiasm only an Italian could possess on this subject, he said, "Roast chicken" and added, "done right!" which we immediately understood to mean *no BBQ sauce*. He gave us his address and warmly invited us to come to his home any time for a great meal, a typical Tuscan one.

Bruno was a wellspring of information. He enlightened us on everything from who was selling their home to what was the best restaurant in Florence to eat *Bistecca alla Fiorentina* (Florentine-style steak). Wanting to further exploit his wealth of knowledge, we asked him where we could find a good *cantina*, another of his favorite subjects. He gave us a few suggestions.

His cell phone rang; he glanced at the number and turned off the phone. It was only business, and now that he was engaged in what he really enjoyed, he didn't want to be disturbed. I joked that perhaps it was his wife calling, but he said that when *she* calls, he answers—this because they have two children, and it could be an emergency involving one of them.

We chatted for a few more minutes, shook hands, and bade him *arrivederci*. We trekked up and down hills for a while, when Bruno suddenly drove up. He had searched and found us and brought us a 1999 bottle of Cortona Chardonnay, a great wine!

"Come to my home for lunch," he said.

"Thank you, but we must finish our walk."

"Next time!" With a wave, he honked the horn and disappeared.

We were touched by the generosity of this stranger. We hurried home to chill the bottle so that we could enjoy it with lunch. Yet after our long walk and so much talk about mouth-watering food, we were too famished to wait for the bottle to chill. We decided to save it for a special occasion.

In the meantime, we accepted the many gracious invitations we received, and as days and weeks went by, our special dinner had to wait.

"Anticipation is the greatest part of any venture," they say, and mine certainly built up as I watched this bottle of Chardonnay chilling in our fridge.

One day Giuliana and Dino, a lovely couple who had been married close to fifty years, invited us over for lunch. I realized that a *casalinga* with this much experience would no doubt prove herself worthy of the title.

After homemade pasta, we were served roast pigeon. I could feel the little bones in my mouth and tried not to think about it. David wasn't a fan of pigeon himself and hadn't been since age ten, when he and his brothers painted their old VW station wagon fire engine red in their garage. They were almost finished when they heard flapping wings. They had forgotten about the pigeons above them, and, suddenly, hundreds of feathers fell down. They tried to pick them out of the fresh paint, but it was too late. Feather imprints remained. David has never forgiven those pigeons.

Admittedly, Giuliana's pigeon was quite tasty. Along with it, she served stuffed zucchini and roast potatoes with wild fennel. These flavors were enhanced by a wonderful bottle of red.

As we ate dessert, Giuliana surveyed the gifts we had brought and left on the counter. I was about to place another spoon of gelato in my mouth when Giuliana said, "Oh, a wine from Cortona. Thank you."

Cortona? David had taken the wrong bottle of wine from the refrigerator! I felt my face flush. David, also realizing his error, flashed me a look of surprise and defeat. I, conversely, realized we had another bottle of wine in the car and wondered, *Would there be any way we could somehow switch them?*

The two other guests, Barbara and Roberta, whom we'd told about this special bottle of wine that Bruno had given us, realized what had happened. They insisted we tell our hosts. They would understand. Besides, Dino didn't drink at all, and Giuliana drank very little. Moreover, they generally thought any purchased wine was full of chemicals.

I egged my husband on, and he went to the car, to have the other bottle on hand when he presented the story. He returned and was about to start explaining when Dino interrupted and changed the subject. Mentally, I willed David to be brave. He tried again, and just as he was about to speak, the subject was changed again. The anticipation was killing me. I saw David losing courage.

Suddenly, Giuliana said, "David, did you want to say something?"

Burying all sense of tact and propriety, David explained our situation.

"Of course, you must take the wine and try it," Giuliana said. "If the man asks if you liked it, what would you tell him?"

I was touched by her sweetness and understanding and began to feel like a heel. Dino, recognizing how much we liked our wine, went downstairs and returned with a bottle that resembled one found in the remains of the Titanic.

"This is a twenty-year-old bottle of Chianti." He explained precisely how long it had to be decanted and a list of other instructions that were necessary to fully enjoy this bottle. We were surprised that he was willing to part with it, for he evidently recognized its value. We profusely thanked them for their generosity.

At a dinner party that night, we tasted a seven-year-old Chianti Classico. Noting our enthusiasm for this particular bottle, our hosts insisted that we take the remainder home with us. It was truly a great day for wine.

Our long drive home through the Tuscan countryside gave us the chance to reflect on the sheer Chardonnay sweetness of our Chianti-plied life here.

QUEL CHE C'È C'È RISTORANTE (WHAT'S THERE IS THERE RESTAURANT)

I CHOOSE MY RED LINEN dress and a long necklace of silver and pearls to wear to the *ristorante* tonight. Inspired by Italians, I put on heels so high; a broken leg is guaranteed if I trip. Heavy eye shadow, bronzing powder, and shiny lip gloss complete the look. I give David the once-over and request only one wardrobe change. Now we're ready to meet up with Beniamino and Claudia.

This restaurant is very popular, we're told, so Claudia has made reservations. I'm looking forward to the air-conditioned comfort and to being served. And to seeing and being seen. The *ristorantes* back home in Canada are hip Italian dining establishments with white linen–draped tables and well-dressed people engaged in lively conversations. Surely, a *ristorante* in the heart of Tuscany will be even more fascinating.

After driving through several small villages and over a bridge that is supposedly the one in the *Mona Lisa* painting, we approach the *ristorante*. It's just as I pictured it, a restored old stone building with an abundance of red geraniums in pots. As we get closer, I see that the flowers are plastic. *A bad sign.*

The place is empty, even though it's eight-thirty. We walk up three stone steps into a *cantina*-like room, see a table set for four, and assume it's reserved for us. On it are three types of *crostini*: Tuscan liver paté, red pepper paste, and white bean. Completing the spread are a platter of prosciutto, other local salamis, a delicacy called *lardo* made of pure pork fat with herbs and spices, a giant basket of bread, two large bottles of unlabeled wine—one white, one red—and two bottles of water.

We await the maître d' and soon are greeted by a very skinny waitress. She bids us, *"Buon appetito."*

We eat and drink, while Beniamino enthusiastically tries to sell us on the virtues of *lardo*. "It's specially pressed between marble, seasoned Tuscan style," he says.

Therein lays the secret. Had he used the name of an impoverished region where people ate lard . . . but ah, not so when it's Tuscan style! Soon we gobble it up, and I wonder what I can begin to export under the brand "Tuscan Style." Back in Canada, I once saw an ad for Tuscan cat food. *Surely, I can make some money this way.*

The waitress arrives with two huge serving bowls of pasta. She plunks them down and disappears without a word. One dish is drenched in wild boar sauce. I try to forget Chiara's warnings about eating meat sauce in restaurants. The other dish is *farfalle* pasta with pesto sauce. We pass around the never-ending bowls of pasta and enjoy our lively conversation.

Lively conversation is a relative term, I soon discover, because we are no longer kings of the castle. The group of scraggly looking hunters who reserved the large table behind us now arrives. Each one greets us on his way in. I feel even more out of place and casually remove my silver-and-pearl necklace.

We can barely hear ourselves think over the rowdy hunters' noise. We speak louder and louder, and they overhear us and realize we are *Americani*.

"Hey, Miami! Hey, Miami!" they shout.

We smile and wave and keep eating our pasta.

The volume gets louder as the wine bottles get emptier. We can no longer even attempt conversation. Yet soon we are rescued, when the owner of this "fine" establishment approaches and asks, "Would you mind moving into the other room?"

"Not at all," we respond.

"Good," he says. "I wouldn't want to upset the hunters, because I forgot they'd requested a room of their own."

On my way out, one tipsy red-faced hunter yells, "Hey, Miami!" and enthusiastically pats the bench beside him, winking.

We are then seated in a quasi entrance/eating area, and the food keeps coming: mozzarella and tomato salad and two platters of grilled meat.

"Is everything okay?" the owner asks. We compliment him on his food and wine, and he returns with another large bottle of rosé.

"You must try this one, too, though it's been a *very* bad year for rosé wines." He puts the bottle down and heads off to entertain the hunters.

Up the giant stone steps is an electronic keyboard. The owner, a tall man, must duck to get through the entrance. He sits down, and even when he hunches over, his head almost touches the curved ceiling. He plays some typical Italian songs, but as he gets braver, I recognize English words. He belts out a Beatles song and looks at me for approval.

I smile and give him a thumbs up, and he gets louder and more confident, singing an old do-wop song from the fifties. Yet his musical career comes to an abrupt end when the electricity goes out. The hunters groan, then clap and whistle boisterously when it comes back on. This continues throughout the evening.

The only "air-conditioning" being two open doors, my heavy perfume now begins to attract mosquitoes. The Germans outside on the "patio" seem oblivious to the swarms of bloodsuckers. I'm the only one bothered by them or by the mangy, matted black dog that ambles in and out, occasionally lying down by my feet.

A dry, crumbly chocolate *crostata* is served for dessert, and we wait a while for our espresso, because the hunters ordered twenty of them before we did. The waitress brings us bottles of grappa, *limoncello,* and *Vinsanto* (holy wine), along with *cantuccini* (hard almond-flavored biscuits) to dunk into the wine.

Our espressos eventually arrive, and despite the late hour, I have one because I'll be driving the "twenty or so minutes" home.

Afterward, we stroll in a nearby park, where couples are dancing to romantic music under an immense white tent. I feel as if we're living in an Italian film.

Quel che c'è c'è. What's there is there. And we got what was there. It has been an experience, just not the one I expected.

And on that note, David says, "Goodnight, Miami!"

To Pay or Not to Pay

WE COME TO REALIZE THAT our popularity is largely based on our postal code. The Tuscan villa we aspire to own one day now includes a separate guest house. David's brother Giancarlo arrived a week ago, and with him sleeping in our combined kitchen and "living room," I remember why I'm grateful I don't have a teenager.

Giancarlo isn't without his redeeming qualities. He loves good food and wine and has no problem with all of us enjoying these in a restaurant. We spend leisurely days wandering through the Tuscan countryside and hilltop villages, Montepulciano being one of our favorites.

Where else can you walk into an *enoteca* and browse through bottles of wine that vary in age from two years to more than forty? In one *enoteca*, Giancarlo gleefully announces he has found a *Vino Nobile* from 1969—David's year of birth.

He's amazed to find such vintage wine. Getting more excited by the minute, he clumsily grabs another bottle, while I worry that the entire shelf and a half century of *vino* will come crashing down on us.

"Look, I found my year, 1963! We'll drink this with dinner tonight!"

He holds both bottles, suddenly quiet and reflective. Then he returns his birth year wine to the shelf and explains that while David has been living in Tuscany, he has been fighting a bitter divorce battle in Canada, in freezing cold weather, so 1969 surely was a better year. He places the chosen bottle by the cash register. I admire its deep ruby color in the sunlight.

Seeing that we are serious customers, the gentleman in the store plies us with samples. With a gleam in his eye and passion in his voice, he pours choice after choice. We chat about life in Italy versus life in North America. He complains about Italy's terribly high taxation.

"We don't actually begin working for ourselves until August twelfth," he explains. "We are taxed at a rate of 72 percent!"

We find this hard to believe. Italians are beautifully dressed, eat well, have giant apartments lined in granite and marble—albeit located above their parents, but nevertheless—and they seem to enjoy life more than most people do. We ask him for the secret of how Italians survive, then, if they are so heavily taxed.

"Ah," he says, "truth be told, we just don't pay the taxes."

We all burst out laughing, realizing that therein lays the fundamental difference between us and them. Italians are not anxious to participate in the crazy government scheme that we Canadians simply refer to as *income tax* and accept as a fact of life.

The samples continue to flow, but Giancarlo takes over and now pours them for himself. The store owner doesn't seem to mind Giancarlo's acting as sommelier, while David and I are embarrassed. Giancarlo soon discovers another wine he enjoys, and like the proverbial bull in a china shop, he slams it onto the counter. Two bottles of wine and ninety euros later, we walk out of the store.

We get into our sun-baked car and drive through the glorious countryside to Pienza. We feel like millionaires in our nineteen-year-old BMW, and with no native Italians on board to complain about drafts, we pump up the AC to the max.

After a short walk around Pienza, we look for a restaurant. Most of them have signs posted: "Closed for Vacation." We soon have to agree with the Minister of Tourism, who declared that "Italy is like a man driving a Ferrari at sixty kilometers [thirty-seven miles] an hour." Being unable to find an open restaurant in Tuscany in the middle of tourist season is a case in point.

At last, we find one. It's bustling with activity, though we aren't sure whether this is due to its being a good restaurant or being the *only* restaurant open for business.

We are ushered to our table and sit down in the "coolness" of Italian air-conditioning (which is never really that cool). We start with a platter of typical appetizers and, naturally, a bottle of the house wine. The boys order their next course, gnocchi with wild boar sauce. I opt for the liver. The waiter makes certain that I know what I'm ordering.

"Of course, liver," I say. "I love liver."

"Okay, fine." He ambles away.

I soon discover the reason for his lack of enthusiasm. My liver looks like three black balls from the nether regions of a bull. The waiter drops the plate in front of me with a look that says, "I told you so."

The boys can't contain their enthusiasm for their gnocchi: soft, moist, wonderful. As I watch them smugly devour their gnocchi, I'm tempted to tell Giancarlo about the dangers of eating meat sauce in restaurants. Yet I remain silent and try to eat my dried-out bull's balls. They must be overcooked, for they are literally inedible. The waiter comes over, and I ask him whether this is how the dish is normally prepared.

"Oh, yes, diced pork liver wrapped in caul fat and then cooked until black and dried out."

"Ah, just checking," I say. Not wishing to lose face, I smile and declare my newfound love for overdone pork liver wrapped in caul fat.

The restaurant is not without its amusements, though. A deeply tanned, handsome, well-dressed Italian playboy type waltzes through the place, grabs a drink from the bar, and helps himself to dessert with an air of confidence. Giancarlo scowls, and I note a hint of jealousy as he describes the man's life for us.

"This guy just woke up," he begins. "After making coffee in his automatic espresso machine, he leaves the extremely large apartment that his father built and completely equipped for him."

I say that Giancarlo is wrong: prior to coming here, the guy spent his morning by the pool, wearing big sunglasses and sipping cappuccino.

Giancarlo impatiently rolls his eyes at me and continues, "Then he gets into his expensive sports car, makes a quick stop to pick up cigarettes, and is now sitting here, in his father's restaurant, which he will one day inherit but will, of course, hire other people to run." Giancarlo finishes this last sentence in a huff.

Again, I think Giancarlo is wrong. On his way here, the man stopped at the Armani store and picked up the blue linen shirt that he's wearing, along with the white linen pants.

The boys are not amused.

"Don't say you would actually fall for this playboy type if you weren't married?" they demand.

"Nah," I lie.

Giancarlo insists on paying. He leaves a large wad of cash on the table and heads to the bathroom. The waitress returns with his change. Not sure how much of a tip Giancarlo wants to give, we leave the funds on the table. The proprietor, suddenly eagle-eyed, spots the "extremely generous tip" the *Americano* has left and encourages the waitress to grab the money. Before we can say a word, she takes all of the bills and the change. Smiling, she drops the money into a tip jar on the counter.

Shocked, yet embarrassed, we aren't sure what to do. Giancarlo returns, and we explain what has taken place. Giancarlo, though shocked, is *not* embarrassed and knows exactly what to do. He wanders over to the tip jar, does the math, and leaves her an ample, yet, by comparison, much smaller tip. Then he shoves his huge hand into the jar and retrieves the rest of his funds. Without waiting around, David and I sneak out.

After a day of essentially doing nothing, we're exhausted. We have no other recourse but to go home and take a *pausa*—but first we must stop for a gelato. The locals briefed us on which are the good *gelaterias* and which ones have simply hung out a sign stating *Artigianale* (homemade). We find a place that serves unusual flavors: cheese and pear, celery and lemon, and other interesting combinations. After much contemplation, I get my regular: pistachio and hazelnut.

Giancarlo orders two scoops, melon and vanilla. His request is denied, because this is an inappropriate combination. My brother-in-law insists, but the teenager behind the counter has been duly trained and will not mix an ice base with a cream base. Giancarlo finally chooses two cream-based flavors, and the smiling kid behind the counter scoops them out, now a hero in his own mind.

As we drive home in the searing heat, we pass a very old lady in a bikini working in her vegetable garden.

When it's time to drive Giancarlo back to Abruzzo, we plan to first stop in Rome to visit relatives. We haven't seen them for two months, and Giancarlo hasn't seen them for an entire year.

Rome is excruciatingly hot and humid. Our regular lodgings at "Hotel" *Zia* and *Zio* are now closed for summer vacation, because they've gone to their cool mountain home in Abruzzo. We'll stay at another uncle's home. As a result, we are now traveling on the Grande Raccordo. The definition of *anarchy* should be: "this highway." Adding to my woes, Giancarlo is showing David, our driver, something in a book. Naturally, David looks intently at it.

There is hope ahead, because I see brake lights. I must be the only human being alive who is grateful for traffic. The traffic is so bad that a man with a cigarette dangling out of his mouth is leaning out of his car window and asking other drivers for a light.

I sit in the backseat, smiling. I relax and doze off while traffic crawls. But soon that smile will be wiped off my face.

We arrive at *Zio* Natale's home, and he decides to take us out to dinner. We get into his shiny black Mercedes, and, much like a tour guide, he explains each spot on the road that has special meaning for him. This is where he rolled over into the ditch. See that missing piece of stone wall? The time he went over the edge and landed in a tree was awful, because he couldn't get the car out and had to stay overnight in a barn. Here is where those dirty cops stopped him for driving 120 kilometers in a 50 km zone (75 mph in a 30 mph zone).

As he finishes describing each unfortunate episode, he assures us that he really is a very safe driver. How I pity the poor unsuspecting soul who one day buys *Zio*'s not so gently used Mercedes!

The pizzeria is crowded and lively, and we sit on a spacious outdoor terrace. Even though it's nine o'clock at night, the air still feels stifling. The Romans are sporting their tans and the latest fashions. For women, it's cowboy boots paired with the tiniest of tops, because they have evidently also discovered the minimum-coverage, maximum-support bra.

Swarms of well-dressed children laugh and play in the courtyard, throwing stones at the fence and inadvertently hitting the fancy BMW illegally parked at the entrance.

Television sets abound, though it appears that no one actually wants to hear anything the scantily clad models onscreen say. I order a large alcoholic drink with my pizza, planning to sedate myself for the harrowing ride home. After the first few minutes in the car, I realize I should have ordered a double.

We arrive at *Zio*'s and try to fall asleep. I close the window to block out the sounds of *motorinos* whizzing through the city and put up with the oppressive heat.

We cut short our trip to Rome, because it's positively too hot. Even the lure of summer sales isn't enough to keep me here.

The next day we drive to Abruzzo on the Salaria, the old road they used to deliver salt to Roman soldiers as a salary, hence the English word. We drive peacefully through mountains and villages until we realize we're running out of GPL—propane for cars. We look for a gas station that is open, but it's Sunday in Italy, so it will be difficult to find one.

A sign curiously indicates the distance to the next gas station; 26,000 meters (28,433 yards). When we get there, we find that it, too, is *Chiuso Domenica* (closed Sundays). Luckily, we make it home.

Mamma and Papà are waiting for us with open arms, beaming faces, and half a dozen freshly made ricottas and pecorino cheeses. They have been on a cheese-making mission, their garage transformed into a small factory.

The following morning we wake up to find Briciola, the little dog from down the hill, outside. She has patiently been waiting more than two hours for us to wake up. She plants a lick on my face, attempting many more. In no time, we hear loud meowing from a safe distance across the street. The cat from next door has also realized we are back and wants our affection. Then Leone lumbers into the yard. David's parents are shocked, because none of these animals have been anywhere near the house since we left.

Feeling like a criminal, I sneak down to the basement and get the pet food we had previously bought and hidden. David stands on guard while I feed the animals.

As expected, on Day One we visit family. Despite the heat, *Zia* Franca is wearing her classic black sweater. *Zio* Luigi is not in his usual farmer's get-up but looks rather sharp: fresh pressed shirt, dark jacket, and nice pants. He is tanned and trim. On holiday from his farm, he has been hanging out at the beach lately. With an umbrella and a gallon of wine, off he goes every day to the seaside with his friends.

Now *Zio* puts on a pair of giant funky sunglasses and poses. "I bought them from a black guy selling them on the beach." He adds, "Really, really black."

He has also made other acquisitions. Glumly, he shows us the remainder of a tattoo on his right arm. "It was supposed to last three weeks, but it's almost all gone in a week. I should have known better, because I bought it from a Chinese lady."

Had he not been in his seventies, I would think he is going through mid-life crisis.

Tomorrow, we'll visit more relatives, the owners of "Hotel" *Zio* and *Zia* in Rome, who are now vacationing in Abruzzo.

"Which Saint Is Looking Down on Us?"

WE ARE EN ROUTE TO *Zio* Mario's and *Zia* Rosa's when we make a sudden stop. Giorgio has seen a sign: "wood for sale." My father-in-law is no fool; he'll take advantage of his two strong sons being here to stack the wood for him.

Giorgio and Maria exit the car, but soon they return. The man selling the wood appeared too cunning. They're convinced that he spends his days dousing the wood with water before weighing it. Shadowing the man when he weighs the wood and delivers it to your home would not be enough of a precaution. You would have to stalk him for weeks before buying the wood to ensure that no funny business was taking place.

We drive up to a dozen houses built close together, with nothing but land and forlornness around them. *Zia* and *Zio* are outside sitting on plastic chairs with their neighbors, awaiting our arrival.

It's close to twelve, and we must rush inside to eat. We say a hurried good-bye to all of the neighbors and enter the kitchen, pushing aside the hanging bead curtains on the door. Giancarlo sits on a chair but is told that this spot is reserved for me, because I'll be the one serving. He reluctantly sits on the hard bench, squeezing in next to my husband.

The assembly line begins. David's aunt, mother, and I start serving the four seated men. Smug smiles appear on David's and Giancarlo's faces, as I put heaping plates of pasta in front of them. They begin to push their luck, asking for extra salt, please, more water, and so on. I flash them a warning look. *Zia*, disappointed in me, hurriedly gets up to fetch the boys whatever they desire.

To enhance our lunch, hemorrhoid preventions and cures are discussed at length. I tune out and instead begin to mentally redecorate this house, no easy task. I start with the floor. The garish tiles have been firmly laid down. Even an earthquake wouldn't dislodge them.

"Enough talk about hemorrhoids," says *Zia* and instructs everyone to take a nap. We obey. We spread out all through this house and the one across the road, on three floors and in four bedrooms. Just before falling asleep, David looks up and jokingly asks, "Which saint is looking down on us?"

At one minute past four, we are awakened by loud drilling, signaling that *pausa* time is officially over. *Zia* has the key to several apartments in the area and gives us tours of them. They all lack evidence of a designer but are solid as a rock, discouraging any attempts at improvement.

In the minuscule square outside is a long garden hose, hooked up to the village fountain and no doubt leading to a garden—despite the watering ban. A satirical sign in the middle of the square honors *Zio* Mario as "the worker of all workers."

On our way home we stop to get some spring water, which will supposedly give us long and healthy lives. Thick black smoke from forest fires just over the mountain pollutes the air, no doubt negating any benefit the water provides.

David and I are ready to vacate the nest once again, leaving Giancarlo to battle his parents alone. His parting words are "When I can no longer stand it, I'll be calling you."

We make bets on how many days it will be before we get his call.

AN *AFFARE* TO REMEMBER

NONNA IS LEAVING TODAY. AFTER we'd slept with her for two weeks, it will feel odd to have our bedroom all to ourselves again. She actually slept in the room next door, but it sounded as if she were in our room.

Every morning her deafening, manlike voice made me jolt upright in a panic. Her granddaughters would immediately shush her, but their shushing was louder than *Nonna*.

Our landlords had brought her here to recuperate from bronchitis, which they felt she'd acquired from the air-conditioning recently installed in her bedroom. In Naples, temperatures soared higher than 110 degrees Fahrenheit (44 degrees Celsius), so *Nonna* happily spent a lot of time in her bedroom. They advised her against such "air-conditioned" folly in the future, banishing her to the blistering heat of the living room.

Our phone rings, and caller ID alerts us that it's Giancarlo. Fourteen days have passed. His father's accordion playing finally got to him. He'll be arriving tomorrow. He lasted longer at his parents' house than we expected and far longer than we could have.

Our friends Beniamino and Claudia told us they'd found us a house in the Tuscan hills with lots of privacy, for that's what we *Americani* oddly seem to like. They assured us that the old stone house was fully restored, surrounded by twenty acres of land. Beniamino's sister bought it years ago, but now they want to sell it.

The price was reasonable, they confided, and it was only a short distance from Arezzo. We planned to see the house Saturday afternoon. That would also give them time to clean it up a bit, because it hadn't been inhabited lately. We assured them this wasn't necessary; we could visualize its potential, and a few dust bunnies wouldn't affect our opinion.

Saturday arrives, and Giancarlo joins us on our real estate hunt. In the customary Italian manner, we'll first meet Beniamino and Claudia at one location, then follow them to another spot to meet Beniamino's sister, Luisa, and his brother-in-law, newlyweds of only two weeks. We're surprised to see that the groom is about seventy-five, and we learn the couple has been together for more than thirty years.

The three-car convoy will then proceed to our destination. While David drives, Giancarlo and I stay on the lookout for Beniamino's Mercedes ahead and his sister's bright yellow Fiat Panda behind us.

Finally, we're close to our turnoff, and we change the order of the cars. The yellow Panda will take the lead as we drive up the mountain. Soon I realize that "not far from Arezzo" was based on the Italian "more or less" formula. We follow the speeding Panda. As the old guy drives through each mountain curve, he leans on his horn, beeping away. We follow suit, and the few villagers probably think a wedding procession is en route. We continue our ascent, and our hopes are dashed that olive trees will be on our property. At this altitude, they would never survive.

It doesn't bode well when the owners drive right past their property, apparently not recognizing the entrance. We all back our cars up, even though no house is in sight and certainly no driveway. Nor is it especially reassuring when the old man gets out of the car, puts on thigh-high rubber boots, and grabs his sickle. I now notice that his wife doesn't have an inch of skin showing, which is highly unusual for an Italian woman in midsummer. She's wearing long pants and hiking shoes. I look at my knee-length skirt and open-toed flip-flops and then at the ominous path the old man is vigorously clearing. I let everyone go ahead of me, having heard one too many viper stories.

After much trekking, we can't see a house anywhere, only a thick forest overgrown with bramble. We come to a sudden halt when we encounter a bog. The men decide that we'll have to slog through the mud. At least, the prickly bushes can't grow in this soil. We carefully make our way through the bog, and on exiting, we see a beautiful old stone house.

"How old is the house?" I ask.

"Old," the elderly man replies.

We wait while he cuts another path with the sickle. His face gets redder and redder, and he breathes as if he's about to have a seizure. *Luisa may have married him just in time; the pension is secure now.* With sweat pouring down his wrinkled face, he continues, relentless. Finally, we spot old stone stairs. We're anxious to see the inside of the house, but the couple wants to show us the stone woodshed. They point out that it has been restored and add that "It's in better condition than the house."

Finally free of the hateful bramble, my legs look as if I fought with a vicious cat and lost. We climb up the steps, and the old man pulls out a giant key. Before entering, they apologize for the condition of the home, reminding us it hasn't been inhabited for some time. As he opens the door, though, we immediately see that the house *has* been occupied—by bats, mice, and a host of other critters.

"When were you here last?" I ask. They argue a bit, not remembering exactly when. Finally, they notice a calendar on the wall, and point to it. August 1994. Thirteen years ago! The condition of the house confirms this; animal droppings are everywhere, along with their pungent odor.

Luisa starts sweeping as we tour the house. It *does* have potential, and with several hundred thousand euros and a lot of sweat equity, it could be turned into something quite grand. The boys start their contractor talk. This wall could go out if a beam were put in. The floors could be leveled if . . . the doorways seemingly built for Snow White and her dwarves could be raised. . . .

I leave them to figure out a solution for the bathroom, as I go outside to look at the back of the house.

The owner, still red as a beet, is clearing a path through the waist-high bramble that will lead to the ground floor of the house. I walk around the other side, imagining what I could do with all of this land.

The bramble gives my legs fresh scratches that instantly turn into welts. When I see a square piece of metal on the ground, I'm grateful to step onto it to avoid the bramble. Suddenly, the metal piece slips from under me, and I slide straight into a well. My feet get soaked as I hit the water. I grab onto the sides and grasp the ridge with my hands.

I scream. David runs out, catches sight of me, and calls for help. The two men pull me out. I survey my wet and muddy feet and inspect the new scratches on my legs.

But the tour isn't over. Appearing near death now, the would-be seller has finished clearing the path to the ground floor. We enter through another child-size door into two large rooms, separated by a beautiful stone arch. The floor is dirt, and a long wooden animal trough runs the length of the room. Again, with a few hundred thousand euros, this area could be spectacular. The men see themselves playing billiards here and watching soccer on a big-screen TV in the next room.

I go outside to wait in the sun, taking in the forested views, quite sure it's for the last time. Finally, the boys are ready to go, and off we all trudge through bog and bramble to our cars.

Earlier, Beniamino had told us they were asking two hundred thousand euros, but since the house had been on the market for years, he told us to offer one hundred thousand, because they were anxious to unload it.

Thus forearmed, my husband pulls the old man aside to discuss the price.

"It was recently appraised at three hundred thousand, but the price is negotiable. For example, if you give me three hundred and fifty thousand, I won't say no," the old guy says. He repeats, "Three hundred and fifty thousand," and collapses in an uncontrollable fit of laughter.

The following day we find out that the old rascal had hiked up the price, reckoning we were rich *Americani*. He wasn't fooled by our nineteen-year-old car. After all, anyone who can take a year off to live in Italy is surely filthy rich.

I vow never to judge a book by its cover again.

Over a glass of wine that evening, we describe our real estate fiasco to Robert, an American living nearby.

"Ah, that's normal around here," he says. "My house was listed for 400,000. I offered 350,000. Now I expected the old chap to go down to 390,000. Instead he says, 'Fine, 410,000!' This is how it kept going! Finally, I say to him, 'Hey, this is *not* how it works!' The old guy doesn't care, and the lower I go, the higher he goes! Finally, our agent, thankfully an ancient man, who feared not earning his commission prior to dying, intervened and helped us agree on a price. The contract was drawn up, and I waited for him to provide banking information so I could send the funds to him. At this point, I had to tell the old scamp that I couldn't send money to his mattress."

"It's the honest truth," Robert says, pouring himself another big glass of wine.

Only now can we believe him.

ONE BEDROOM AND SEVEN PEOPLE

THE PHONE RINGS ON MONDAY evening.

"This Saturday?" David asks, surprised. Giancarlo is still with us. David covers the receiver and asks what we should do.

I shrug and answer, "How can we say no, since we invited them to visit us any time?" We *had* expected a little notice, though—which is quite likely what the De Lucas feel they have given us.

"See you Saturday for lunch, then," my husband says.

I looked forward to showing them Tuscany. "A beautiful land, far, far away," as Alessandro described it, anxious to please us with this detail. He heard about *Toscana* in school. Despite being born and raised in Italy, they have never visited Tuscany.

The "beautiful land far, far away" is but a three-hour drive.

In four days, seven of us will share one bedroom and one bathroom.

Despite knowing about Sofia's overwhelming obsession with all things Italian, I've decided to let them experience the North American way of life. I won't be ironing the sheets, the pillowcases, or even the dishtowels. Being an *Americana* has some privileges.

I try to prepare everything in advance, knowing that the minute Sofia arrives, she will shadow me the entire time. Personal space is a North American concept. Despite my best efforts, I'm still cleaning the lettuce when their car pulls up. David runs out to greet them.

Before Sofia is even out of the car, I hear her ask, "Where is your wife?"

We exchange warm greetings, and I take them to the bedroom to unpack. Within minutes, Sofia is standing right next to me, ready to help.

"Everything is done and on the table outside. Go and relax. I'll be there in a minute."

"I'll stay with you," she insists. "We can walk out together."

"I'm just running to the bathroom, and I'll be right out," I say.

"No problem, I'll wait for you here." She begins her vigil outside the bathroom door.

When I emerge, she grabs my arm, wraps it in hers, and we walk the short distance together to the picnic table. Everyone is already seated, and I'm relieved that her seat will be across from me and not beside me.

We sit down with the glorious backdrop of Cortona behind us and the not-so-glorious pig smell enveloping us.

I'd carefully chosen the dishes in this Italian meal. No pairing of sweet and sour this time, and for them, the meat is perfectly overcooked. They compliment me and seem genuinely surprised that I was able to cook a good Italian meal.

Earlier, we'd picked some figs, and I serve them. They look at the figs as if they are poisonous.

"You don't like figs?" I ask.

"Figs are very fattening. Eating two of them is like eating a large plate of pasta. And I'm still on my diet," says Massimo.

Looking at his physique, I won't be taking diet advice from him.

They grab their camera and present us with two beautifully wrapped gifts. "This is so you never forget us," Sofia says.

We're touched by their generosity, because they live on a tight budget. They have bought each of us a sterling silver bracelet. With the big dark sunglasses and now the bracelet, my husband will be fully Italian!

After lunch, we take them to Montepulciano because we're completely out of wine. We go from one closed cantina to the next, until we find one that's open.

When David and I sip our sample, we conclude that it's too acidic. I diplomatically invent the phrase, "We're looking for something sweeter."

"Then you're in the wrong area, *signora*. Montepulciano doesn't have sweet wines," the owner says and writes us off as crazy tourists.

In another cantina, we find a wine worthy of parting with 1.50 euro a liter ($7.50 U.S. a gallon).

We visit the compelling historic center of Montepulciano, which stands imperious on its high ridge and seems to have been positioned by a landscape painter. We also visit more cantinas. If Alessandro turns into an alcoholic later in life, it will be entirely our fault.

When we get home, I make a Tuscan meal: *pici*, thick spaghetti-like pasta, with meat sauce. Again they compliment me, astonished.

After hours of what seems like an Italian cabinet meeting, I'm ready for bed. David and I will sleep on the lumpy couch in the middle of the kitchen, while Giancarlo will bunk next to the gas stove. I ensure that the stove and the oven are off, and that it's safe to go to bed.

Giancarlo leaves early in the morning. I don't hear him because I'm dead to the world. Soon, though, I sense the pitter-patter of feet. Dreamily, I see Massimo's heavyset body passing by. He waves and goes out the kitchen door. Before long, I hear someone else trying to sneak past. It's time to wake up before I'm surrounded by all four De Lucas.

David will take them to Cortona, while I stay behind to make lunch. They have heard of the book *Under the Tuscan Sun*, and we tried to see the movie together. Sofia begs for me to come to Cortona, and I beg for her to go. Then they frantically wave good-bye and blow kisses, as if leaving me behind for a lifetime.

In no time, they're back, deeply disappointed. Cortona is just another hilltop town. I'm not sure what they were expecting, thanks to Frances Mayes and Hollywood.

After lunch, I ask whether they prefer espresso or American coffee. They decide to be open-minded but are as disappointed with American coffee as they were with Cortona. Displaying the "American Coffee" container, I notice *"Gusto Classico Italiano"* emblazoned on it. American coffee boasting classic Italian flavor! They laugh hysterically and admit that Italians have gone too far this time.

Massimo's phone rings. His boss has agreed to give him the day off tomorrow, so they'll stay with us tonight. I take out some meat to thaw. They insist they will eat only a tomato; that's all they need. I ignore them and go to the miraculously unoccupied bathroom to get ready for Arezzo. Minutes later, I emerge and find a tablecloth draped over the defrosting meat. I remove the cloth to discover a few bowls underneath as a decoy. They'd put all of the meat back in the freezer. I scold them and take the meat out again, wondering what on earth I would have served them tonight if I hadn't uncovered their ploy.

They decide that they'd like to see the piazza in Arezzo where *Life Is Beautiful* was filmed. David and I get into our car, while they insist we take only one car.

"But there are six of us," we object, "and your car only seats four comfortably and five legally." They grab our arms and insist. We finally give up. The two men, of course, will sit up front, while the four of us cram into the back. Sofia is stuck against me, holding my hand, and Massimo says, "See, there's plenty of room for everyone."

Sofia, though, is freezing and says, "Turn off the air-conditioning!"

Thankfully, Massimo ignores her continued complaints from the backseat.

On our way to the square, Sofia asks me three times if I've seen the film. Each time I answer yes. I'm ready to show them the square, but they take a quick look around and decide it's time to go. According to them, "Once you've seen one Italian hilltop town, you've seen them all."

We hurry home now, because everyone is starving.

Like a pack of hungry wolves, we eat everything in sight; not a piece of the rescued meat remains. I pray that they'll soon leave the kitchen, which also currently serves as our bedroom. They keep remarking on how tired we all are, especially David and I, because we keep yawning. They, too, begin to yawn. Massimo lies down on the couch and begins to fall asleep. Alessandro can barely stand now, his eyes red from fatigue. The daughter is never too tired to text message and is happily doing so, as I'm about to fall over. Finally, I tell them I'm going to brush my teeth and prepare for bed.

"Go ahead," they say, making themselves comfortable.

David is reluctant to offend our guests, but I tell him that unless they leave our kitchen pronto, I'll fall over and go to sleep in the middle of the floor. This gets him to his feet, and he heads to the bathroom, hoping they'll get the hint now that we're both wearing pajamas. Thankfully, Alessandro falls asleep. As they carry him out, I quickly close the kitchen door and yell goodnight.

The next day, we encourage them to see Florence but let them know we won't be able to join them. They debate forgoing Florence and spending more time with us instead.

"No, you must see Florence!" I say, almost too quickly. Though unwilling, they leave us behind and head off. We go back to bed, and the phone wakes us up at 11 a.m. They're standing in front of the Duomo; they made it in record time and are appalled that people have to pay to use the bathroom!

Florence has left a memorable impression on our guests: over dinner, they can't stop talking about how it cost 70 cents to use the bathroom.

Finally, little Alessandro says, "I've heard that you have to appreciate art to like Florence, but I know nothing about art, and still I liked Florence."

I decide that the kid is the only non-Philistine among them.

After dessert, they prepare to leave. An hour and three positions later, they drive away. We wave until they're out of sight and we hear the toot of the horn.

We go inside and count the days before our next guests arrive.

It's close to 11:00 p.m., and Massimo calls to let us know that they made it home safe and in record time.

The following morning I sleep till noon. Though we love our friends, their visit has taught us that we are still very much North Americans. I wonder if we'll ever feel completely at home here. Then I sip my hot cup of American coffee, with real Italian flavor.

All Good Things Must Come to an End

IT WILL SOON BE TIME to depart. Our one-year visit is almost over. Our glorious view of Cortona will be replaced by the back of my Canadian neighbor's aluminum shed and an abundance of all-season plastic red roses that I inspired her to "plant" after she saw my flower garden.

"Do I really have to return to the land where money never sleeps?" I ask David, regularly.

No amount of pleading has convinced him to stay in Italy.

Chiara will throw a going-away party for us on Sunday evening. All of our friends will attend, but we won't be there. She assumed we'd be free, but we aren't.

Chiara is distraught and begs us to ask the family who invited us over to come to her place instead. We're too embarrassed to do this. Since we aren't able to make it to our first going-away party, they will throw another one on Thursday evening. This is extremely thoughtful; however, we're leaving Tuscany on Thursday morning. Again, they invited everyone else first, assuming that we were available.

The day of departure arrives, and it's time to say good-bye to our landlords. Smiling, they watch us load luggage onto our roof rack. They give us an enthusiastic send-off, as David honks the horn several times. We're heading back to Abruzzo, for one last visit with his parents.

We arrive just before one o'clock, and Maria is on the front porch, eagerly expecting us. Giorgio is sitting at the table, eagerly expecting lunch.

I look at the sky and its ominous dark clouds and our suitcases piled high on the roof rack. Nonetheless, we rush inside to have lunch.

Zio Luigi has dropped in to greet us. *Zia* Franca wanted to as well but was too tired. They harvested olives yesterday and took them to the mill where the oil-making process began. But because the press kept breaking down, *Zia* Franca had to stay with their olives, guarding them faithfully, until five in the morning.

"A necessity," according to *Zio*, for who knows whose olives they would be pressing and trying to pass off as his?

We have brought some Tuscan treats: a costly bottle of Brunello, pricey cheeses from Pienza, and wild boar sausage.

I watch in horror as *Zio* lifts a bottle of water and pours it into his glass of wine. After David's parents and *Zio* sample the expensive pecorino cheese, the final consensus is that it's not nearly as good as *Zio*'s homemade one. Yet connoisseur that he is, *Zio* considers the watered-down Brunello drinkable.

The phone rings. It's Giancarlo calling from Canada, counting down the days before our life of leisure is over, and we must return to reality.

"Six," he says and hangs up. I can almost hear his sinister laughter on the other end.

The days pass quickly, and we need to visit all of the relatives before we leave for Canada. Fearing this may not be possible, Maria decides we should visit them according to age, starting with the oldest. Each time we say good-bye, they say it's probably for the last time. Knowing that *Zio* Roberto, age seventy-four, is healthy and agile enough to climb down a rope to the steep valley behind their home just to clear away some garbage, I feel certain it won't be the last time I see them. They all have tears in their eyes as we say good-bye. We must hurry—Giorgio is already waiting in the car, because one o'clock is fast approaching. Apparently, he's not afraid this will be the last time, either.

I try to remember the good things about going back home: friends and family I love, stores open throughout the day, enforced traffic regulations, and, more important, we can eat lunch whenever we want.

The phone rings.

"Two," Giancarlo gleefully says. That's something else to look forward to: an end to these phone calls.

The house is packed with relatives and neighbors, and only the barber is missing. We're tired, and a long journey awaits, but the merry voices keep us up late.

The alarm rings frightfully early the next morning. We insist that Maria go back to bed, but she scurries about packing huge quantities of food and drink for our two-and-a-half-hour bus ride to Rome. As we say good-bye, she clutches onto us and only lets go when she hears Giorgio's restless tooting outside.

Our year in Italy has proved to be a "relative" experience.

"Home" Is Where the Heart Is

We return to Canada and pick up our lives where we left off. I go back to work at the investment firm, and David goes back to making furniture. We try to look on the bright side: no more hiding from relatives, and when we invite eight people over, only eight come. People give us specific addresses for social events; no more high-speed chases.

Yet our experience has changed us. Home no longer seems like home.

"I can't believe it, but I actually miss Italy," David finally says.

The well-intentioned, yet terribly overbearing, relatives, the bureaucracy, the absence of customer service, and other inconveniences suddenly became insignificant. The stunning landscapes, the great food and wine, and the leisurely, simple way of life were now what we remembered. Italians earn much less than their North American counterparts, yet are better dressed, take more holidays, and spend more time enjoying meals with family and friends. The hustle and bustle of life in a big city are now unbearable. We simply can't stay in Toronto.

Though anxious to return to Italy, we must wait several months to ensure that my foot is healing, because I'd tripped on some uneven pavement and injured it while carrying items to our garage sale.

We book our flight with a German airline, and, finally, we are back in Italy.

At the airport in Rome, we wait patiently for wheelchair assistance, then I give up and limp along with my broken foot in a cast.

Papà Giorgio and Francesco wave madly as they catch sight of us. They rush us out to our car, which they'd illegally parked in the no-load zone, inciting loud honking. The parking patrol tries to enforce law and order but is ignored by the masses. The incessant honking continues. Francesco slowly fastens our luggage onto the roof rack, arguing with Giorgio about how secure it needs to be. The parking patrol takes pity on us, perhaps due to my broken foot or our now twenty-year-old car with its homemade roof rack making us look dirt-poor.

Giorgio still doesn't possess the patience of Job and eggs Francesco on to pass slower cars. Blind curves don't dampen his enthusiasm for overtaking. Giorgio keeps telling us that the suitcases are tied precariously, and I'm certain that if one falls off, we won't be going back for it.

Ironically, even though we're rushing home for lunch, within minutes of getting onto the highway, Francesco, the driver, begins to serve us snacks: fresh picked figs, roasted chestnuts, and juice out of a large jug. He keeps looking back for our nod of approval. I smile and keep my eyes on the road.

Due to Francesco's simultaneously serving snacks and driving, we experience a few near misses. Giorgio and Francesco get all riled up, yelling at the other drivers, and launch into a tirade about just how many dangerous drivers there are in Italy.

After what seems like a lifetime, we arrive at their home. Maria comes running out in her traditional *casalinga* apparel and welcomes us.

"How was your trip? How is your foot?" she asks.

"No time for questions, let's eat," says Giorgio. David and I look at each other and already start counting the days— even more so after lunch, when the accordion comes out.

Nonetheless, with so many relatives to reacquaint ourselves with and presents to hand out, the days pass quickly.

David runs some errands and becomes the proud owner of an *auto d'epoca*. Now our twenty-year-old BMW is no longer an old piece of junk but is a vintage car with privileges, greatly reduced car insurance and yearly fee, and invitations to join the antique car races. Wait until they hear our Ferrari BMW!

We visit the older relatives, in the prescribed sequence, all of whom have survived another year. We listen to as much accordion music as we can humanly stand, and tomorrow we'll leave for the life that awaits us in Tuscany.

We prepare for the many well-wishers who will arrive, because we may not see them again for a couple of months. The *festa* goes on well into the night. Exhausted, we finally head off to bed. In our sleepy state, we hear, "Don't worry, we'll come and visit you soon."

In the morning, we console ourselves that perhaps it was just a bad dream.

"STRANIERI GIUSTI" (THE RIGHT TYPE OF FOREIGNERS)

"FOREIGNERS?" THE *SIGNORA'S* SHRILL, AGITATED voice emanates from the rental agent's phone.

He looks up and smiles at us, while calmly assuring the *signora,* "*No, questi sono stranieri giusti.*" (No, these are the *right type* of foreigners.)

Her tone seems to change, and she agrees to bring the keys pronto and show us her place.

We are in Monte San Savino, a classic Tuscan hilltop town graced with hilly terrain, groups of cypresses, and abundant vineyards. Our plan to stay here depends on finding work and a home to rent, and we're anxious to keep our Tuscan dream alive.

The moment *Signora* Donatella spots us, a radiant smile lights up her face. She looks at Stefano, our agent, and nods. Evidently, we are the right type of foreigners after all.

We exchange a few minutes of pleasantries, then hop into Stefano's car and soon arrive at our destination: a group of elegant townhouses that in the past had beautiful views overlooking the Tuscan landscape. Now, however, the views are blocked by town homes being constructed directly across the street. The idyllic views will belong to them.

The roar of construction machinery nearly drowns out *Signora* Donatella, who at full volume informs us what a nice, quiet neighborhood this is. Judging by the stage of construction, we're certain it will be several months, if not years, until the noise ends. We immediately decide this location won't work. Yet *Signora* Donatella is anxious to show us her home, regardless, and we don't have the heart to say no to this elderly Italian lady.

The four of us huddle in the entryway, while *Signora* Donatella gives us a tutorial on its charms. I never realized one could find so many glowing things to say about a small entrance.

She provides a similar lecture as we traipse through each room. We are trying to do a quick walk-through, just to be polite, and then make our escape. As we enter the kitchen, we realize we may have found our "out," for there is no kitchen—only a few pipes jutting from the walls.

"What about the kitchen?" David asks.

A brief look of confusion passes over *Signora* Donatella's face. "Well, of course, there is no kitchen. The place is not furnished. Kitchens are a very personal matter."

Our minds are made up, but *Signora* Donatella is intent on giving us a painstaking tour of the entire house. She even includes the basement, which has no windows or electric lights. In her haste, she almost trips down the dark stairs, while I and my recently healed broken foot nearly follow suit. We politely stand in the blackness as she points out the many virtues of this room and its infinite potential. I sense that Stefano is also getting impatient.

We thank *Signora* Donatella, and she looks at us in disappointment, because to her we really were "the right type of foreigners." Stefano, too, realizes we won't be taking the property. As a result, braking for stop signs on the way back becomes optional, and we make it to his office in half the time it took to reach our destination.

Because time is of the essence, we vow to be more ruthless about future houses if we're not interested. Tuscany apparently has no such thing as a multiple listing service, so we hope and pray that each agency we call might have a listing to match our specifications. We will pay one month's rent for this service. I visit several real estate offices to get their latest brochures. As the full-color back pages of each brochure attest, combining your search for a house, a prostitute, and a strip club are somehow related.

After spending several days calling agencies in the area, my husband is getting frustrated. "So you don't have anything at the moment. Can I leave you my name and number so that if something comes up in the next few weeks or month, you can give me a call?"

He scowls and heaves a loud sigh. "Okay, then I'll keep calling you back to check." He slams the phone down. As a final injustice, moments later, his phone rings and a text message informs him exactly how much that last call to the unaccommodating agency cost.

Yet like many of the other foreigners here, bumbling through the bureaucracy, we aren't ready to give up our fantasy.

One agent is very interested in helping us. He says he has exactly what we're looking for and can take us there immediately. Unfortunately, he is the only agent we have been warned about. Rumor has it that he shows you a certain place, then, after you pay him, he gives you the keys to another house. He hasn't been arrested, because his contract apparently has something in the fine print . . .

David is getting wiser, though. When he speaks to agents now, he includes his Italian last name. He says that we are foreigners, from Canada, but that he has Italian parents. *Stranieri giusti*. This gets us a bit further, because the agents think we may have money.

After one more call, David hangs up the phone and smiles. He has located another agent with a few homes in mind for us. We can meet him tomorrow morning at 10:00

a.m. at the gas station near Castiglion Fiorentino, a little town halfway between Cortona and Arezzo.

Due to traffic, we arrive fifteen minutes late. The agent has been anxiously waiting for us in his white Suzuki 4-x-4 jeep. He waves as we pull up, but there is no time for introductions.

"Follow me!" says the man, who has to be at least eighty, surely the world's oldest real estate agent. He peels out of the gas station. He has the driving finesse of someone escaping the law after shooting a cop. We speed through the town's narrow cobblestone streets, and I'm thankful that most children are in school and no one has stepped out of his front door without looking twice.

Signor Lippi is just getting started, though. It will soon be time to use top gear, for we are now entering the Val di Chio on an open country road. In shock, I watch the speedometer needle quickly rise. I hold my breath, as two cars pass in a narrow space that I'm certain can accommodate only one vehicle.

Signor Lippi is undeterred. He disappears over a steep bridge, and we wonder if we can catch up. As we fly over the bridge, I'm reminded of why I hate roller-coasters. I also wonder how *Signor* Lippi has managed to live so long.

I try to concentrate on the lush, fertile valley. The green forested hills interspersed with olive groves, the occasional Tuscan villa standing majestically on the hillside. Golden vineyards. Persimmon trees full of bright orange fruit hanging like Christmas tree ornaments. We hurtle over another bridge, this one surely built by drunken engineers, for it rises in a huge hump, and, as we drive over the peak, we immediately encounter a dangerous curve. Clutching the steering wheel, David swerves into it at full speed. I tell him to slow down. I no longer care if we lose *Signor* Lippi and possibly our only chance to find our ideal house.

David reluctantly taps the brakes, and just ahead we see our agent pull into a driveway. Mercifully, we arrive.

I peer up at the grandeur of the ancient stone villa, surrounded by abundant gardens. Not one neighbor is in sight. Perhaps the drive has been worth it, after all. That, or maybe there has been some mistake.

Dante, the gardener, has been waiting for us. That was what the mad rush was all about. I vow never to be late getting anywhere again. Dante is a lovely older man, mild mannered and sweet as can be. He lives close by.

He greets us with a warm smile. "We'll be neighbors," he says.

Dante is evidently a man of the land, because his first priority is to show us the vast grounds. The "terrace" is a large cement pad with an open metal structure at one end. He informs us that this is the *concimaia*, where the pig manure was kept to season it before use. I notice two enormous floor covers. He lifts one and explains in graphic detail how the manure and juices were ladled up and then spread onto the adjoining fields. I avoid looking down into the pit. How many giant terra cotta pots would I need to make this area look presentable? Otherwise, our future guests might realize their lounge chairs are perched over a manure heap.

We would have three acres for personal use, but with twenty-five acres surrounding the house, there would be plenty of privacy. Dante points out where we could plant our vegetable garden and gives us a synopsis of what will undoubtedly be lengthy lessons on gardening if we move in.

"On Santa Lucia, when the moon is good, it will be time to plant fennel, but you want to plant . . ."

I walk back to the "terrace" and admire the lovely view of the hilltop town, thinking about the garden parties we could have.

Yet my daydreams are shattered as we enter the house. At 150-plus years, the villa is showing its age. The kitchen, furnished with only a small stove, a sink, and a rusty fridge, has no countertops to prepare the vegetables I'll grow and no cabinets to store the dishes and pottery I'll collect. The rest of the house is a mish-mash of rustic antiques and hideous wicker furniture. Pastel-colored paintings and large rattan fans decorate the walls. It's Miami dazzle meets Tuscan "chic"—truly an interior decorator's worst nightmare. The landlord's philosophy of "more is more" has evidently reigned for a very long time.

The layout also leaves much to be desired. The best views, which would include sunsets and a stunning view of the hilltop town, are visible only from the bathroom.

With mixed feelings, we leave.

But *Signor* Lippi, who has by now mentioned that his title is actually "*Ingegnere* [Engineer] Lippi," has more homes in store for us. Since he is the only agent with any prospects, we have no choice but to follow him.

We drive at a more reasonable speed to the next destination. Immediately, we see that it won't suit our purposes. Despite the rural country setting, the property consists of several town homes attached together.

Just as we are about to voice our objections, we see a couple standing by the door to greet us. The elderly man appears very fragile, and his wife also shows signs of advanced age. With their distinguished clothing, they appear to be upper-crust. This is confirmed when greetings are exchanged; our agent and the couple address one another with a profession, followed by a surname.

"*Buongiorno, Ingegnere* Lippi."

"*Buongiorno, Avvocato* [lawyer] Rossi." They reminisce for a while about old times, while we plot our escape. Yet again, their warm eyes cast a spell on us, and we are helpless to leave. The neighbors are out now, keenly eyeing their potential new neighbors, the *stranieri giusti.*

Ingegnere Lippi takes us on another grand tour. This one is almost heartbreaking, because the house is perfect, newly restored, with beautiful terra cotta tile floors, roughhewn wooden ceiling beams, and an American-size kitchen with all of the amenities that expatriates cherish. Four spacious bedrooms upstairs, three bathrooms. I am torn, as I fantasize about all of the possibilities. But then I remember all of the neighbors. Everyone watches us with anticipation, and our excuse this time is that the house is not furnished. And we don't have any furniture, because we just arrived from Canada.

Our excuse is not successful. The *signora* smiles. "Oh, I'm sure we could come up with some furniture for you."

Ingegnere Lippi adds that anything we need, we can find in his storage room. I have no doubts of this, having seen many a cantina full of enough unused furniture to furnish a large villa and then some.

David nudges me. We thank the *avvocato* and the *signora* for their time.

As we leave, I wave good-bye to the neighbors. They all return the gesture, confirming to us that we have made the right decision.

Back at the cars, we chat with *Ingegnere* Lippi, or, rather, he chats at us, rarely allowing us a moment to express our wishes. He clearly wants us to take the *avvocato*'s house, despite the fact that it isn't what we're looking for.

David again tries to explain. "We want an isolated house in the country, for just us. We don't want any townhouses."

Ingegnere Lippi decides he will try another tactic. "The first house you saw was very isolated, and this you may enjoy for a while." He lowers his voice and leans toward David. In a warning tone, he continues, "The thing is, while you may like it at first, after you get a job and go to work, your wife will be all alone in that house. She will then become lonely and soon look for friendship elsewhere."

"What?" we both yell.

"What are you insinuating?" David says, offended.

Ingegnere Lippi sees that his warning advice hasn't been met with the results he expected. He backtracks hastily, putting on an equally shocked look. "What did you think I meant? I meant she will go out and find some ladies to be friends with."

We decide that it may be time to go.

Realizing we might not take either home now, *Ingegnere* Lippi returns to singing the praises of the first one. "It is quiet and peaceful and has lots of land. Dante is a very good neighbor, and I, too, live in the Val di Chio. . . . we would be friends."

David takes a chance. "We may consider it, but not for eight hundred euros a month. We could only offer six."

Ingegnere Lippi reflects for a moment and then says, "Ah, you want it all. You want your barrel full, and your wife drunk."

We don't even bother to reply. David is firm. "If they're interested, let us know. If not, thanks for your time, *Signor* Lippi."

I notice that *Ingegnere* has now been demoted to *Signor.* No doubt, so does he.

And so the search continues. Agents regularly take us to the exact type of home we have specifically told them we are *not* looking for. We drive from small town to small town, walking into agencies, hoping to find *the* one. Finally, an agent promises she has a house that will suit our requirements. It's only a short drive away; we soon arrive and, indeed, it's true. A lovely villa awaits us with stunning views of classic Tuscany. As soon as we step out of the car, though, disappointment is in the air. Could it be? We take another whiff.

"Yes, David, it's the pig smell."

We remember the picnics going awry last summer, as this scent wafted into the scene. The ridicule of my brother-in-law as we sat, picnic table loaded with gorgeous, untouched food, the stench ever-present, the backdrop of Cortona's glory ignored.

"I knew it was too good to be true," I say. We can't leave at this point, so once more we suffer through a long tour of a home we know we certainly won't take.

We now mention *no pig farms nearby* as another item on our "not wish" list. Our criteria are getting longer, the list of homes is getting shorter, and our time is running out—yet as we drive through the beautiful Tuscan countryside and picture the cold Canadian winter just ahead, we keep faithfully searching.

Our next agent resembles Fabio the model. Perhaps that's why he has never had to become a good agent.

The agent after him seems very skilled when we first meet him in person, but he is averse to returning phone calls.

The next agent thinks I'm young and beautiful and kisses my hand each time we meet, calling me "Blondie," but he doesn't have the type of home we're looking for.

The only agent left in the running is probably the only one who doesn't need to be, for at his age he is surely loaded. *Signor* Lippi has his flaws: he never listens to anything we say and always cuts us off. He never explains anything, and if we insist, he gets annoyed. He never returns calls, either, but waits for us to call him again. He doesn't trust us but insists that we trust him. Still, in our desperation, we admit he has some possibilities.

David now permanently demotes him to *Signor*, no more *Ingegnere*. "*Buongiorno, Signor* Lippi," David greets him, smiling. If this is keeping David sane, I'm happy to allow him his one small vice.

We'll take another look at the first house he showed us, with new eyes this time. Perhaps we can make some small renovations to render it habitable. Besides, there are no other contenders. The owners of the farmhouse have been contacted, and before they make any agreements, they, too, want to meet the *stranieri*, though no doubt they have been informed: we are *stranieri giusti*. They are driving up from Rome, a two-and-a-half hour trip, to meet us.

We dress suitably, not wanting to disappoint our prospective landlords. They, along with our insufferable agent, are waiting for us. In scrupulous detail, we are instructed on a number of items about the house, and then we finally sit down at the table to wheel and deal.

Signor Lippi tries his sales pitch again: "Anything that you may need in the way of extra furniture, I can help you out with. I'll give it to you for practically nothing!"

I can just guess what his version of "practically nothing" is.

The landlords thank *Ingegnere* Lippi, while we thank *Signor* Lippi. He'll draw up the revised terms of the contract, and we'll meet him and the landlords next week for everyone to sign the agreement.

"I'll call you when they're ready," are his last words to us.

"Now that his exorbitant fee of one month's rent is imminent, he may just call," I say.

David advises me not to hold my breath.

CRASH COURSE

AFTER LOOKING AT MORE THAN thirty house rentals, thankfully we have settled on one. Now we have to make the long trek over the Sibillini Mountains to my in-laws' house to pick up the rest of our possessions.

"You'd better clear a space in the backseat, so you can see out the rear window," Giorgio says. "If the *carabinieri* stop you . . ."

Yet whenever Maria finds a tiny space in the back seat, she views it as an opportunity to shove in one more item.

"Can't you push things closer together?" she implores.

For there are many things staying behind—bottles of recently made tomato sauce, a large hind of Parma prosciutto, tomatoes, onions, peppers, and potatoes, all from their chemical-free garden. She inspects the car again and notices an empty space in between my feet.

"Your snack can go right there!" she says triumphantly.

It's 12:30 p.m., and we've just finished eating. Our drive back to Tuscany will take no more than three hours. Yet she looks so hopeful, I can't disappoint her. I assure her the snack will come in handy.

Giorgio continues his rant. "I'm telling you for the last time . . ."

David shrugs and says, "What can I do now? What if I drove a panel van with no rear windows? That's what side mirrors are for."

Giorgio gives up, annoyed. He waves good-bye and disappears, certain that we'll get stopped by the *carabinieri*.

If only my mother could see us now with our old BMW: two patio tables strapped on the roof rack, along with anything else that Maria can scrunch in. Maria doesn't understand that you can't fill holes on top of a car the way you can inside. She adds items on one side, while David removes different items from the other. Like most Italian mothers, she has no fear of the *carabinieri*, no fear of packages of pasta, potatoes, or other foods flying off the roof. Her fear that we won't have enough food far outweighs worrying about the long arm of the law.

Frustrated, David tells her in no uncertain terms, "*Basta!*" (Enough!)

I squeeze into the car, and once I'm seated, Maria places the items David pulled from the roof rack around my feet, on my lap, and to the left and right of me. I'm buried in food, and strange odors fill the air. I pray that I won't need to escape in case of emergency, and bathroom breaks are out of the question. Maria inspects the car one last time and realizes there won't be enough room for the bag of potatoes. Dejected, she shakes her head and waves good-bye, eyes brimming with tears, though I'm not sure whether they're for us or for the bag of potatoes left behind.

We blow her a kiss, and David madly honks the horn, announcing our departure to the entire little village.

Thanks to all of our goods, the weight of the car, and our obstructed vision, David drives very slowly and carefully. I sink back into the bags of pasta and hazelnuts and relax. Able to enjoy the mountain views at this leisurely speed, I secretly thank Maria as the bags of *rigatoni* dig into my side.

On the highway, cars whiz past us at incredible speeds. Even an old white Fiat Panda, complete with elderly couple, passes us. This doesn't go unnoticed by David, so he risks the tables on top, rather than our lives. He presses on the gas, and the sound of plastic flapping above, combined with the roar of the engine, creates the sensation that we're about to take off.

We get off at our exit, grateful that we and our roof rack have survived and that we've managed to avoid the *carabinieri*. Happily, we drive along the back road, now certain that we'll make our appointment with our future landlords on time. We'll meet them at *Signor* Lippi's office to exchange signatures and finalize our contract.

A small Fiat Punto approaches the intersection. At first, I'm not concerned because Italian drivers usually edge out into traffic before stopping. This woman's complete disdain for stop signs, though, soon becomes evident. I scream, and David tries to swerve but cannot, with oncoming traffic in the other lane. We brace ourselves for the inevitable crash.

After the impact, we wait a moment to see if we're okay. The lentils have served as an air bag, and no doubt Maria's other packages all around me have cushioned the blow. We get out of the car, and David is impressed with the cheap cords he purchased, because the tables have slid forward only a few feet and now dangle over the hood.

"Wow, only one of the cords broke."

We make sure the other driver is all right and ask her, "Why didn't you stop?"

She tries to blame us, saying that we were signaling right.

"Why would we signal right when we were on the main road going straight? That's not true," David says.

She refuses to accept the blame. I angrily say that we'll have to call the *carabinieri* but then meekly ask to borrow her cell phone, having forgotten ours. I look at our car and remember Giorgio's last words to us, and I wonder if we should risk calling the police after all. Incredibly, the lady has also left her cell phone at home—no doubt a statistical rarity, two Italians without cell phones.

I run to a nearby house to call the *carabinieri* and *Signor* Lippi.

I head back to the scene of the accident. The police officers have arrived and are trying to figure out what happened.

"It is one hundred percent her fault," David says.

But she is unwilling to take all of the blame. The *carabinieri* stare at the three of us a bit longer, perhaps hoping to scare someone into a confession. They have no choice, so they mark the scene and commence measuring and drawing to determine guilt. They work slowly and methodically and regularly remind us that if they figure out who is to blame, then they'll have to issue a fine, but if guilt is confessed beforehand, the guilty party will avoid the fine.

The lady suddenly yells, "Fine, by force I will accept one hundred percent blame." She acts as if she's doing us a favor, somehow forgetting that she never even slowed down for the stop sign.

"Okay!" the officer says, rather pleased, and helps us fill out the paperwork.

A large tow truck appears, having been called by the *carabinieri*. A man with long white unruly hair named Giovanni emerges, wearing fluorescent orange plastic overalls and rubber boots. He speaks in an unrecognizable dialect and looks at us and laughs loudly. Perhaps that should have been our first sign.

Before we know it, we're sitting in the truck beside him, trying to decipher what he's saying. The other driver gets into her car and, as she irately pulls out into traffic, narrowly misses colliding with another vehicle. Now even more furious, she peels away.

Back at *Signor* Lippi's office, our future landlords, Vincenza and Enrico, have received word of our misfortune. Though they feel terribly bad for us, the paperwork must be signed. They offer to drive over to the mechanic's, and in haste we foolishly agree.

David has meanwhile called our former landlord, Rocco, who lives just around the corner.

The hoist is raising our chock-full car when Giovanni appears with a big crowbar. The sight of a crowbar near our precious "vintage" vehicle makes David nervous, as does the loud banging that immediately follows. Giovanni smiles and announces that we'll have to leave the car with him for several days. David wonders if he can trust his car to Giovanni. Surveying the BMW, its contents, and the two tables dangling precariously on top, we have no choice.

Rocco now appears with an entourage, friends we had met last year who are visiting.

"Are you okay? Can we take you to a hospital?"

"We're fine, but our car is not so fine," I say and point to it. "And my sister is coming from Canada soon, so we need the car in order to fix up the house we'll be moving into."

As I say that, our future landlords and *Signor* Lippi's secretary arrive.

After ever so briefly inquiring about our health, she pulls a sheaf of papers from her bag. Despite ten of us crowding the room, with eight people talking at once, we manage to have the presence of mind not to sign anything rashly.

Anna, one of Rocco's entourage, had just warned us: "You'll never be able to understand how much we don't trust each other here in Italy."

"We would like to read through this pile of documents," David says.

The secretary appears surprised but reluctantly tells him, "No problem."

Our future landlords look at us with confusion and suspicion; perhaps they should no longer trust us. We certainly no longer trust the mechanic, whose all-purpose tool of choice seems to be the crowbar. We hear more banging. We're not sure whether to trust our future landlords, with their pile of seemingly unnecessary paperwork, but at least we know we can count on Rocco and our friends. So we start the colossal task of emptying the groceries from our car and removing any items of real value, such as our newly purchased automatic espresso machine. The mechanic catches us unloading our valuables, and he undoubtedly senses we don't trust him. The courtesy car that was previously offered suddenly becomes unavailable.

We load up all of the cars with homemade tomato sauce, Giorgio's famous sausages, and hunks of Parmesan cheese. Vincenza and Enrico will drive us partway, and then Anna and her husband, Francesco, will pick us up and drive us back to where we're staying in Arezzo.

We soon realize that Vincenza is indeed not to be trusted—at least, in regard to her driving. I've never before seen David search for a seat belt in the backseat. She carelessly enters a roundabout, narrowly escaping a collision. She doesn't blink, perhaps being accustomed to this. With my eyes closed, I nervously chat with them and again wonder how drivers like this make it to a ripe old age. We somehow arrive at our destination and are transferred to the other car that's waiting for us.

Days pass, and our car isn't ready, so David convinces Giovanni to lend us a courtesy car. When I see it, a nice VW Golf, I think that Giovanni has forgiven us.

He hands us the keys and says, first in dialect and then in Italian, "The locks don't work, and there's a loud rattle in the engine, but don't worry about it."

David starts the car, and the banging sounds as if a person is trapped and trying to escape from under the hood. With his mad scientist's white hair, Giovanni walks away, and I expect to hear fiendish laughter. I realize he hasn't forgiven us after all.

"Do you think we can trust a mechanic whose courtesy car doesn't work?" I ask.

David is silent. No doubt that thought had also crossed his mind.

We drive over to *Signor* Lippi's office, because the documents were deemed safe to sign. A detailed list of every item in the house is attached, to ensure that at the end of our lease we don't make off with the cheap rattan fans or other ghastly knick-knacks. Anna's words about lack of trust ring true.

David holds out a check, and *Signor* Lippi protests, "No, no! We deal only in cash at this office," as if using checks is a clandestine activity that he certainly would never take part in.

"Your secretary told me a check would be fine. Besides, I have no cash on me."

Perhaps fearing he may have to wait to get paid, which is a justified concern at his age, *Signor* Lippi reluctantly agrees. David proceeds to write the check out to *Signor* Lippi and asks for the exact spelling of his name.

"C-A-S-H," replies *Signor* Lippi. David ponders for a moment, then makes the check out to CASH.

The check now safely in his possession, *Signor Lippi* shakes our hands. David thanks him and asks for a receipt.

"But we're friends now, we can trust one another." Meaning, there will be no receipt for us.

David loudly sighs and bids *Signor* Lippi, "*Arrivederci.*"

We drive back to Arezzo and try to ignore the loud rattle coming from the engine.

When we return, the phone rings, and David answers it. I can hear yelling from the other end of the line, and David paces in a frenzy, as he yells back, "Calm down. Okay, speak slowly and speak Italian." This tells me it is the car mechanic. "I don't know what happened with the insurance company. Of course, you'll get paid."

David slams down the receiver. He calls the insurance agency and identifies himself as David, the Canadian.

"*Ah, si, si.* Can I call you back in a couple of minutes?"

David waits several hours, and, fearing another call from the mechanic, he calls the agency again. Apparently, the secretary inadvertently left our paperwork in a pile on her desk two months ago and never registered our insurance. The agent acknowledges the company's error and insists it will right the wrong.

Meanwhile, the old fox *Signor* Lippi made his way to the bank, where the cashier informed him the bank no longer accepts checks made out to "CASH," and try as he might, he cannot get around it. I regret that we weren't there to see the look on his face.

No doubt within seconds of exiting the bank, he calls us in a panic. David sees his name on the cell phone but decides to let *Signor* Lippi stew a bit, whatever the reason for his call. It seems *Signor* Lippi has forgotten we are now friends and can be trusted, because he calls repeatedly.

Finally, David answers.

Signor Lippi blames David for his current predicament. "If only you had given me cash, this never would have happened! You should have trusted me, I know banks don't like dealing in checks."

David points out that it was *Signor* Lippi who said to make the check payable to "CASH." This logic is lost on *Signor* Lippi, as he continues to gripe and doesn't let David get a word in edgewise.

"We're in Arezzo, and we'll be coming back in a few days. I'll have your cash for you then." *Signor* Lippi objects, so David reminds him, "We're friends now, you can trust me."

Dead silence—the old fox has been trapped.

A few days later, we head back to Castiglion Fiorentino to the farmhouse we have rented. Though it's on our way to pass by *Signor* Lippi's office, David goes directly to the house. "We have lots of work to do."

David rather enjoys making the old guy squirm. By early afternoon, *Signor* Lippi's name appears on the cell phone. David quickly answers it, which surprises me. "Yes, sorry, we are so busy here; we'll try to come later today if we can." David pauses and with an evil smirk says, "Or if you want it immediately, you could drive by and pick it up."

A minute later, *Signor* Lippi is on our doorstep, indicating that the call was made from our front gate. David hands him the wad of money. Apparently not trusting us, he slowly and carefully counts it, twice. We know better than to ask for a receipt, because we are friends now. The amount is correct, hence there's no need for further chitchat among friends, so off he goes.

After much cleaning and organizing, we're tired. Nonetheless, we go to the mechanic's to check the progress on our car, because my sister Vesna will soon arrive, and we want to pick her up in Florence.

Giovanni begins wheeling and dealing. Repairing a dent will be too time consuming, so he'll give us one hundred euros, and we can take it to a body shop and have it fixed. We agree to that. He also doesn't want to work on the fan; perhaps we can get that fixed elsewhere, too. Maybe he only knows how to work with a crowbar. David is getting frustrated. We don't want to get the car overhauled piece by piece at several shops. We also doubt that the amount of money Giovanni gives us will cover the cost of the work to be done. After much debate, we say we'll be responsible for the dent, and he grudgingly agrees to repair the fan.

And indeed, the cost to fix the dent will be two hundred and fifty euros. We suspect that Giovanni will charge the insurance company for a lot of work he doesn't feel like doing. In Italy, they foresee this problem and have a local *perito* (assessor) drop in on mechanic shops. David says he would like to meet the *perito*. Knowing that we're staying one hour away, Giovanni calls David whenever the *perito* is supposedly there and says, "But if you don't make it here within a half hour, he'll be gone."

In the following weeks, Giovanni calls repeatedly, demanding that we return the courtesy car because he has promised it to another client. Angry, we drive almost an hour to return the courtesy car, hoping to pick up our semi-finished car. The vent fan is now *almost* working.

"You no longer have any variable settings; now it is just on or off."

To the right of the steering wheel, there is a new makeshift switch, and Giovanni has likely charged the insurance company an outrageous price for this hack job. The air conditioning doesn't work either, though Giovanni assures us that "it just needs to be charged with the proper gas."

Every time we return, it's the same scenario. Vesna arrives and spends more time at Giovanni's shop than touring Tuscany.

Each time Giovanni swears, "I need one more part and twenty more minutes, and your car will be done."

Finally, the part arrives. David stands over Giovanni, watching the mechanic like a hawk as he clumsily replaces it. The part is not on straight, and David foolishly points this out. Giovanni, not pleased, grabs his faithful crowbar and, with a swift hard hit, knocks it on straight.

Weeks pass with no word from Giovanni, so we drop in to see if we can pick up our money to fix the dent and for him to flush the air conditioning. Giovanni sees us and starts shouting.

"What's going on?" David asks. "Why are you so upset?"

"They didn't pay me! I won't finish the rest of the work until I get paid."

"Why didn't you call me?" David says.

Giovanni, with a face to match his mad hair, paces back and forth, trying to calm down. I fear for David's life; this man is truly crazy. David promises to call the insurance company and get the problem resolved.

In a mad huff, Giovanni wanders off and shouts, "You'll get your money when I get mine!"

Shocked, David gets in the car, and we drive away. We try to guess how many calls he'll have to make to the insurance agent before everything gets settled.

Days pass. The phone rings, and it's Giovanni. I fear the worst.

"Come get your money," he says.

David mentions he would like two hundred euros, because that's what it will cost to fix the dent.

"Fine," Giovanni miraculously agrees, adding to our suspicion.

I now envision a gun with a silencer on it, pointing at David's head. A team of burly men in custom-tailored black suits stand nearby to dispose of the body. It may just be my paranoia, but David, too, is perplexed.

"Why would a man who doesn't call us when he wasn't being paid now call us to come and get our money ASAP?" he asks.

"I think he's going to kill you," is my reply.

We drive over, and my suspicions are confirmed that David is also nervous, because he says, "Wait in the car, but leave it running." Then he adds, "I love you," and walks into the shop. Moments later he emerges, jumps in the car, and quickly drives off.

Grateful that he returned without a broken leg, I ask, "What happened?"

"I went in. He said wait a minute and walked into his office. He came back, handed me two hundred euros, and walked away without saying a word."

We didn't get the air conditioning flushed, nor do we dare try.

We also never heard from *Signor* Lippi again, despite his promise that he'd call us the minute the documents were finalized.

And we didn't get to meet the *perito*, either. Only later would we find out that he didn't actually come to the shop.

"You'll never be able to understand how much we don't trust each other here in Italy."

Perhaps we will, Anna, perhaps we just will.

CAREER CRISIS

BILLS AND CONTRACTS FOR SERVICES start to arrive with utmost efficiency. David surveys the large pile. "We'd need a team of lawyers to decipher this. I give up! I'll send them off as is; hopefully, it's good enough."

As he folds the wad of paperwork for the electric company, so thick it won't fit into the return envelope, he notices that a fine of 103 euros will be imposed if the documents aren't filled out properly. This motivates him to start over.

There is a knock on the door. Dante and an older lady are here to welcome us. He looks very sweet and distinguished in his crisply ironed shirt.

I assume that the woman is his wife, but Silvana explains that she is not and that Dante's wife died several years ago, as did her own husband. Then she mentions something in regard to a survivor's pension.

"Come on in," David says.

Reluctantly and shyly, they enter the house. Dante looks around at his former home and points to the open fireplace. "We used to do all our cooking in there, and then after dinner we put our chairs on the platform next to the fire to keep warm. Having cows below us also helped," he says almost longingly.

They invite us to join them in attending church each Sunday and then say good-bye.

Thanks to the mounds of paperwork, we're still at home when the *vigile* comes by to confirm that we're renting the house. He is a very proper man, befitting his official uniform. He sits down and slowly and methodically asks David questions, taking a long moment to reflect after each answer before carefully writing it down. The *vigile* now turns his attention to me, though he directs his questions to David. "And what about the *signora?*"

"We're still doing the paperwork, but she will have residency here soon."

The *vigile*'s eyes shift from David to me and then back again. He writes something else and stands up and says, "Good."

He shakes our hands and, rather soldierlike, exits the premises.

"Maybe he thinks we are *stranieri giusti*," I say. "Good thing you didn't mention the slight problem we're having with the Questura with my documents."

"Some things are better left unsaid," David wisely replies.

As I look at the pile of bills, it becomes evident that part of the charm of living here the last time had to do with my large severance checks being deposited monthly. I now realize that the books I've read on the joys of living in Tuscany were written by retired people. Reality sets in, as we try to look for work.

Each day David wakes up early, grabs his portfolio, and heads out to furniture-making shops located within a one-hour radius of our home. Though impressed by his ability, they are not impressed by his age. Our friend Giuseppe was right.

"Thirty-nine is too old?" David had asked incredulously.

"Of course, thirty-nine is too old. You'll just have to face it, you're too old, and there is no work here for you!" Giuseppe said matter-of-factly.

Finally, David puts his portfolio away.

We check the want ads again. A school is looking for mother tongue English speakers and is willing to train us, so we head off to Florence. Our fellow classmates are made up of young Americans seeking fun and adventure in Italy, along with an American man our age, on the run from U.S. authorities. His attire confirms that he has never owned a suit in his life. He is currently sporting clothes that appear to be borrowed from three different people of three various sizes, living at the height of fashion in different decades. We figure it's best not to ask this fugitive any more questions.

David spends three grueling hours preparing for his first class. He possesses virtually no knowledge of English grammar, although the school assures him this won't be a problem. Yet this English school apparently does have a problem with math, because the pay is far less than was originally promised.

We go to the employment office. The receptionist looks at us and, without an ounce of optimism, nonchalantly says, "There is no work here. Hasn't been any for a while, nor will there be any for a long time."

Perhaps she is related to Giuseppe.

Despite the complicated tax laws, which are based solely on distrust of both parties, David looks for some independent woodworking jobs.

Giuseppe, the prophesier of doom as far as our job search is concerned, sums it up: "The government knows that most people cannot be trusted." He makes the gesture Italians use for *stealing*. "The people know that the government cannot be trusted." He makes a gesture that denotes *cunning*. "So each party must come up with new ways to confirm this extreme distrust of each other. Honest people, it is assumed, do not exist."

Despite Giuseppe's speech, David picks up a job installing a railing for an American man, Paul. The owner of the metal shop promised it would be ready last week, but we have yet to hear from him. David calls on Monday to find out that the man had to take his aging father to the hospital.

On Tuesday David calls again.

"The railing isn't ready today, because my young daughter was in an accident."

We next fear for this man's son. David will also have to come up with excuses when he calls his client to postpone, once again.

But Paul has lived in Italy for a while and reassures David, "You're being far too conscientious. We're in Italy. I never actually expected it to be done when you said it would be."

By word of mouth, I find my first job in Italy. Taking a 90 percent pay cut from my brokerage job, I humbly go to clean the home of a hovering eighty-year-old *signora*. She shadows me the entire time. I clean the living room, while she sits on the couch, inspecting my every move. I smile at her, but she doesn't smile back. It's nerve-racking, so I become clumsy and knock things over. The vacuum bumps into doors and furniture. It's just as the old *signora* suspected: I need supervising and she feels vindicated with each slip-up.

I take my cash, and as I drive away, I feel liberated to leave behind those suspicious eyes. I will not return. This is too high a price to pay for the "Tuscan dream."

I send my resume to English schools in the area. Though I couldn't explain present perfect tense if my life depended on it, I miraculously get hired and will teach three groups of children the following week.

How hard can it be? I tell myself.

Two little live wires sit in the classroom. "*O Dio!*" says Leonardo, again. He rolls his big blue eyes with long lashes and asks his classmate, "What did she say?"

I'm about to answer when they engage in another game of rock-paper-scissors. I sigh, but they don't mind, no doubt rather proud of themselves for their ability to exasperate the new teacher.

They are completely unruly until Leonardo hears the loud siren of an ambulance; he calms down and crosses himself.

"Just in case," he explains.

Paolo grabs Leonardo and starts making fun of him. To change the subject, I say to Leonardo. "That's a nice watch you have. How much did it cost?"

"Five euros!" he answers.

"That's a great price!" I say.

"*Si, è Cinese!*" (Yah, it's Chinese!) he affirms.

I barely survive one hour with these clowns and wonder how I'll get through the next two. I fondly remember my stressful brokerage job.

Fortunately, the next class redeems my faith. Giancarlo Andre is wearing a navy blue Ralph Lauren sweater and has the sweetest demeanor. His accent borders on British, and he already speaks English rather well for a twelve-year-old. His friend Greta, a pretty little eight-year-old girl, dressed in expensive clothes, smiles and shrugs coyly, because she can't grasp even the basics. On occasion, Giancarlo Andre looks impatient, but for the most part he carefully and patiently explains the lesson to her in Italian. They should be in different levels but are best friends and refuse to attend separately. I imagine them marrying one day.

"Have you learned English from watching movies?" I ask Giancarlo Andre.

"No, everyone speaks Italian," he says.

"But American movie stars speak English," I say.

"They speak Italian, too!" says Greta.

Giancarlo Andre explains, "Not just any Italian voice can be used for dubbing. They find a guy who really sounds like the movie star, and then he is used for all other movies."

I review colors and ask him, "What color is your car?"

He takes a moment to contemplate and unpretentiously and innocently replies, "The Mercedes is black, and the BMW is blue."

Only one of my students that evening has a brother and a sister. In every other family, it seems the parents have saved their money to send their child to English school and apparently to buy a Mercedes and a BMW.

I move on to conversation skills and ask, "Would you ever like to travel elsewhere and leave Italy?"

They look at me with frightened expressions and emphatically answer, "No! Never!"

Thus ends my conversation on travel.

I then ask sweet Giancarlo Andre what his father does for work.

"He's not working at the moment," he says.

"Because of the crisis?" I ask.

He looks up at me with sad eyes and says, "No, because he is dead."

I lose confidence in my conversation classes.

My next group arrives; this time, it's two more live wires. Both of them have brought a snake and try to terrify me with it throughout the lesson.

Francesco suddenly puts the snake down and says, "*Maestra*, I have a really important question to ask you."

"What is it?" I say.

"Do you believe that God made everything, or do you believe Big Ben did?"

I smile at his mangling of the Big Bang theory, while the other student adamantly says, "Of course, I believe in God. If I didn't, I'd go straight to *inferno!*"

A deep and rather heated discussion ensues between the two eight-year-old boys, ranging from belief in Jesus' miracles to the possibility that everything came about by Big Ben.

I survive the evening, if only barely.

"*Che noioso!*" Francesco repeats throughout the lesson.

Fortunately, my Italian is limited, so only later do I realize he kept saying, "How boring!" in my class.

I collect my rather measly pay and drive home exhausted. *Retirement is how many years away?*

"Get Off Your Butt!"

With no other options, I muster all of my strength and go to teach mostly unruly students a language they don't want to learn.

The Questura has inexplicably canceled my "permission to stay" document, which I require for my part-time teaching job.

With as much enthusiasm as we'd have going for root canal, we head over to the Questura.

Many young African girls are accompanied by elderly Italian men hobbling by their sides. Their cases are simple: Italian citizen, married in Italy, pension. No one asks where they met.

Our case is different. Though David is an Italian citizen, we were married in Canada, and he doesn't have a one-year job contract, earning a minimum of seven thousand euros.

"Can we get our marriage certificate translated into Italian?" we ask, hoping to put an end to our excruciating visits here.

"No, for how do we know you didn't get divorced six months ago?" the official says.

"Because then I wouldn't be here with this woman," David replies. "Are you saying that my wife of eleven years will have to leave the country, even though I'm an Italian citizen?"

"She can stay here, just illegally," the immigration official says. "No one will kick her out." She disinterestedly shuffles the paperwork we brought, based on our last visit. She adds, "What you really need to do is to get off your butt and find a job!"

Mussolini would be proud.

Though his Italian blood is now boiling, David remains silent.

Assuming he is deaf, the *signora* repeats, "You need to get off your butt and start looking for a job with a one-year contract, earning a minimum of seven thousand euros."

"Haven't you heard there is a crisis in this country at the moment? And are you saying that even if I was a billionaire, I would need to get a job with a one-year contract paying that much?" David indignantly asks.

"Yes," she robotically answers and says, "*Arrivederci*."

We have been dismissed. David stops asking questions, because he no longer trusts the answers. We reluctantly leave and wish that the *signora* would lose her comfy government job and have to get off *her* butt to find work!

Weeks go by, and we try to resolve matters. We arrive early at the Questura to ensure that we don't get any workers near lunch hour. We provide an ever-increasing pile of documents. I watch as the official flips through them. The question of health care now arises.

Tears well up in my eyes, for it seems as if our Tuscan dream won't become a reality. Perhaps feeling some empathy, the *signora* offers to check with Italy's health care system, because it is up to them.

Sadly, I leave, and David graciously thanks the *signora* for her help.

A week goes by, and we receive good news: I will receive my "permission to stay" document, and I'm entitled to health care if I'm married to an Italian citizen!

David tells the *signora* he could kiss her!

She says, "Give the kiss to your wife."

He does, and we hope that now we can start enjoying life under the Tuscan sun.

THE TRUFFLE TELEMARKETER

THE CHILDREN AT SCHOOL ARE driving me crazy. Plus, with preparation time, I've calculated my earnings to be three euros an hour. Hence, tomorrow I will go on an interview for the job of selling truffles, the venerated fungi. They advertised that they want a woman. Why a woman would be better at selling truffles doesn't concern us. We just hope they don't mind that I'm slightly overweight and probably don't have enough cleavage to get the job done.

I ring the bell and take one last look at myself, hoping I can pass as young enough. David helped me pick out my outfit: a floral blouse with a skirt that would be considered so cutesy back home, no one would consider wearing it to a job interview. That confirmed it would be perfect here.

Looking through the politically incorrect want ads has left me nervous. Blonde Italian, twenty-eight, searching for office job. Youngish Romanian lady, searching for cleaning job. Here, if you're over thirty, you've missed the boat; in Canada, we call thirty-something "experienced."

David and I find the address; the location is a private house. There's no company name on the door or on the intercom. I fear I may be sold into slavery, and I leave a note in our car stating our last whereabouts.

My concern is not alleviated when the door is answered by a very young, very thin girl, with long dark hair and thong underwear showing above her low-waist jeans.

"*Salve.*" ("Hello.") Sizing me up, she says, "Marina will be with you in a second."

What am I doing here? At least, I do smell the strong aroma of truffles.

She leads us into a quasi boardroom and then sashays out of the room, providing us with another glimpse of her black thong.

Posters of truffles are clumsily taped on the wall. Only two of the four rickety chairs match. The plastic table, a cheap brown imitation wood, is broken. I remind myself not to lean on it during the interview. We hear the chatter of many women in an adjoining room and try to figure out what they're saying. I catch the word *tartufo* (truffle), and I relax— though I still think it was a good idea I left the note in the car.

Marina arrives and dismisses David. "This is not how interviews are conducted." She tells him there is plenty of literature for him to read in the waiting room. "We will be a half hour."

He looks at me as if asking, "Will you be okay?"

I nod but wish I could convey, *Don't leave the waiting room, not even for a moment.*

Marina is very serious and with pen and paper in hand begins her interrogation. "What are you doing here in Italy?" is her first question. "Do you have plans of learning Italian proficiently, rather than speaking as you do?' Her next question is "How many job interviews have you gone on?" She asks, "Do you own or rent the home you are living in here?" I answer while she scribbles furiously. "Do you own your house in Canada and collect rent? How much money do you *really* need to earn per month?"

I've had enough of her interrogation, and I begin my cross-examination. "Is this job based solely on commission, and what exactly would I be doing?"

Marina takes a moment for this to sink in, because I'm not the one who is supposed to be asking questions. She maintains her composure and assures me that this will be discussed during the third interview. "That one takes three hours, because we want to ensure you're the right person for the job."

Quite certain I'm not the right person for the job, I tell Marina one last time, "If this job is based solely on commission, I don't want to waste your time or mine."

She's in a quandary, because this isn't supposed to be discussed until the third interview. She is speechless.

I finally blurt out, "I can do the job. I have worked for high-profile executives and extremely demanding customers. I can sell your truffles. I just want to know what I will be paid."

I don't even realize it, but I've raised my voice a little. It gets Marina's attention, and, lowering her voice, she now reveals the top secrets of the third interview, which are normally reserved for only the worthy. "During that interview, we would tell you that it is on a commission-only basis but at the same time let you know you can make lots of money. This is a very prosperous company."

She waits for my response. I glance around but refrain from suggesting what some funds from this prosperous business should be set aside for. I explain that I'm not the employee they're looking for, and they are not the company I'm looking for. Marina is confused. I thank her and shake her now rather limp hand. The roles have been reversed, and I leave poor Marina quite bewildered, her world momentarily turned upside-down.

As we return to the car, David asks, "How did it go?"

"To become a truffle telemarketer in Italy requires more interviews and interrogations than it did for my prestigious investment firm back home, where one needs to be bonded. In fact, I think it would be easier to become Prime Minister of Canada."

David is not remotely surprised.

I crumple up the note I'd left on the dashboard, hoping David doesn't notice. I've had enough interrogations for today.

UNDER THE TUSCAN CLOUDS

CHANTAL, OUR FRIEND FROM CANADA, wrote to us, "If you aren't really lounging in the Tuscan sun, don't feel you have to try too hard to disillusion us. We rather like to think that somewhere life is wonderful."

We'll have to keep several secrets from Chantal.

The thermometer in the hallway reads fifty degrees Fahrenheit. There is no sun, and we're enduring the wrath of dark Tuscan clouds, showering copious amounts of rain on us. The days are damp and dreary. Our kitchen resembles a badly dressed store window: laundry hangs off chairs, hooks, and knobs, attempting to dry.

The post office has run out of stamps and won't have any for two months. We have been labeled "difficult clients" by the phone company for complaining that its turnaround time of one week has become ninety-three days and counting. We're learning that "the customer is always wrong."

The mouse in the cantina has eaten more prosciutto than I have this week. David once again battles small furry gray enemies and once again returns, defeated.

His job prospects look bleak, too. His last job involved installing paper towel holders and soap dispensers in newly built office buildings. He was assigned a partner to work side by side with. This twenty-something young man was full of frenetic energy and shadowed David with the tenacity of a personal stalker, even when they weren't working. Finally, David escaped to the bathroom and slyly hid inside the stall, while the kid, having lost sight of David, anxiously shouted, "David, David, where are you?" Needless to say, the young man was truly disappointed that his hero, David, decided to pass on this great job that paid minimum wage.

As a result of our fruitless job search, spending money for "frivolous things," such as heating with gas, will be kept to a bare minimum. David carries a bucket full of hot coals into our bedroom to take out some of the chill, because our small, inefficient, smoky wood stove is not able to keep up. I now understand why, in period films, they wear hats to bed.

We climb into our "guaranteed not to pill" flannel sheets covered with pills. The house is silent, except for the loud drip of water falling into a metal bucket in the open fireplace. According to our landlord, it's normal to have reasonable amounts of water puddle on one's kitchen floor. The pitter-pattering is getting on our fragile nerves; we have been introduced to the Dark Side of Tuscany.

The next day, the morning light filters through the ancient gray-blue shutters. I hope for sun. There is none. Small clouds of my breath form as I speak.

I long for a warm villa, knowing it is reserved only for the rich. On our current budget, we'll be heating with wood and only the rooms deemed necessary. Books written about Tuscany are written by the warmth of the summer sun or by wealthy expats. We won't mention this to Chantal and will let her think that all we do is sip Chianti "under the Tuscan sun."

As far as relatives are concerned, we're more famous than Tuscany. We thought that living three hours away would be safe; none of them had ever ventured this far north before.

Yet soon *Zio* Natale will be coming with Giancarlo, who has taken a year's sabbatical and returned to Italy. I hurry to ensure that lunch will be served pronto at one o'clock, because *Zio* is both an elderly Italian man and related to David's father.

Zio has been having a difficult time lately, so we extended this invitation to him. We were surprised that he accepted so readily. Last year we could barely coerce him into coming for one dinner; now he wants to stay for several days.

The minute he steps in, I can see that he is terribly ill, coughing, sneezing, and blowing his nose relentlessly.

"Oh, *Zio*, you're so sick! You should be at home resting," I sympathetically tell him.

"Nothing I can do about being sick—might as well be sick here," he says, in between fits of coughing. Spreading germs is not something he's concerned with.

As he hacks away, I feel affection for him. His first wife died years ago, and due to inheritance laws here, he has strained relations with his six children. *Zio* has built a real compound in suburban Rome. It's four stories that consist of several apartments, some of which his children live in. Strained relations or not, the kids need somewhere to live. He has recently separated from his second wife. Thus, despite my concerns about catching his undoubtedly contagious illness, I'm glad he can have a few days' respite.

I hear more hacking as Giancarlo enters. He, too, is sick! David hasn't been feeling well, either, and I can see my immediate future: caring for three sick Italian men.

They sit down to lunch, and I serve them. Despite their illnesses, their appetites are fine as they polish off plate after plate of food. *Zio* has finally sold an apartment he had on the coast and used in the summer. The buyers didn't have enough money to also buy his garage. Though he originally regretted it, *Zio* is now thankful they didn't buy the garage, because he will turn it into a summer place: a beach "house" for himself. He'll install a bathroom and possibly put in a window. I smile, as I picture the other residents parking their cars to the sound of a flushing toilet.

After the men enjoy a couple days of repose, I'm completely exhausted. I suggest that we go out to eat. *Zio* is frightfully embarrassed, because in his haste to get here and pack us an extravagant supply of groceries, he left without getting money. We offer to take him to a bank machine, but he doesn't trust them.

"I have at least five thousand cash in the house at all times," he says. No doubt, *Zio* isn't the only one in this country sleeping on a lumpy mattress.

"*Zio*, we'll be happy to treat you for a change!" we say.

He is highly uncomfortable with that idea. Obviously distraught, he says, "It's better to be without underwear than without money."

I'm not sure I agree.

We drive to Montepulciano through pastures turning a glowing green as the new wheat grows. *Zio* has never been to Tuscany before. He was a home builder in Abruzzo and is quite surprised that cypress trees grow so close to houses here, something he never thought possible.

We take *Zio* to all of the *cantinas* in town, where he poses with barrel after barrel. We stop at the historic Art Nouveau Caffè Poliziano for lunch. *Zio* pulls out a postcard of Montepulciano and addresses it to the wife he is currently separated from. At least, she'll know he's having a great time without her.

Afterward, we head to the thermal spa. I drop off the ill men and go into town to do some window shopping.

When I return, I spot the three of them exiting the spa, happy as can be! *Zio* loved the experience and swears it has cured him. The eucalyptus and other aromatherapies have opened up the men's breathing passages, and they all feel much better.

"If I lived close by, I'd go once a week!" *Zio* says. I suspect we'll be seeing a lot more of him.

Giancarlo and David loved the mud room. "You lather on hot mud, then you let it dry," David says.

"Only pigs like to bathe in mud," *Zio* informs me. He had refused this treatment. Nor did he enjoy the womb room— where you sit in a dark room, in a round chair, in silence. As he sat in it, he explained in between loud coughing to everyone within earshot how all of the germs they exhaled were being sucked in by others and vice versa. David quickly ushered *Zio* into the next room, so that the other customers could enjoy the "spa" experience.

Zio and Giancarlo will be leaving soon, so I prepare a special four-course meal. As we're eating our *Caprese* salad, a fight breaks out. *Zio* is adamant on a certain topic and cannot be swayed. He is manifesting one of the worst attitudes of certain "old school" types in a patriarchal culture. The two boys vehemently disagree with him. *Zio* has worked himself up, and any minute now I expect him to stand up and throw the table over, toppling the four-course meal I'd spent hours cooking.

I reflect on all of the books I've read that glamorize hosting dinner parties in Tuscany: sitting on candlelit terraces, sipping fine wine, while discussing how to distinguish between a wine's aroma and a wine's bouquet, everyone picture perfect with their big smiles. What a contrast to my "dinner party" tonight! *Oh, Chantal, if only you knew . . .*

Finally, *Zio* calms down, though he keeps erupting with occasional flare-ups. David and Giancarlo refuse to discuss this issue anymore, and I sit there eating, though I've lost my appetite.

I fear for Giancarlo having to drive back with *Zio*, who is already a maniacal driver when he's not upset. We bid them farewell and a safe drive back to Rome.

In no time, we receive a call from Giancarlo.

"Where are you?" I ask.

"I'm in Rome," says Giancarlo. "Once *Zio* hit the *autostrada*, he drove a hundred and eighty the whole way home!" (Note: 180 kph equals 110 mph.)

"Weren't you scared to death?" I ask.

"What could I do? I stayed quiet, put my seat back, and went to sleep."

I shudder—an elderly man driving like that! I wonder if *Zio* will soon get another speeding fine to add to his impressive collection.

Now I really begin to worry—not because of the hefty fine he may receive but rather that *Zio* may be back sooner than we think. After all, he can get here in practically no time!

On that note, I pour myself another glass of wine, grateful we have survived, if only barely, these last few days.

Bar Congo

It's already dark, so we're surprised to hear a knock at the door. A man is holding the flier we recently distributed that says we're looking for work.

We really have been "getting off our butts."

The flier advertised cleaning and home maintenance services; thus, it is with great trepidation that we invite Eric inside. Tomorrow, we'll be having twenty Italians for lunch, and I've already started cooking a meal worthy of them. Food-encrusted pots and pans are strewn about the kitchen. Dead wildflowers I picked a week ago droop in a vase. We've just finished dinner, so dirty plates cover the entire table. I'm afraid there is no chance we'll be hired.

Eric, despite being a lawyer, isn't the judgmental type, nor is he a serious drinker. Thus, it's rather fortuitous that we offer Eric a hefty glass of strong red wine the moment he enters our home.

He needs help with the finishing touches in a house he recently purchased and is in the process of restoring. He also owns another home in the village, and he and his family are here on vacation from Belgium. "The house is two hundred meters down the road, and you can start work tomorrow morning at nine o'clock."

Eric, sitting relaxed amid the mounds of unwashed dishes, explains why he loves life in Italy. "It's like living in the fifties. The way life was thirty years ago!"

I refrain from mentioning the current year and that it's closer to *sixty* years ago. Regardless of the math, we feel that he is correct.

After two hours of filling us in on local village gossip and the everyday curiosities of Italian rural life, interspersed with pouring out his soul, Eric gets up to leave. "If I don't get home soon, my wife will think a wild boar has eaten me!"

We like him. There's a certain eccentricity about him, and we're certain he'll be a wellspring of fascinating, though highly suspicious, information. We head off to bed, grateful.

Knowing Eric is not Italian and thus perhaps keeps to a schedule, David and I ensure that we'll be ready for him by 9:00 a.m. At a quarter to nine, we hear wild pounding on the door. It's Eric, along with his eight-year-old son. He apologizes for being early and, walking away, says, "See you in fifteen minutes; if you cannot find the house, two hundred meters away, you're fired."

We get his point and quickly finish dressing, grab our things, and hope we can locate his place.

Buttercups are abloom in the meadows, along with miniature daisies. I feel the sun on my neck, ever grateful as I walk the two hundred meters to my new job and remember the one-hour commute on the crowded bus back in Toronto. At the first fork in the road, we turn left, and there stands his house.

Eric tells us it is five hundred years old and adds, "I know you don't believe me, but it's true." Full of enthusiasm, he wants to show us the house and the mill that the river used to run through. The formation of the bricks confirms this. Eric has brought a virtual mill from Belgium, by van, and would like to set it up for nostalgia's sake. Eric is a man with vision and many plans.

On the ground floor is a kitchen. The walls and the floors have been finished, but the plumbing and other hook-ups still need to be completed. From the kitchen, a small ladder leads to the second floor, kind of like a tree house. Eric scurries up this tiny, steep ladder, which is most likely not up to any safety codes. I climb slowly and cautiously. The second floor consists of a living room with a large open fireplace, a bathroom, and two bedrooms. To enter the second bedroom, one must walk through the first one. Eric is convinced that's why this house wasn't snatched up sooner.

"Belgians don't mind that," he says.

I am here to clean; however, all of the rooms have mounds of construction materials scattered about, many of which still need to be used. Yet Eric is a man on a mission and would like me to wash the newly tiled terra cotta floors, despite the fact that there is so much stuff piled all over, I can barely see them. I oblige him, and after I spend a long time moving furniture, without washing any tiles yet, he calls me to come downstairs.

"Break time!" announces Eric, with the authority of an army sergeant. He has set up a quaint, rickety old table and equally rickety chairs in the tall grass near the house.

"Sit down and take a break," he demands. I examine the tall grass and hope there are no snakes. I follow David's lead, literally, because he sits on the wobbly chair and falls over, and then I do the same. Eric laughs and asks if we would like beer or wine. It's only eleven o'clock, but since he hasn't brought anything else, I opt for the white wine. David and Eric each have a large bottle of beer. Quinten, Eric's son, joins us and tries to balance himself on the unsteady chair on a slight incline.

We are quite the sight, drinking and taking turns falling over, when Franco, the Italian neighbor comes by. Franco has a vacation home next to the old mill, even though he lives in town about three kilometers away (1.8 miles). Each day he and his wife drive over to their vacation house. He's a friendly man, and he never misses an opportunity to chat with someone.

He saunters over and says, "What? You're drinking alcohol this early in the morning, without eating?" He lectures us on how one should have something to drink only at mealtimes.

Eric takes another sip of his beer, smiles, raises his glass, and yells, "Cheers!" Then, with the same drill sergeant tone, he hollers, "Back to work!"

Quinten hops up like a gazelle, no doubt accustomed to his father's commands, while David and I stand up with due caution, fearing that if we fall this time, the Italian neighbor will conclude we are drunk. Eric has seemingly levitated inside and is upstairs getting my next project ready, though I haven't even finished my first one yet.

Before we continue working, Eric is ready to talk pay.

"How much do you want to be paid?" he asks.

We hesitate, then ask, "Do you think nine euros an hour is okay?"

Because he's a lawyer, we're surprised at his response: "Fine, ten!" With that settled, he has a new job for me.

"What about the floors?" I remind him.

"Oh, yeah!" His memory is suddenly jolted. "Fine, finish the floors then, as you wish, Madame."

I get down on my hands and knees and scrub the impossible-to-scrub floors. Eric doesn't care, for he's already anxious for me to start on my next project: hanging curtains. I'm realizing that Eric is a lawyer cum mad scientist. Construction materials are scattered about, doors still need to be painted, old dressers need cleaning, and the windows are filthy, but Eric would like the curtains hung!

"Do you think it might be better to wash the windows first before we hang the curtains?" I ask.

Dismayed by this lack of progress, Eric concedes, and I clean the windows.

David is putting together the modern IKEA kitchen that Eric chose for this five-hundred-year-old home.

Quinten is a sweet boy, with long white-blond hair and a big smile. He has been assigned the task of repainting the message Eric had impulsively scrawled. A lovely shade of bluish gray has been mixed to paint over the big letters spelling out BAR CONGO. Quinten industriously paints over these words, no doubt unaware of their origins.

Months earlier, when Eric and the crew of men he'd brought from Belgium were in the middle of repairing the ancient stone oven, a cantankerous neighbor remarked, "Do you think you are in the Congo and can do anything you want?"

Soon thereafter, the *carabinieri* put a stop to Eric's aspirations of restoring the wood-burning oven. There would be no pizzas baked in this one.

In revenge, Eric tauntingly wrote the words BAR CONGO on the oven's metal door.

As Quinten finishes painting, he looks up at his father for a nod of approval. Staring at the freshly painted oven door, Eric shrugs and sighs.

Eric now decides that rather than finish any of the construction projects upstairs, he will first hang pictures and other items on the walls. Having already quashed his vision of white curtains flowing in the wind, I remain silent and let him happily hang pictures that will undoubtedly need to be rehung once the pieces of furniture are put in their respective places.

"We will have the three masters in this room!" he says, hanging dusty pictures and explaining details about each print.

Next, he whimsically hangs bunches of fresh rosemary from the ceiling, again ignoring the cobwebs and mounds of work yet to be done.

One by one, more blond heads appear. It's approaching lunchtime, and Eric's wife has enlisted the children's help to get her work-obsessed husband to come home. First, his eleven-year-old daughter arrives. Minutes later, his other daughter shows up. Seeing that Eric still isn't making plans to head home, the reinforcement finally appears: Eric's oldest son.

"By the time the fourth one comes, I know I'd better be home quick!" With lightning speed, Eric turns off the lights, and they're gone in a flash.

David and I look at each other.

"Well, that was most interesting," I say.

Despite all of the confusion and disorder, we agree that we like Eric and his children.

It's April; the sun is finally shining. I pick myself a bunch of buttercups on the walk home.

Two older women greet us; one appears to be in her seventies and the other in her eighties. On their backs are tied two large bundles of wild asparagus. "We had to climb high, high to get all of this."

I regularly climb the hills behind our home but have yet to find more than a few spears of asparagus.

Inspired by the two elderly ladies, that afternoon I climb higher than all of the eighty-year-olds in our village and find some wild asparagus plants that were not picked over. I happily head home with a dozen of them.

Luciano, our neighbor, laughs at my small bundle. Despite our objections, he has just finished plowing under a patch of our grass with his tractor, insisting we need more land for our garden. He shows off his tractor, explaining its features and pointing out the air conditioning, though I highly doubt he has ever used it.

Another neighbor wanders over to inspect our newly plowed tract of land. Both men give us pointers on how and what to plant. They have seen that Eric is back, so they give us their version of the latest village happenings. We fear there will be plenty of unsolicited advice and information as the months go by.

Soon after Eric returns to Belgium, he receives a registered letter. In an email to us, he explains, "My enemy has started a legal case against me. Suddenly, Italy has become a dangerous place. This is no longer fun. I'm looking forward to our next glass of wine together."

We think he'll need it!

FOURTEEN FERRARIS AND A FIAT PANDA

IT'S THE END OF JUNE, and I'm still alive, though barely. We've had company since the end of April. My hips, thighs, and stomach haven't escaped all of the hearty Italian meals unscathed. Many of our guests were generous, appreciative, and gracious; however, no one wants to hear about them. The others fall into one or, on occasion, more than one of the following categories:

The Problem Solvers: Are ruthless in their ability to figure out a solution when we object to their staying with us. Not enough bedrooms? No worries, we can bring blow-up mattresses. You have a contagious disease? No worries, we can quarantine you. Ironically, their problem-solving skills seem to fall short when the dinner bill arrives, and they have to figure out just how much they owe.

The Mathematically Challenged: These guests originally tell us two people will be staying for three days, but then four of them arrive and stay six days.

The Self-Assured Guests: These guests are convinced that their mere presence is more than I could ever want, and specialties from Canada or other monetary tokens would only pale in comparison.

The Grocery Store–Averse Guest: They are averse to entering grocery stores and much prefer waiting in the infernal confines of our ancient car on blistering hot days, thus avoiding any possible encounter with a pesky bill.

The Servantless Guests: They have unfortunately, for one reason or another, left their entourage of personal servants at home and are now at a complete loss when it comes to simple chores, such as doing their laundry, ironing their shirts, washing dishes, or taking public transport of any sort.

The Expert Guests: These guests have read one too many books on Tuscany and have come to fill us in on what the Tuscan experience is *really* all about, according to Jamie Oliver. They also freely lavish their "expertise" on the chefs and the producers of olive oil and wine whom they encounter.

The Guest Who Describes My Life as a "Vacation": Elegantly dressed, they sit there as I wait on them hand and foot, even though I haven't had time to take a shower or make myself presentable. They once again declare just how fortunate I am, as they leave me with the dishes and go to take a *pausa*.

"The Bird That Has Eaten Flies Away": These guests are ever so grateful for everything we have done for them, they will never forget us, and they declare this trip a life-altering experience, only to never be heard from again—unless, of course, they have inadvertently left something behind that needs to be mailed back to them.

And finally, the "Crashers": These types don't place themselves in the category of "guests," because they are only asking to "crash" at our place, implying, but certainly not expecting, that they can simply sleep on the floor, and no effort whatsoever will be required to put them up; I will hardly notice them! They feel this ploy will guarantee a "yes" from us, because how can we say no to anyone who just wants to crash?

Our last guests left this morning, and John and Debbie, whom I'm certain will fall into the "gracious" category, should arrive shortly. The house is a mess, the meal only half ready, and I'm filthy and sweaty. I look at the clock and contemplate suicide.

I think of Martha Stewart, cool as a cucumber, hosting dinner parties for upward of thirty people, graciously welcoming them. And Frances Mayes in Cortona, all made up, awaiting her guests, sipping a glass of Chianti, and chopping fresh basil and rosemary as she waits.

I take a "luxurious" two-minute shower, barely rinsing all the soap off myself, and hurry to finish the dishes and wash the floor. I leave my hair to dry on its own, and I look like the Bride of Frankenstein with pink lipstick.

A car pulls up in the driveway. They're earlier than expected, so I send David out to greet them. "Take them to the terrace and start plying them with drinks."

Their bed is not yet made, and the rest of the house is far from perfect. I recall all of the preparations I made for our first guests: I ironed their sheets and pillow cases. I arranged large blossoms of pink roses for their nightstand. I lit lavender-scented candles. They were indeed privileged. But that was then, and this is now. For these guests, I barely manage to clean their bathroom in time. I quickly finish up inside, and though frazzled, I greet them as if I've waited a lifetime to see them.

I pile on the food, and they eat like there's no tomorrow.

We're on the terrace when the *carabinieri* arrive. We run over to see what it's all about.

The *carabinieri* always seem very official, and their uniforms alone are imposing. They size you up, as if to determine what crimes you may have committed. They take your documents and unhurriedly walk back to their car. Though I'm the most law-abiding driver in all of Italy, they never fail to make me nervous. Thus, I'm surprised that one of them greets us, casually saying, "Nice place you got here. Really, really nice."

He looks around and asks a few inappropriate questions regarding the house. His partner is not amused.

The serious one demands, "Documents, please."

We wonder what this is all about, as undoubtedly do our guests. David goes to get our documents, while the jovial *carabiniere* chats with me. He really is impressed with the house and the grounds, and I won't be surprised if he takes a self-guided tour soon. His partner is visibly embarrassed. I mention that we're renting it and could never afford to buy a house like this one. Now they both become sympathetic.

David returns with our documents and answers their questions. The serious one writes down all of our information. They are confirming that all is in order for me to receive my "permission to stay" document and that I do indeed live with David.

"How did you find our place?" I ask. "Most people have a hard time locating us."

"It took us two hours," they confess. "We went to several homes looking for you."

I have a sneaking suspicion the locals didn't want to betray us by reporting our last-known whereabouts to the *carabinieri*. The village will have its gossip for the week. Perhaps people will no longer think we are *stranieri giusti*.

Their official business finished, the *carabinieri* head off.

We look forward to our week with John and Debbie and to receiving my "permission to stay" document. Yet each day of "glorious vacationing" under the Tuscan sun tests John and Debbie's marriage. Each sharp curve of the road is an ordeal for her nerves and, consequently, his as well.

One morning they leave to explore the countryside and are gone all day. I fear for them, for they are proficient at getting lost.

When they return from the stunningly beautiful Chianti area, it isn't the rolling hills covered in lush green vineyards they describe. It isn't the castles, the *cantinas*, and the fine wines they stumbled upon, or the quaintness of the small towns. Rather, we hear about the curves that made them both terribly sick, the fights over John's driving, and getting lost on the way there and back, turning a one-hour trip into a three-hour one. My Italian lessons earlier that morning, for "straight," "right," "left," and so on, had not helped. We soon realize we had better get them a GPS navigator, or one day they simply will never return—or, at least, not together.

Even taking the train to Florence doesn't prove to be stress free. They are running late and arrive with one minute to spare. John quickly parks the car, while Debbie buys the tickets. As the train pulls out, John tries to recall the parking regulations and fears he has left his car in a one-hour parking zone. They will be gone all day before returning to get the car.

Then their train car fills with smoke, and panic sets in. Everyone is yelling in Italian, and poor John and Debbie have no idea what is taking place. After a while, the train continues its journey, and the smoke subsides. Seeing that the Italians are no longer panicking, they sit back but can't relax, thanks to the smoke and possibly a huge parking fine awaiting them.

It's four o'clock. I've spent the day cleaning the house and doing their laundry, and I'm just about to rest a bit when I see their yellow Fiat Panda pull into the driveway.

"We saw Florence!" Debbie says.

"Did you get to the Pitti Palace and the Boboli Gardens?" I ask, because I knew Debbie had longed to visit Florence for years.

"Nah, couldn't find them! So we just came home." She adds, "We're so glad we saw Florence the way we did. Imagine, friends of ours stayed three days!"

The next day I really start to worry about them. They will be touring the Crete area, just south of Siena, full of hairpin curves and without one straight road. I hope they will arrive safely—and still happily married—at the thermal baths and will enjoy the stunning view of the Val d'Orcia valley, complete with an ancient castle in the background.

I prepare them breakfast that includes protein, for the Italian breakfast was not to their liking. I want to avoid any more complaints about the "spa diet" from my guests. Breakfast is preceded by at least two espressos and is followed by the same number or more. If Debbie eased up on the caffeine, she would be far more relaxed in the car.

By five o'clock, they are already back. I make them Campari-and-orange-juice cocktails, accompanied by fried zucchini flowers.

They had barely survived the curving roads of the Crete area. They enjoyed the baths, if only for an hour, and loved the picturesque medieval village of Bagno Vignoni, with ancient stone houses clustered around a large pool that functions as a central piazza, water bubbling up from the natural springs.

"On our way home, we followed fourteen Ferraris for more than an hour through winding roads," John excitedly says.

Could this be true, and if so, how did their marriage survive it?

"We're part of the Ferrari family, because FIAT owns Ferrari! The cars were all different colors, and we were the last ones in the convoy! We kept up and waved at everyone as if we, too, were in a Ferrari. It was so much fun!"

This story will definitely be going home with them.

After appetizers and cocktails, Debbie takes a nap, while I clean up and get ready for a night on the town. John insists we take his Panda, because our BMW is not in the Ferrari lineage, whereas his car obviously is. Not wanting to ruin the excitement of the day, we concede.

John carefully and slowly drives to the restaurant, yet Debbie keeps reminding him to drive even more carefully and slowly. She lets out an occasional blood-curdling scream as we approach intersections, fearing that the Italian motorists won't stop. This fifteen-minute drive makes me doubt that they really could have followed fourteen Ferraris for an hour and still be married.

We have reservations for eight-thirty at the elegant Ristorante Preludio in Cortona, where the coffee-flavored ravioli stuffed with mascarpone and ricotta is certain to please their palates.

After dinner, we take them to our favorite place for coffee, Nessun Dorma, named after a Puccini aria that translates to "no one sleeps." We have an espresso, and they have two, while we sit under the stars in the piazza. The summer festival will soon take place, where people can listen to an opera in the ancient square under the night sky.

We stroll back to the car via Parterre Park, and John and Debbie suddenly exclaim, "The Ferraris!" and make a beeline for the cars. They mention to one of the men that they had been in their convoy for more than an hour: from Bagno Vignoni until Bettolle. A distinguished-looking man with a lovely British accent confirms that was the route they took. They really did follow fourteen Ferraris!

This amicable man tells us they are all from Dubai, and we note the Dubai plates. They had shipped the cars to a port town in Italy and then driven to Switzerland, where a few drivers were heavily fined for extreme speeding, and some also lost their licenses. They drove through the glittery towns of Gstaad and St. Moritz, then on to Italy.

The boys examine the cars, each one a special limited edition. I'm fascinated by the man's stories, and he offers to take me for a ride. For a brief second I consider it, but the thought of traveling at high speeds through curvy mountain roads brings me to my senses—even more so than getting into a car with a man I don't know. Besides, I'll still have bragging rights; I was offered the ride. I run over and tell David. Jealousy immediately sets in—not because I was offered a ride by a charming, filthy rich foreign man in a Ferrari, but because David wasn't offered one.

It's late, and John says he'll drive us home "in the family of Ferrari," his Fiat Panda. The man laughs heartily. We wish him a good stay in Tuscany and walk past the armed security guard, hired to safeguard the Ferraris overnight.

John drives home, as cautious as ever and Debbie as nervous as always. We are going so slowly, I fear we may be rear-ended.

A week later, we see a write-up in the newspaper with details and pictures of the Ferrari tour. I will mail it to our friends, for, after all, they were part of the "Ferrari family" and no doubt will truly appreciate this one last souvenir!

OCCUPATIONAL HAZARDS

THE BROCHURE FOR THE TUSCAN retreat advertises "Away from the everyday hustle and bustle, steeped in the uniquely beautiful Tuscan countryside, where old stones and bricks have been turned today into wonderfully restored country houses to offer the visitor top of the class comfort and relaxation."

Cypresses line the long driveway, lush lavender cascades down ancient stone walls, abundant rosemary grows above it. Prolific blooms of red roses complete the picture. A bona fide paradise; "a memorable experience," the brochure promises. And so it will prove to be . . .

It's eight o'clock in the morning, and, one by one, the privileged children arrive at the retreat. Deeply tanned mothers, sporting extreme high heels, skin-tight jeans, and low-cut tops, drop off their darling children and kiss them before entrusting them to us. For the next five hours, they will be ours to entertain. Three teachers will oversee twenty-three children. The odds are not in our favor.

Eight-year-old Carla is accompanied by her grandmother, who is determined to update me on the school system here. "A little *Marrocchino* boy in Carla's class failed last year."

Carla shakes her *nonna* by the cuff of her shirt and says, "*Nonna*, he's not called a *Marrocchino*, he's called a *straniero.*"

Nonna looks at me and shrugs, apologizing, "The children must be so politically correct these days."

Carla continues, "The teacher was upset with him, so she told him that she has reserved a camel for him to return to Morocco if he doesn't want to learn in her class!"

David and I can't believe our ears!

Nonna, however, wants us to agree that there is nothing wrong with taking notice of someone's nationality. *Nonna* asks Carla, "If you saw that someone was Albanian, what would you say?"

"I would say Ciao!" the little girl innocently replies. We smile.

We chat with *Nonna*, while the last of the sexy moms drops off her child, and we are ready to proceed.

Welcome to Kids Summer Camp. The flyer promises both sports and creative activities: games, songs, and English lessons to encourage your child to explore his or her imagination, dreams, and emotions.

The first day David and I will work together until 10 a.m., so that the parents can meet both of us. Then we'll alternate days.

The director asks the children to draw some pictures and answer some questions—a type of psychology test, we are told. The children rapidly scribble and color away. Handling four children apiece until 10 a.m. is quite manageable for David and me, and the kids aren't drawing anything that would lead us to believe they are psycho killers in the making.

Minutes after David leaves me alone with the eight children, each child *does* appear to be a psycho killer in the making. I barely survive the morning; my head is ringing with the sounds of twenty-three boisterous children: "*Maestra! Maestra! Maestra!*"

That chant will haunt me to my grave.

The parents pick up their little darlings, cooing and aahing at their projects, and a staff meeting is held to discuss the groups. There is a family feud going on, and Gianni's mother absolutely does not want him in the same group with his cousin Matteo. Giovanni has lied about his age; the maximum age is eleven, and he is thirteen, so we'll have to adjust his group. Daniele is too hyper, so we'll have to move him. The two sweet six-year-olds want to be together. The rearranging is relentless. I'm tired, and the positive, high energy of the American teacher is getting on my nerves. Her big fake smile annoys me, and I've had enough of her long lectures on child psychology. *The brats have gone home; why can't I?*

The American has further words of wisdom, accompanied by a toothy grin: "You must assume they know no English, for they don't. Also, Italian children are very spoiled, just something you'll have to get used to."

I'm teaching kids in a country with one of the lowest birth rates in the world, I know they will be spoiled!

Finally, the staff meeting is over, and I drive through the somewhat diminished beauty of the Tuscan hills until I reach the peace of our country home. I feel the sun on my face, while I drink a glass of table wine from Montalcino and gaze at the quaint hilltop town in the distance and hillsides dotted with olive groves. Perhaps I can do this after all. A second glass of wine, along with the hot sun baking my brains, convinces me that I can. Besides, tomorrow is David's turn. I go into the house and take a well-deserved *pausa*.

David wakes up early, anticipating his first day of classes. He prepares a few lessons and games and leaves with the same positive high energy of the American teacher who grates on me.

Perhaps it's just me, I think.

It is approaching two o'clock. Certain that David will be starving, I prepare a lovely meal for him.

Yet the minute he comes in the door, I see that his positive high energy has vanished.

His first words are "I'm sorry I didn't have any empathy for you yesterday. I'm very sorry."

He staggers off to bed, apologizing for being too tired even to eat, and within seconds falls into a deep sleep.

I eat lunch alone and snicker, feeling rather vindicated! Two hours later, he wakes up, still groggy and still tired. I wear that sly smile the rest of the day, until the realization hits me that tomorrow is my turn.

I vow to be better prepared. I surf the Internet looking for instructional outdoors games that will allow kids to release their pent-up energy and also teach them English. Finally, hours later I'm ready. I avoid doing the math on exactly how much I'm making per hour. The fact that I haven't killed myself tonight trying to prepare the lessons with our super-slow Internet connection makes me think I might survive tomorrow.

The first hour is fine, because the children sit calmly doing crafts. I attribute this to their still being half asleep and slightly dazed. By eleven o'clock, however, I wish I was back in Canada working for my high-strung stockbroker. Hours of painstaking preparation have not yielded the results I expected. Instead, a fight has broken out, and I'm grabbing Giacomo by the scruff of his T-shirt and demanding that he calm down. He is a beautiful eight-year-old boy with long curly blond hair and an enthusiastic personality. But being so beautiful is difficult; the two six-year-old girls evidently have crushes on Giacomo and tease him relentlessly. The older boys are jealous of him and hence also taunt him.

"Little blond boy," they all chant.

"Stop teasing me," he yells and escapes my grasp. I chase after him, as the others chant and run after both of us. He finds a big stick and charges at the children. I grab him by the back of his T-shirt and forcefully announce, "Outside time is over!"

While I hold the kid by the scruff of his neck, separating him from the relentless mob of screaming children, my friends all across North America think I'm living the high life in Tuscany!

We return to the stone building that the brochure refers to as a wonderfully restored country house where visitors enjoy comfort and relaxation. I wonder if the current guests agree, as they sit by the pool hearing all of the ruckus and watch me furiously chasing groups of unruly children.

The first craft session went well, so I do another one with the children. Soon I hear the thirteen-year-old say, "*Non ho voglia*" ("I don't want to").

I control myself, because I want to grab him and yell, "Listen, kid, do you think I want to be here? Working for minimum wage? *Anche io non ho voglia* [I don't want to, either], but I am here! So sit down, do the craft, and be quiet!" Instead, I smile and try to coax him to do the craft. When that fails, I provide him with a variety of other options for his personal enjoyment and satisfaction.

The other two teachers and their groups have now returned. The room has a high-domed terra cotta ceiling, and the noise level is unbearable. My only satisfaction is that the American teacher's unrelenting cheerfulness has evaporated.

"Do you have any children?" one of the kids asks.

"No, I don't," I respond.

With a big smile, he says, "Bet you're glad you don't have children, aren't you?"

I laugh. "At this very moment, yes, I am glad, really glad."

Thrilled that they have managed to take away my desire to reproduce, they go back to fighting.

The day never seems to end. My only other consolation is that I'm done for the week; poor David is next.

I drive through the ever-diminishing beauty of the Tuscan countryside. I have no energy to appreciate it. Dealing with the children has taken away the rows of cypresses, the scent of lavender, and the bright red roses. The children have worn me out, and gone are the splendors of my surroundings.

The following morning, David leaves with a justified sense of trepidation. He returns home in far better shape than I expected.

Without an ounce of shame, he smiles and says, "Blackmail. Yup, I've started blackmailing the children. Today, Daniele went over the page and drew onto the table; a black smudge stained the antique wooden table. I asked who is going to pay for the damage. Daniele looked at me, finally with fear in his eyes, and with great concern said, 'It was an accident.' I then sternly replied, 'It doesn't matter, someone will have to pay for the damage. If you are good, I won't phone your parents, but otherwise I'll have to.' The poor hyperactive kid actually managed to behave for a while. The minute he didn't, I took out my cell phone and pretended to call his parents or the *carabinieri*—I alternated! It was tremendous! He calmed right down and joined in the activities! I have to admit, it's a low blow, blackmailing children, but I love it, and I wouldn't hesitate to do it again!"

Proud as a peacock, David needs only a one-and-a-half-hour nap today.

Days pass, and we both miraculously survive. Notions of returning to Canada to my stressful job diminish as the end of week two approaches.

I prepare a zoo project and give hope to several travel agencies as I collect brochures advertising safaris to Africa. I capture the children's attention, until they start fighting because they all want the same picture for their African Safari photo album.

On Wednesday, I get a sore throat, followed by a fever and a severe cold. My Italian friends attribute this to the hot weather, combined with the air conditioning that has been turned on in several stores. By Thursday, David has caught the same bug. We call the school in the morning before he leaves, warning them of his and my illness.

The director of the school kindly tells us, "Don't come in if you're sick. We'll manage without you."

Had we won the lottery, we could not be happier. Delirious, we both lie in bed, grateful for our unbearably painful sore throats and the debilitating flu-like symptoms.

I'm supposed to work one last day, Friday, but, fearful of our illness, the school director sends us a text message that we don't need to come teach if we're still sick. It feels great to win the lottery again.

My only regret is that I missed seeing the smile permanently disappear from the American teacher's face, because she was undoubtedly entrusted with our little darlings, as well as her own, for the last two days!

Two weeks later, I still have a cough that sounds as if I've smoked three packs a day all of my life. David is also hacking away, and we go to the doctor, fearing we may have bronchitis. We're also both on the verge of a nervous breakdown, because our countless phone calls and emails to the school have been ignored. There is no way we'll let the director forget to give us our "danger" pay for the eight days of torture we endured at Kids Summer Camp!

When you receive health coverage in Italy, you're given a choice of three doctors in your area. David did an evaluation and picked the one with convenient and, even more important, *free* parking.

Il dottore pokes his head out, and it's our turn. We state the reason for our visit and are offered anecdotes, jokes, and on occasion some relevant medical advice. *Il dottore* seems to be in no rush and appears oblivious to the line of people waiting outside his door. He is a fan of wine but says that "Hard liquor is not for us Italians. Hard liquor is for the British."

He says that David will be a lot healthier with the Italian diet. "I used to date a Canadian girl, and I know the junk you eat in Canada."

David agrees. "I used to eat a lot of junk food in front of the TV."

Il dottore suddenly becomes indignant and says, "If you ever buy a TV here, never, never, give them your real name. Give them your neighbor's name, your priest's name, anyone's name but yours. Only in this country do they make you give out your name if you buy a television and make you pay an annual tax for watching it!"

He rants and raves for a while, then returns to his pleasant self, gives us a prescription, and concludes the visit with a joke. "So there's a guy in a bar . . ."

Our high blood pressure issues are resolved when we receive this text message: "You can come by the school Monday morning to pick up your pay."

We're thrilled! Though the job was hazardous to our health, the funds will come in handy.

LIVING LA VITA LOCAL

TODAY'S MOUNTAIN WALK WAS QUIET. Luciano has taken a break from his chain-sawing expedition, which began more than two weeks ago. He says one does not need a permit to cut down trees: only a chainsaw, a tractor, and a willing wife as your helper. Consequently, for the last two weeks I have no need of an alarm clock; the illegal felling of trees begins promptly at 6 a.m. Soon thereafter, my neighbor Enzo guarantees my wake-up call with his weed-whacker. He has lots of weeds and lots of land. He doesn't use the weed-whacker every day. He alternates with his power mower, riding and mowing his vast empire. Thankfully, he's already attacked every weed and blade of grass, and I will get a week's repose. Even the excruciatingly loud hunting dogs, which bark and howl in unison for hours on end as they battle wild boars in the night, seem to have taken a *pausa*.

I love my mountain today.

As I ascend, sweat drips down my face, for without my wake-up call I have left far too late in the morning, and it's hot already. My efforts are rewarded by the vision of vast fields of bright yellow sunflowers blooming in the valley below. Next to the sunflowers is a heap of building supplies that Eric's arch enemy, Mauro, has been stockpiling for years in an empty field. The corrugated metal roof on a hideous iron structure has caved in, becoming even more of an eyesore. Mauro is past fifty and still lives at home with his aged parents; thus, it seems unlikely that all of this hoarded and no doubt stolen material will ever evolve into a house. It will merely mar the landscape for years to come. Tourists are probably more than a little shocked, because the drive to their idyllic Tuscan rental is littered with terra cotta roof tiles, sewage pipes, rusted machinery, and other debris that doesn't belong under the Tuscan sun.

I return—hot, tired, and glowing red. I make my village rounds, briefly chatting with all of the elderly people as they work, seemingly effortlessly, in their gardens. I greet the older man who daily asks me, "Going for a walk, are you?" I wave at a group of older men who sit alongside the stairs of their ancient stone homes for hours on end, watching passers-by— not a rewarding endeavor in a town of only a dozen people.

My walks are becoming much longer than I intended. There simply is no appropriate place to interrupt a man who is explaining that he has had "four bypasses and now lives with only half a heart." Who says that every day of life is precious to him . . . as he shows me his unsightly scars and tells me his heart is about to break at the mere sight of me. I can't interrupt my ancient neighbor who gives me a walking cane that appears older than he is, but he claims to have bought it just for me. Nor is there any quick escape when a farmer is intent on showing me his prized tomatoes, his award-winning eggplant, the superior quality of his zucchini. I'm so out of place here, yet ironically I feel so at home.

At home, I pick up the cantaloupe Luciano has dropped off on our stairs. There are also several eggplants that Enzo has placed in his regular drop-off spot.

Outside, the hot sun shines relentlessly. The multicolored butterflies flutter around, and the barn owl and her chicks are at home on our roof. A moth resembling a hummingbird flits from one bright flower to the next. The cicadas chirp noisily away.

Lunchtime approaches. I look at the defrosted chicken and realize I have lost my marbles; a sane person does not roast a chicken in this scorching heat. I head out to the garden to see what has multiplied overnight. I pick a lettuce and some ripe red tomatoes; they even smell good.

The blazing sun has made it unbearable outdoors now. The breeze feels like a hot blow-dryer. I close all of the windows to prevent the hot air from flowing in. Doing any work at this time of the day is out of the question, so I put on my bathing suit and go outside, for we have devised a "poor man's swimming pool." It's a shower hooked up to our well, and I cool down under the cold water and then laze away in a lounge chair. I am now refreshed, despite the heat, and as I gaze at the views around me, I feel like a million dollars.

I fall asleep and don't wake up until I hear a weak beep, beep. A Fiat 500 is parked on the grass in front of our steps.

It's Eric. He and his family have returned from Belgium for their summer vacation. With their presence, they have greatly reduced the median age of the village.

Eric found this car abandoned in the woods and has since lovingly restored it. The engine works perfectly, and the outside is immaculate, painted a shiny bright blue. Strapped onto the back of the car is an antique leather suitcase.

"Does your wife want to go for a ride?" Eric asks David.

"She recently turned down a drive in a special edition Ferrari, so I don't think she'll be interested."

"What's the maximum speed?" I ask.

"Fifty miles an hour, but usually it goes much slower," Eric regretfully says.

Smiling, I get ready for my first ride in a Fiat 500. David laughs at me for refusing a ride in a $200,000 Ferrari, yet meanwhile I gladly hop into the Fiat 500.

Since David is on the terrace, I run up to the house to lock the door.

Eric scolds me. "Who will steal anything here? Leave it, let's go."

I put to rest my landlady's warning about marauding bands of gypsies and their larcenous children.

My drive in the Fiat 500 is quite short-lived, thus so are the chances of the gypsies robbing us blind. After driving two hundred meters, Eric catches sight of his wife. Three hours ago, he promised to take her shopping, and she is still waiting. He apologizes to me, and I get out of the car. As I head home, he begins apologizing to his wife.

David is on the terrace and appears panic-stricken. "We've been called back to teach Kids Summer Camp the last two weeks of August! What should we do?"

Weeks ago, we were grateful for that horrible flu that rescued us from teaching the last two days of classes. Now, as the euro continues to head north and the Canadian dollar south, we feel we have no choice.

He texts back, then pauses, glancing at me for reassurance.

"We have no other work, the stock market sucks, so we have no choice," I say.

He knows I'm right. David again fantasizes about being wealthy. Italy has a way of inspiring us to wish we were filthy rich.

I break the news to my sister. Relieved, she laughs and says, "The way you sounded when you said you had news to tell me, I thought for sure someone had died."

Hasn't she read *Under the Tuscan Sun?* Frances Mayes describes her partner "in the piazza every afternoon, gazing at the young couple trying to wheel their new baby down the street. They're halted every few steps. Everyone circles the carriage. They're leaning into the baby's face, making noises, praising the baby." Ed tells Ms. Mayes, "In my next life, I want to come back as an Italian baby."

The instruction manual for our Italian espresso machine includes a picture of a baby crawling across the coffee machine, with a big X marked across this scene.

These are the same children who attend Kids Summer Camp.

I pray that the stock market recovers and soon we can sell our bank shares. Incidentally, Ed could also have stated that in his next life, he would like to come back as not only an Italian baby but an Italian child, an Italian teenager, a forty-year-old Italian man, a newly married Italian man, and so on. The level of being doted on doesn't change substantially with age.

"Fantastic. I'll be in touch real soon," the school director replies.

I think of all of the rich Americans living the high life here in their villas. I wonder how long it would be before they high-tailed it back to America if they had to teach even one morning of Kids Summer Camp. Readers beware.

In harmony with the news of going back to teach, for the first time I see a scorpion in my kitchen sink.

The phone rings soon thereafter. It's my mother-in-law. She would like us to come and visit, and then she can come to our place when we drive back.

"How long do you want to stay with us?" David sheepishly asks.

"I don't know, a week or two," she says. "I'll see how I feel."

At least, our overseas friends can stop being jealous.

SEVEN DAYS, SEVEN ROOSTERS

WE ENTER MY IN-LAWS' HOUSE, and I'm immediately apprehensive: four accordions are displayed on the mantel. I imagine what awaits us. It isn't long before I find out.

David's cousin drops in and with great pride presents her eight-month-old baby, who on catching sight of us begins to cry and cry and cry. My shiny beaded necklace doesn't console her. David tries bouncing her up and down, but this only proves she can vomit on demand. Hence, Giorgio tries his hand at calming her down, and he succeeds, mesmerizing her with his accordion. She stares at him while he plays on for what seems like a lifetime, and not one tear falls from her little eyes.

Cry, baby, cry! I silently urge, because it's far more appropriate that she cries before I do. But alas, little Erica loves the accordion. There is no need to cut their visit short; both Erica and Giorgio are so happy.

Then Giorgio carefully chooses which accordion will serenade us tonight. I manage to feign enthusiasm, despite having heard this melody for the umpteenth time. Maria, now his accomplice, puts in a CD of accordion music. As the CD plays on and on, so does he. I pour myself another glass of wine. With the chorus of accordion music blaring, I finally tell everyone goodnight.

Full, tired, and hot, I return to our room. I will sleep in tomorrow morning and will try to convince David to defy his father and bring me my coffee in bed.

***

Seven roosters crow loudly just outside our window, and there's definitely a competition taking place.

I distinctly remember my elderly grandmother grabbing roosters by their wings and carrying them against their will to be slaughtered. I watched through eyes covered half of the time and gasped as I saw their fate. Having done her deed, she chucked them into a large basket, one after the other. Their bodies thrashed about until finally they were dead. I swore I could never do that.

At 5 a.m. this morning, however, I vaguely contemplate it. At 6 a.m., in a sleepy stupor, I visualize it in detail. By 7 a.m., I'm certain I can do it.

What has come over my in-laws? It's a miracle their neighbors haven't killed them or their roosters. I get up and angrily close the shutters and the windows. The cool morning breeze no longer enters the room, and soon it is stifling. I try to go back to sleep, but the cock-a-doodle-do contest continues for the next few hours.

Much to my father-in-law's delight, we rise early this morning.

I sleepily ask my mother-in-law, "How can you stand it? Don't the roosters wake you up?"

Smiling, she replies, "Yes, of course, they do. But soon there will be only six of them—one is for you."

I'm not sure whether she means he'll be joining us dead or alive; either prospect doesn't appeal to me much.

Because it's early and a walk is still bearable, I go down the mountain, hoping to find my little dog Briciola. The views are truly stunning, the city of Ascoli Piceno in the background and the green mountain covered in wild flowers in the foreground. I call, "Briciola!" and she comes running as fast as her legs can carry her. We walk past Franco's place and see that the gas company has made its way through his property, and the hill is covered with signs warning "Gas line here." The olive trees that were seemingly planted with such care lie abandoned next to the gas structure.

Briciola happily follows me the rest of the way and refuses to return home.

Emma, on seeing me, rushes over to congratulate me on my pregnancy. I knew my weight gain was obvious when my mother- and father-in-law saw me this time and said I was just perfect now! I am not pregnant, thus will have to intensify my leisurely walks.

David and a posse of uncles have gone to collect bamboo. It grows abundantly here, and in Tuscany you have to buy it in hardware stores. Being completely Italian now, my husband refuses to pay for bamboo when he can harvest it free of charge. He puts the roof rack on again, and I picture us and one hundred stalks of bamboo making our way back to Tuscany. To think my mother was embarrassed over a few mismatched suitcases!

I begin to prepare my onion and rosemary focaccia. Maria's sister from Rome has arrived, and we'll be one big happy family. During lunch, *Zia* Luisa doesn't hide her disdain for the pasta once she learns it isn't her favorite brand: De Cecco. She puts her full plate aside and mutters under her breath, as she watches the rest of us finish our non–De Cecco pasta. She's quite an outspoken character, and I can only imagine how much fun we'll all have together during the next few days.

I used to think that Italian families merely sounded as if they were always fighting; now I realize that they actually *are*, a good part of the time.

Everyone is currently "discussing" Singer sewing machines. Apparently, thirty years ago Singer sold its name, and Giorgio insists that ever since then, all of its parts are plastic. *Zia* vehemently defends her sewing machine, and a heated argument ensues. Finally, Giorgio stands up and loudly threatens to take the entire machine apart, piece by piece, to show her all of the plastic.

I sigh. *And American movies portray us in Italy discussing art and history and the finer things in life.*

Thankfully, *Zia* changes the subject and in so doing saves the sewing machine. She asks, "Who is going to farm this land when all of the old farmers die?"

Half jokingly, and perhaps stupidly, I try to get a rise out of them and say, "The Albanians or the Romanians."

Zia replies, "They're all drunk all day, so how can they?"

I gladly retire to the kitchen to do the dishes. *Zia* follows me in, to supervise, and says, "You don't know how to wash dishes."

Having seen how excited she got over the sewing machine, I obediently and humbly change my mistaken ways and pretend to accept her advice.

I dry the dishes. Yellow sticky notes are on the shelves, labeling all of the glasses: "glasses for water, glasses for wine, and glasses for beer." Oddly, all of the glasses are practically identical; some are perhaps an ounce bigger than the others. I return the glasses to their appointed spots and head off for a well-deserved *pausa*.

However, we soon discover that roosters don't take afternoon *pausas*. "He that crows best is king" is still their motto well into the late afternoon.

After my *pausa* without any actual sleep, I receive some "good" news. David's aunt will be going back to Tuscany with us for a week, along with my mother-in-law. I surely will be adept at washing dishes after spending a week with her. David's cousin Francesco and his wife and two children insist on coming to pick up David's mother and aunt. Another cousin reassures us she will come and visit us very soon.

We receive several phone calls from neighbors back in Tuscany, proving that the Italian neighborhood watch program is alive and well. Someone was stealing our tomatoes and other vegetables, and the perpetrators were apprehended in the very act.

Luciano recorded all of the pertinent details for us. "They were driving a gray Fiat Uno, license plate number . . . "

I visualize him shaking his head as he considers the enormity of the crime, which he describes with great zeal. "They said they were your friends and that you had told them to take some tomatoes while you were gone."

It seemed an unlikely story to Luciano, who then closed and locked our high metal gate, preventing any more of our so-called friends from getting in!

Shortly thereafter, we receive a call from our friends, who tell us they were caught by Luciano while picking our tomatoes. David and I laugh at the thought of calling the *carabinieri* to report tomato theft and having Luciano as our key witness to prove our case beyond any reasonable doubt.

We'll be leaving soon, so Maria is downstairs squirreling things away to bring with us. It appears she has been doing this for months now. I survey the shelf on the wall, brimming with goods, and wonder how on earth we can take all of it. And that was before she pointed to the freezer. I have visions of myself, the bamboo, and the rooster riding on the roof rack.

It's our last night here, so I have to endure only a little more accordion music. Tomorrow morning should be somewhat more peaceful because rooster number seven— apparently, the loudest rooster—is now in the fridge, awaiting transport to Tuscany. His feet and head will remain in Abruzzo, strewn across the lawn for the dog to eat.

I sure hope he *was* the ringleader.

REVENGE OF THE ROOSTER

THE BAMBOO, THE ROOSTER, AND the four of us make it safely back to Tuscany from Abruzzo. Thankfully, we all ride in different parts of the car, while *Zia* Luisa enthusiastically gives David driving lessons from the backseat.

The moment we arrive, Luciano is quick to let us know, "Those aren't friends you have! Those are thieves! They stole twenty kilos of tomatoes, peppers, absolutely everything in sight!"

Luciano has definitely missed his calling, and the CIA pays quite well. However, Luciano cannot keep a secret. Wherever I go for my walk that evening, it's the talk of the town: "Heard how your friends stole everything." "Unbelievable the quantities they made away with." "Next time, better make sure you lock your gate!" The only thing missing is the WANTED sign with a police sketch of our friends posted beside the recent death notices.

After a few days here with not much to do, *Zia* Luisa and my mother-in-law are getting restless. Relaxing with a cup of tea or simply enjoying our Tuscan views is not exciting enough for them, so I decide that a bit of fruit picking might be a nice excursion.

David, too, is pleased that I'm taking them away for a while. At least for that short time, he'll be spared their relentless bickering. This may also keep his aunt from picking grapes and berries on obviously cultivated land that belongs to our neighbors. I don't want to become the center of village gossip, as our tomato-picking friends now are.

Besides, we found a fruit tree on the hillside of an abandoned road, so I assume it belongs to no one.

Now I watch from below in dread as the branch sways. I hear a slight crackle and can no longer take it. "*Zia*, come down!"

Not only is she up in the tree, but the tree is on a hill, and I have visions of her falling out of the tree and down the slope.

She angrily yells at me, "*Silenzio!*"

There are too many plums left to pick, and despite the fact that we have nowhere to go and nothing to do, our newly purchased fruit-picking device is not picking them fast enough. It's a long adjustable pole with a cloth bag on the end, specifically designed to pick fruit on high branches. This must be only for people who don't have a seventy-seven-year-old aunt. My mother-in-law, also in her seventies, doesn't blink an eye; she's too busy scouting which plums *Zia* should pick next. I watch *Zia* and shudder.

They are relentless; every last plum must be picked. If I dare to voice my concerns, I am immediately shushed. "*Silenzio!*" currently seems to be *Zia*'s favorite word.

Zia is now swaying right, left, and center, contorting her body in ways I thought impossible even for a much younger person. I can no longer watch.

Zia picks obediently, as my mother-in-law shouts directions for another lone plum. "Over to the left, a bit higher, no, higher . . ."

We hear a roar as a helicopter flies low overhead, taking photos to ensure that no one is doing any illegal building. It scares the heck out of me, but *Zia* pays it no mind, too consumed with the task at hand.

Finally, the tree has been picked bare, and *Zia* comes down to tell me off. "You kids these days are all the same! Just like my son—screaming for me to come down. If I didn't go up the tree, who would? That's why I have to climb the cherry tree after my son goes to work. You kids don't go up and pick the fruit. What am I supposed to do, let it all rot?"

I wisely refrain from replying to that forceful soliloquy by an elderly woman who has the strength and agility to climb a tree.

During the next week, I become a bastion of silence and bite my tongue on several occasions. I'm silent as my dozen elegant glass candle holders in the kitchen now double as tomato holders, a large freshly picked red tomato balanced on top of each one. Dish towels have escaped the drawer and adorn much of the kitchen furniture. Extra terra cotta pots now overflow with potatoes, decorating various posts in the kitchen. The front balcony has been turned into a tomato sauce–making plant, with *Zia* Luisa and Maria feverishly producing jar after jar. Traces of tomato sauce can be found on almost everything now. They process the plums and prepare some for the freezer, while simply flinging the pits and the rotten ones onto my lawn below.

They remove the wool rugs, because apparently no one needs them in the summer, and they reorganize and interchange many items to *their* liking. The few rugs that they miraculously don't take away are switched, because blue, beige, and brown don't match, according to this design duo. I keep silent and count the days . . .

David, however, is losing his patience. He listened to suggestions on his garden. He let them assist with the watering and the weeding. He didn't balk when they rearranged all of our flower pots, the whole time muttering how we foolishly spent money on terra cotta pots when plastic ones look just as good and would have sufficed. We obeyed when they sent us to our room at two o'clock for the obligatory afternoon *pausa*. We didn't dare to breathe, not wanting to wake them and give them more time to indulge their vices.

Thus, I'm surprised to hear that Maria will be taking the bus home tomorrow. We'd slept longer than they had, but how much trouble could she have made during that time?

"Plenty!" says David. "She completely rearranged my *cantina*!"

Now Maria had crossed the line. I understand his furor, because he had spent many long hours sorting and organizing his beloved *cantina*. His tools were in perfect order, and the *cantina* was just the way he wanted it. David can no longer remain silent.

Neither can *Zia*. At dinner, she announces her disdain for our newly purchased fruit-picking device. "With that stupid contraption, ten hours later we would all still be there!"

Recalling the recently rearranged cantina, I realize that wouldn't be a bad thing.

Maria laughs off the whole incident. She has no real intentions of taking the bus home. Her task was accomplished, and she is proud. She insists on showing me the newly organized *cantina*, trying to get my nod of approval on each "improvement" she made. She has no remorse.

Poor David. For the rest of her visit, I hear him yelling, aggravated, "Ma, where is . . . Ma, where is . . . ?"

With a sly smile, she then wanders down to the *cantina* to show him the new and improved place for his hammer, knives, power tools, and so on.

Soon, my mother-in-law has not only taken over the *cantina* and the interior design of our home but has also taken over the kitchen. It also becomes apparent that I cannot escape roosters. It's broiling hot outside; the heat is absolutely oppressive. I do everything I can to keep the heat out, hoping the extremely thick walls will help, while my mother-in-law insists on cooking the rooster for lunch.

"Roosters are tough and need to be cooked on the stove for at least two hours," she says.

That's certainly what we need during a heat wave. Yet I soon discover that Italian mothers are tougher than roosters, and after a short debate, I admit defeat.

In no time, the kitchen resembles a steam bath. It's unbearably hot outside and now, thanks to the rooster, even hotter inside. I suggest having lunch on the terrace to escape the inferno indoors, but Maria feels there is no need to carry everything out when we can simply eat in here.

Yes, we can just have lunch in the sauna instead.

We eat the rooster for what seems like hours in the insufferable heat, and we don't even make a dent in the huge bird.

This won't be the last I see of this rooster. The leftovers will last for days.

Zia Luisa has decided to take the train home and will leave tomorrow morning; replacing her will be Francesco, his wife, and their two children. Although they're coming to pick up Maria and take her back to Abruzzo, she isn't sure she wants to leave yet. She will decide later whether to return with them or not. I love Maria, but I want my candleholders back, and the terra cotta tiles on our balcony cannot handle any more tomato stains.

David drives *Zia* to the train station. I wave good-bye and feel a sense of relief, because I no longer need to worry about *Zia* climbing trees and breaking her neck on our watch. But alas, it is not to be; the scheduled train has been canceled. I'll have to keep watching *Zia* like a hawk until the next train comes to town.

Soon thereafter, we hear the toot of a horn. Francesco and his family have arrived, with lots of luggage and a gift for us. I take the heavy package and graciously thank them. His wife apologizes that due to the long journey and the extreme heat, it is now unfrozen and hence will have to be cooked.

I look inside the bag and almost scream out loud in horror. It's another large rooster! I cannot escape them and will be forced to cook another one in this heat!

I thank them again, rather insincerely, and try to find room for the rooster in our minuscule fridge. I clear out a spot next to the other rooster in the pot and let the two of them rest side by side.

Tomorrow, while they broil in Florence, I will broil in my home. The rooster must be cooked.

Maria, not satisfied just to be a chef, an interior decorator, and a *cantina* organizer, has now turned into a tour guide as well. She informs Francesco that if he is going only to Florence tomorrow, he can also visit Montepulciano.

"But they're in opposite directions," I point out. "It won't be possible to visit both."

Maria adamantly disputes me. "You don't need more than a few hours to visit Florence." She offers suggestions on how to do all of Tuscany in a day. I soon realize that Maria has a lot of work to do, and she doesn't want to be bothered with guests. So much tomato sauce to jar, so little time remaining.

Despite there "not being much to see in Florence," the guests nonetheless head there. Maria goes off to work on the balcony cum tomato sauce plant, and I reluctantly begin preparing the extremely large rooster. I chop off the head and any other parts I deem unfit. Maria watches me work for ten minutes, then she insists that I work too hard and there will be no more canning of tomatoes here. Instead, from now on, she, a seventy-something lady with bad health, will prepare them for us at her home and will transport them from Abruzzo.

Now I'm *certain* she is tougher than that rooster, I thank her and head off to relax and read a book. Besides, I'll need all of my strength to bring myself to turn on the stove in this heat and cook the rooster for dinner.

At least, this time there will be eight of us, so we won't have as many leftovers.

MORE FOWL PLAY

MARIA DECIDES THERE'S TOO MUCH for her to do here, so she extends her stay. We wave good-bye to Francesco and his family and face the fact that the three of us will be eating rooster for the next long while and that the tomatoes will continue to ripen on my candle holders.

Maria proves she could run a canning factory with utmost precision. She has taken over the kitchen, the *cantina*, and the balcony and has us making fig jam, *peperonata*, tomato sauce, and plum jam from the fruit *Zia* almost sacrificed her life for, even though we told her we already have enough to last several years.

Giorgio's phone call nicely coincides with the garden being stripped and any fruit trees within a reasonable distance picked bare. He's tired of cooking for himself. It's time to close the canning factory and take Maria home.

Having just come from Abruzzo, we begrudgingly make the drive back. We arrive in what seems like no time at all: for me, because I was asleep, and for David, because I was asleep.

We find Giorgio making grappa. He has a secret formula that involves pantyhose and mint candies. I decide this is a grappa I may want to steer clear of.

After a few days, we're ready to make the trek back home. David suddenly realizes he can't find his wallet with his driver's license. He might have left it back in Tuscany. The drive home won't be pleasant—for me, because I hate to drive, and for David, because he hates for me to drive.

Over morning coffee, David says, "My parents have a gift for us: two hens, their best ones!"

The three of them anxiously watch my response.

"Now you can have fresh eggs every day!" Maria happily says.

Though I had refused several times in the past, their eager faces convince me to say, "Wow, that will be great."

Maria runs downstairs, and although we had just recently visited and returned with a car full of food, an Italian mother knows no bounds.

I bring my overnight bag outside and find the car loaded to the brim. A virtual grocery store has once again taken over the trunk.

The two chickens are in a little box next to the car.

"Oh, I guess there's no room for the chickens?" I conclude.

"Of course, there is—in the backseat," Maria assures me.

I'm supposed to have on four-inch heels and a flowing skirt, coupled with a pretty frilly top. My hair should be long, tousled in a sexy way. My husband should be wearing a crisp white shirt with slim-fit black trousers. This is how we're supposed to look when in Italy. I have seen movies and advertisements!

I stare at our ancient car, full of food and loaded down with stalks of bamboo on the roof. I look at the chickens in the box, and they regard me with equal bewilderment.

Next thing I know, I'm driving through lovely mountain roads to the sounds of clucking from the backseat.

The strong smell of pecorino cheese does little to mask the odor of the chickens responding to nature's call. We're forced to choose between closed windows and air conditioning or open windows and oppressive heat. The chickens poop again and thus decide for us.

We don't encounter the *carabinieri* doing any random checks on the secluded mountain road, so when we get closer to the highway, we decide that it's safe for David to drive without his documents.

He and I switch seats, slamming the car doors, and this sets the chickens off on a clucking spree.

Yet David drives only a short distance before we're shocked to see the *carabinieri* waving us over to the side of the road.

David stops the car.

"*Documenti*," the *carabiniere* orders.

David gives the insurance papers to the officer. I mentally will the chickens to stay quiet, but their little brains are immune to my mind control.

"Driver's license." The *carabiniere* stoops to look through the window, getting a good whiff of chicken poop and pecorino cheese. Frightened, one of our hens starts squawking.

I try not to laugh at the officer's astonished expression, but it will forever be imprinted in my mind. For a moment I can see through his eyes. His preconceptions about *Americani* are colliding with reality—the colorful, noisy, "fowl"-odored reality of the gypsylike travelers in front of him. In the same way, my own preconceived ideas about life in Tuscany, taken from books and movies, are demolished every day that I live here.

And, to misquote Martha Stewart, that's not a bad thing.

ACKNOWLEDGMENTS

I WANT TO THANK MY agent Dorie Simmonds, for her excellent suggestions and assistance, even long before she became my agent.

Many thanks to Patti Waldygo for her superb editing and advice; I couldn't have done it without you!

Profuse thanks to Joe Shepherd for truly captivating the spirit of my book with his cover design.

Grazie mille to my Italian prince, David, who never complained when his Italian world was repeatedly turned upside-down as I continued to write, oblivious to approaching mealtimes. He faithfully made us pasta on these occasions, and I thank him profusely, even though my hips do not. Seems like Nora Ephron got it right when she said, "Secret to life, marry an Italian." I'll add a p.s.: "Even if he is Canadian to begin with."

A special thanks to Vesna for taking care of everyone and everything overseas, giving me the opportunity to write, and to my mother, Anica, for her love of books and the witty stories she wrote throughout the years and for encouraging us to do the same. It only took me forty years to follow your advice!

My deepest appreciation goes to family members and friends who gave me their invaluable input (both solicited and unsolicited) and their continued support and enthusiasm, spurring me to keep writing. Whether it was sincere or not, it greatly inspired me!

And, of course, to my in-laws, whose never-ending generosity is evident in our permanently stockpiled shelves and *cantina* and for providing countless relatives as inspiration for my stories. I sure hope they have a sense of humor!

Last but not least, thanks to our two hens, Barbara and Roberta, who ended up being the gift that keeps on giving!

RECIPES FOR AN ITALIAN PRINCE

These are some very simple, yet tasty recipes,
guaranteed to land your Italian Prince.
Just beware, he COMES with relatives!

Appetizers

Bruschetta with Sausage and Stracchino
Bresaola with Arugula and Shaved Parmesan
Focaccia

Soup

Pappa al Pomodoro

Primo

Trofie Pasta with Arugula Pesto
Maria's Crepe Lasagna
Maria's Gnocchi
Giuseppe's Pasta

Secondo

Rabbit with Pine Nuts and Olives
Tagliata

Bruschetta with Sausage and Stracchino

Serves 4

16 slices of a baguette (or use Italian bread cut into appetizer size slices)
2 sausages
250 grams of stracchino or crescenza cheese

- Preheat oven to 400°F.
- Remove the casings from the sausages and place in a bowl with the cheese. Blend together until smooth. Spread the mixture on the bread.
- Bake until golden brown, about ten minutes. Serve warm.

BRESAOLA WITH ARUGULA AND SHAVED PARMESAN

Serves 4

16 slices of bresaola
1 bunch of arugula
Shaved parmesan cheese

Dressing:

4 tablespoons of olive oil
2 tablespoons of Balsamic vinegar
Pinch of salt and pepper

- Put the bresaola on a plate.
- Toss arugula with the dressing.
- Place arugula on top of the bresaola.
- Generously sprinkle the parmesan shavings on top.
- Serve right away.

FOCACCIA

Serves 8

2 ½ cups of flour
1 teaspoon of dry yeast
1 teaspoon of sugar
1 teaspoon of salt
1 cup of warm water with 2 tablespoons of olive oil

- Mix flour with yeast, salt and sugar. Stir in warm water with olive oil. Mix well and then knead for five minutes, adding more flour when necessary.
- Form dough into ball and coat with olive oil. Leave dough to rest in a warm spot about an hour or so until at least doubled.
- Brush large baking sheet with oil. Punch down dough and fit into baking sheet. Leave for an hour until it rises again.
- Preheat oven to 400°F.
- Punch fingertips all over dough to make indentations. Sprinkle top of focaccia with a mixture of olive oil, water and chopped rosemary. Sprinkle salt on top.
- Bake for approximately 20 minutes or until nicely browned.

PAPPA AL POMODORO

Serves 4

Wonderful summer soup!

¼ cup of olive oil
2 small onions, chopped
2 cloves of garlic, chopped
2 pounds of tomatoes, peeled and chopped
1 ½ cups of bread cubes
Bunch of basil, chopped

- Sauté onions and garlic in oil until soft. Add pinch of salt.
- Add tomatoes and cook for about 15 minutes.
- Add bread cubes and let sit for 10 minutes. Adjust by adding more cubes of bread or water.
- Add basil and adjust salt and pepper as needed.
- Top with freshly grated Parmesan cheese.

Serve either hot or cold.

TROFIE PASTA WITH ARUGULA PESTO

Makes 1 heaping cup.

Arugula Pesto
2 cups of packed arugula leaves, stems removed
½ cup of blanched almonds
½ cup of fresh Parmesan cheese
½ cup of extra virgin olive oil
2 garlic cloves
Pinch of sugar if needed

- Toast the nuts in a pan over medium heat until lightly brown.
- Combine the arugula, almonds and garlic in a food processor. Pulse while drizzling the olive oil into the processor. Remove the mixture from the processor and put it into a bowl. Stir in the Parmesan cheese.
- Boil pasta as per instructions. I like trofie type pasta for pesto recipes.
- When the pasta is done reserve ¼ cup of pasta water and add to pasta along with pesto.
- Serve with additional freshly grated parmesan and fresh pepper.

MARIA'S CREPE LASAGNA

16 crepes

If you really need to impress an Italian Prince this lasagna recipe is for you!

1 tablespoon of olive oil
6 eggs
6 tablespoons of sifted flour
1 teaspoon of salt
Enough water to make the right consistency of batter, should be thinner than pancake batter.

- Mix above.
- Pour a bit of oil in a non-stick pan and heat on medium high hot until pan is hot.
- Ladle batter into skillet, swirling skillet until batter coats bottom of pan.
- Cook until edges are dry.
- Flip over and cook an additional 30 seconds.

Use crepes as you would use lasagna noodles. Maria usually uses a cheese and tomato sauce base and then pours a béchamel sauce over the top that makes for a wonderfully light lasagna.

You can use these crepes for a variety of lasagnas. My favorite is pesto and béchamel sauce between the crepes.

MARIA'S GNOCCHI

Serves 6

Disclaimer: Your gnocchi will never be as good as his moms!

6 large potatoes
1 egg
1 egg yolk
2 cups of flour

- Boil potatoes with skin on.
- When done and slightly cooled, peel off skin and grind in potato ricer. Add a pinch of salt and if you like also a pinch of nutmeg. Let cool then add 1 whole egg and one egg yolk. Then add 2 cups of flour and mix well.
- Roll each ⅛ of dough into a snake-shaped log, roughly the thickness of your thumb. Use a knife to cut pieces every inch. Dust with a bit of semolina flour.
- Add gnocchi to boiling water. Let gnocchi rise and cook an additional minute. When done, drain and add your favorite sauce. (My favorites are: porcini mushroom and truffle oil, or basil or arugula pesto, or homemade tomato sauce.)
- Serve with freshly grated parmesan cheese.

GIUSEPPE'S PASTA

Serves 4

Pancetta or bacon cut into cubes
1 tablespoon of olive oil
1 onion, finely diced
2 cloves of garlic finely chopped
500 grams of cherry tomatoes cut in half
½ cup of olive oil
Freshly ground pepper
Freshly grated parmesan cheese
500 grams of Orechiette pasta (fresh if available)

- Fry bacon in skillet. Remove and drain on paper towels. Set aside.
- Sauté onion in olive oil. Add garlic. Add tomatoes and sauté until tomatoes are softened. Remove from heat. Add bacon, pepper and the olive oil.
- Prepare pasta as per package directions.
- Combine sauce with pasta and add parmesan cheese.

Rabbit with Pine Nuts and Olives

Serves 6

While Italian Princes' love pasta, and can eat it every day, they also expect something to be served after the pasta…sigh, you cannot have it all!

¼ cup of olive oil
2 cloves of garlic
1 dried hot pepper
2 ½ pound rabbit, cut into 6 pieces
One large carrot, grated
Sprig of rosemary, chopped
1 cup of white wine (or more)
2 cups of tomato sauce
½ cup of olives
2 tablespoons of pine nuts

- Place a large sauté pan over medium-high heat. Season the rabbit with salt and pepper and add to the pan with the olive oil. Cook, in batches, for 3–4 minutes, turning frequently, until evenly browned.
- Remove from the pan and set aside. Add the carrot, rosemary, garlic and hot pepper to the pan and sauté.
- Add the white wine and then add the tomato sauce and bring to a boil. Return the rabbit pieces to the pan, reduce heat and simmer, covered, for 1 ¼ hours until tender. If the pan gets too dry add more wine or some water.
- Remove the lid and simmer for a further 15 minutes until the meat is very tender and the sauce is slightly reduced. Add the pine nuts and the olives. Season to taste.

TAGLIATA

Serves 4

½ cup of olive oil
10 garlic cloves, finely chopped
2 sprigs of rosemary
Green peppercorns, smashed
2 pound thick cut steak, Rib Eye or Strip

- Bring the steak to room temperature.
- Sauté the garlic in oil. Turn off heat and add rosemary and green peppercorns. Set aside.
- Either barbecue the meat or cook on high heat in a skillet. When skillet is hot, add the steak. It should sizzle. Turn it over and cook for 2 to 3 minutes. The meat will be very rare. Sprinkle with salt, and then wrap whole piece in aluminum foil.
- Let it stand for 10 minutes before slicing (on the diagonal, against the grain) into ¼ inch thick slices.
- Arrange the beef on a platter and pour the olive oil mixture over the beef. Add freshly ground pepper and more salt if needed.

Made in the USA
Middletown, DE
02 December 2014